Voices of the
Georgian Age

Voices of the Georgian Age

100 Remarkable Years, In Their Own Words

James Hobson

First published in Great Britain in 2022 by
Pen & Sword History
An imprint of
Pen & Sword Books Ltd
Yorkshire – Philadelphia

Copyright © James Hobson 2022

ISBN 978 1 39900 606 4

The right of James Hobson to be identified as Author of this work has been asserted by him in accordance with the Copyright, Designs and Patents Act 1988.

A CIP catalogue record for this book is available from the British Library.

All rights reserved. No part of this book may be reproduced or transmitted in any form or by any means, electronic or mechanical including photocopying, recording or by any information storage and retrieval system, without permission from the Publisher in writing.

Typeset by Mac Style
Printed in the UK by CPI Group (UK) Ltd, Croydon, CR0 4YY.

Pen & Sword Books Limited incorporates the imprints of Atlas, Archaeology, Aviation, Discovery, Family History, Fiction, History, Maritime, Military, Military Classics, Politics, Select, Transport, True Crime, Air World, Frontline Publishing, Leo Cooper, Remember When, Seaforth Publishing, The Praetorian Press, Wharncliffe Local History, Wharncliffe Transport, Wharncliffe True Crime and White Owl.

For a complete list of Pen & Sword titles please contact

PEN & SWORD BOOKS LIMITED
47 Church Street, Barnsley, South Yorkshire, S70 2AS, England
E-mail: enquiries@pen-and-sword.co.uk
Website: www.pen-and-sword.co.uk

Or

PEN AND SWORD BOOKS
1950 Lawrence Rd, Havertown, PA 19083, USA
E-mail: Uspen-and-sword@casematepublishers.com
Website: www.penandswordbooks.com

Contents

Introduction		vi
Chapter 1	Family, Friends and Society: William Hutton 1723–1782	1
Chapter 2	A Picture of England from the Road: Karl Moritz 1782	16
Chapter 3	Man of Feeling: William Windham 1784–1810	32
Chapter 4	The British Grand Tour: John Byng May–June 1789	43
Chapter 5	The London Bubble: Joseph Farington 1793–1802	57
Chapter 6	Plausible Villain: James Hardy Vaux 1782–1801	70
Chapter 7	Walking in Wales: Richard Warner 1797	84
Chapter 8	Dancing and Travelling: Jane Austen 1796–1814	95
Chapter 9	Quaker: Hannah Gurney 1804–1820	105
Chapter 10	A Dull Year?: Fanny Chapman 1809	113
Chapter 11	Body Snatcher: Joseph Naples 1811–1812	128
Chapter 12	Weaver, Luddite, Criminal: Thomas Holden/Holding 1812–1820	136
Chapter 13	Trophy Tourism: Elizabeth Chivers 1814	145
Chapter 14	Respectability: Thomas Lucas 1813–1816	154
Chapter 15	Radical Reformer: Samuel Bamford 1815–1819	165
Chapter 16	Courtier: Ellis Cornelia Knight 1800–1814	181
Chapter 17	Regency Man About Town: Rees Gronow 1812–1820	194
Notes		205
Index		208

Introduction

Nobody puts pen to paper, to use an old-fashioned term, without a motive. Our first Georgian witness, William Hutton, makes this clear:

> None is so able to write a life as the person who is the subject because his thoughts, his motives and his private transactions are open to him alone. But none is so unfit, for his hand, biased in his favour, will omit or disguise simple truth, hold out false colours and deceive all but the writer. I have endeavoured to divest myself of this prejudice.[1]

Hutton claims to be free of the vices that make history difficult to write, while at the same time declaring, correctly, that most bias is unconscious rather than malicious. Hutton also claims to be wiser and more alert than the average person, which is a prejudice itself, and one he does not recognise because misjudgements of this kind are unconscious.

So our diaries, travelogues and memoirs are problematic but no more so than other historical sources; just because they are attached to a named, frail human being does not change anything. All survivals from the past need to be treated with caution, and the normal questions about provenance asked.

Some were commercial endeavours, written to be bought and read, while others were private and reflective. The difference is easy to spot and relatively easy to take into account. One major advantage is that our witnesses are already well-known people; our sources are not scraps of letters or diaries that have survived with no context, but documents that can be interpreted with specific background knowledge.

This is a social rather than a political history, so our witnesses focusing on the small practicalities of their lives is a strength rather than a weakness. We also go beyond their personal reminiscences to paint a picture of wider Georgian society, as, no matter how interesting our seventeen subjects are, they must represent something bigger than themselves to be worth our time and scrutiny. That they are human beings, with fundamentally the same emotions and core desires as us today is obvious, almost a cliché, so it cannot be a focus of the book. It is the differences that tell us much more, and there are lots of them.

The other focus is travel, hospitality and tourism, mostly in England, but also in Wales and Scotland. These activities are meant to be different to normal life, and people record events with fresh eyes and new perspectives when they are on the move. That's useful and interesting.

The witnesses appear in rough chronological order. William Hutton's life spans most of the Georgian era, and we cover his struggles and boasts up to 1782. All of the witnesses have been edited, and events selected from a great number that cannot be included for reasons of space. These kinds of sources are factually very dense and the challenge was to keep them representative, and this is particularly true with Hutton.

Our next witness is our only foreigner, Karl Moritz, who loved England but did have some critical things to say about it. As with all of our voluntary travellers (Richard Warner, John Byng and Elizabeth Chivers), I have not felt the need to follow their itineraries slavishly. Many of our witnesses repeat themselves; when Moritz or Warner were in rapture over the scenery, it has been mentioned once in detail, later in outline and again only for a very good reason.

Next is our only member of the British cabinet, William Windham. He bears absolutely no resemblance to the major British politicians of the twenty-first century, although it has to be said that he bears little resemblance to those of the late Georgian period either. He is hard to understand and appreciate, and his diary is exceptionally hard reading. Some of the sources are a joy to read, others are much more difficult – this one is a challenge.

Our next witness is John Byng, briefly a member of the House of Lords and an acquaintance of William Windham, one of the very few links between our witnesses. He is a grumpy, entitled and rich traveller with a hankering for a return to the past. Neither is he a great believer in 'abroad'. His type still exists today, in outline if not in detail.

Another archetype that still exists is the cocooned, arty member of the metropolitan establishment. Our example is Joseph Farington, a key member of the Royal Academy, who had direct links with the monarchy and the art world. However, he is included because of his interest in money, death and scandal. Gossip is oral, and is therefore a scarce historical resource. It may be a little uncultured, but I have judged the tittle-tattle of the age as more enlightening than the internal politics of the Royal Academy; you can have both if you read the diary.

At this point, you may be asking where are the poor and powerless? The short answer is 'not writing travelogues and diaries'. The exception is James Hardy Vaux, a plausible and highly literate criminal who is completely unrepresentative of his class, criminal or otherwise, but his description of the Georgian underworld is accurate and fascinating.

Richard Warner is next, a semi-radical cleric with an interest in history and archaeology and a determination to be as nice as possible to the Welsh when he visits them, as long as they stay within his assigned stereotype; another kind of person that still exists, except today they fly in by jet to hot countries rather than walk through Wales with a large shabby overcoat.

Our next witness is Jane Austen, a twenty-something member of the middle classes who wrote a series of light-hearted letters to her sister Cassandra. After her is another, less famous member of the same class called Fanny Chapman, who lived in the same part of the world. There are acres of print about Jane and nothing about Fanny, for the fair reason that the latter did not produce novels of genius, but in the book, they are both treated in the same way: as genteel Georgian women who had little agency in life and hours of time to fill.

Sandwiched between them is Quaker Hannah Chapman Gurney and the difference is glaring. Her constant spiritual examinations are not to mainstream modern tastes, but the summary and conclusions are still interesting. With this witness, the past definitely feels like a foreign country where they really do think differently.

The next story is gruesome yet compelling. The appalling crimes of Joseph Naples and his community of body snatchers (not grave robbers) are brutally exposed in his eleven-month diary of 1811–1812. He is our second working-class witness, and second criminal, but an organised, literate one who was clearly running an efficient business operation. If you can forget what he was actually doing, it is possible to admire his skills.

Next is another working-class 'criminal', but his miserable fate merely reminds us who made the law. Thomas Holden was a Luddite, convicted and transported for conspiring to destroy machinery, and was just literate enough to tell his own story. His brief and scrappy reminiscences are sad and sullen, and show the utter helplessness of the working man and woman in the late Georgian era.

Our next diary belongs to the inexhaustible tourist Elizabeth Chivers. Its tick-box, trophy destination superficiality and love of cakes might make you think 'plus ça change, plus c'est la même chose' when it comes to tourism, but delving deeper there are other things going on.

Thomas Lucas of Stirling in Scotland is next. He has new perspectives – he is our only Scot, our only middle-class provincial male, and the only rich person who lived a few streets away from the poor. His strength is his recording of events, big and small, and his opinions, which were sufficiently mainstream to be representative but unpredictable enough to be interesting.

Our next witness also knew about the poor, but unlike Lucas, tried to do something to help them. He was the radical weaver Samuel Bamford. Bamford believed in protest within the law, despite those laws being made by a political class which did not have the workers' interests at heart. His extensive journal has been edited to only include class struggle; his interest in Lancashire folklore, fairies, trolls and spirits has been omitted, but is available for all to read.

We finish with two completely different members of the establishment. Ellis Cornelia Knight was a gifted intellectual, who, as part of a long and interesting life, devoted her time to the Royal Family, with very mixed results. Our last is the Welshman Rees Gronow. He knew about the army, the clubs of London and the fashionable world of the Regency. His reminiscences were a deliberate attempt to make money by shocking people with gossip and interesting stories, and it still does the trick today.

This brings us to accessibility. The work of all our witnesses is available for free on the internet. This book makes no assumption about which, if any, original sources, will be read, and it depends on the interests and stamina of the reader. If they *are* read, this book has been designed as an introduction to each person; these sources are so rich and varied, there can never really be a full and final conclusion about them. I have only scratched the surface but isn't that always the case with history?

Chapter 1

Family, Friends and Society
William Hutton 1723–1782

Our first Georgian witness is William Hutton (1723–1815). He had a successful life as a businessman, poet and author, but his childhood and family background were modest and life was a struggle. Our source is his biography, *The Life of William Hutton, Stationer, of Birmingham and the History of His Family*, published for the first time in 1817 and reprinted in 1841.

Hutton was born on 30 September 1723 and, like most children before or since, his first thoughts were about his mother, named Ann. Unlike most children today, his memories of her were to be limited as Ann was to survive a mere nine years after his birth. For most of that time, she struggled – 'time produced nothing but tatters and children,' said Hutton in one of his many thought-provoking poetic turns of phrase.

In the eighteenth century, the death of one's mother at 41 would bring grief but not much surprise. Ann's husband, William, had been a self-employed wool-comber, but when William junior was 2 years old, William senior's business failed and he became a journeyman – a day worker for other people. Wool-combing was a hot and greasy job which was done at home. Raw wool was straightened with large combs of increasing fineness so it was separated and of equal length. It was a precarious occupation, as Hutton was to discover, but his family were made poorer than they should have been by their father's lack of application. Both before and after his business failure, William seemed to be supine and intemperate. He delayed decisions, drank too much and alienated his wife, and the whole family suffered.

It was a coarse, cruel and often calamitous life. At the age of 2, Hutton set fire to his petticoats, frock and bib – normal clothing for both Georgian girls and boys. These clothes were flammable; he was playing next to an open fire with a paper fan that his sister had given him, and he just avoided self-immolation. Hutton recounts this story in a direct and matter-of-fact tone that suggests his childhood was typical of the time. This is another example:

> My mother observed I was the largest child she ever had, but ordinary – a softer word for ugly – [she was] afraid she should never love me.

In the Georgian era, childhood ended at about 4 to 6 years old. Hutton's ended at the age of 4 when he was breeched.[2] Up to this point, he would have had long hair and petticoats and been indistinguishable from a girl, and the breeching was a rite of passage at which he should have been the centre of attention. Reaching 4 years old was a milestone worth celebrating; Hutton knew this, as his brother George had just died, aged 3 and a half. The eighteenth-century graveyards contained large numbers of 70- and 80-year-olds but average life expectancy was a mathematical calculation, rendered low by the regular death of children before the age of 5. Every family, even the rich ones, knew this fact painfully.

Life wasn't great. Hutton was not at home when he was breeched so had nobody to buy him new clothes. With his mother and father's relationship being in a mess he was moved away, spending his time alternately between his mother's bachelor uncle at Mountsorrel, Leicestershire and his 'three crabbed aunts', all single and living 2 miles away. None of them liked him. They called him ugly, like his father, and Hutton wondered why they would insult somebody with a fault that could not be rectified.

When his mother came to get him, he was dragged out of his bed half-naked by a servant girl, placed on a horse with the uncle and they rode to Loughborough to pick up a goods wagon to take them on to Derby. Hutton had a pillow under him on the horse, but there would be no suspension of any kind on the wagon. His father, seeing him for the first time in 15 months, said two words only; 'Oh Bill.'

Aged just over 4, work became part of Hutton's life. He went on errands, wearing his best suit, cocked hat and walking stick when going to school. He looked after his two brothers when his mother was at work, and gave the family their milk porridge in the morning (one day he completely forgot his father who, characteristically, did not notice or do anything about it.)

'My days of play were coming to an end,' Hutton said; he was 6 at the time. He needed paid work; child labour in the eighteenth century was only regarded as a problem if there was none available. The first job proposed was a domestic occupation like his father's; winding thread around bobbins. The second was in a grocer's, stripping tobacco leaves.

Hutton was one of the first ever witnesses to the Industrial Revolution. The family lived in Full Street, Derby, almost within sight of Britain's first ever factory. Hutton was one of the youngest workers in this new form of employment. The Derby Silk Mill had been operating since about 1717, and was a curiosity and a tourist attraction. When Daniel Defoe visited, he said it was 'a curiosity in trade worth observing, as being the only one of its kind in England.' The new ways of factory working may have been born in Derby, but Hutton hated it. The 5.00 am start, the cruel use of the cane for every trivial infraction, and the foul language and manners of those who worked there revolted him. It was made much worse because he was the youngest of the 300 workers, and needed lifts on his shoes to operate the machines.

The Hutton family were not members of the Church of England. They were Unitarians – nonconformists of a moderately unpopular variety. They denied the Trinity of Father, Son and Holy Spirit and regarded Jesus more as a religious teacher to be admired than part of the deity to be worshipped. They did not attend the local parish church, although Hutton did so because he was bribed a halfpenny to go to divine service; his father knew, but did not mind, or care. When Hutton went to the church, he sat himself somewhere unobtrusive and played 'push pin', a pointless game where one pin is manipulated over another on a flat service. It can only be played properly by two people, and was a metaphor for Hutton's lonely and aimless early life.

Aged 4 and a half, Hutton's teacher grabbed him by the hair and smashed his head against the wall. The fact that it was worthy of only one sentence says a lot. Extreme violence against children was commonplace. At Christmas 1732, Hutton was beaten so badly that his father's walking stick was smashed into pieces. His crime was two-fold; he lost a halfpenny when he was flipping and tossing it, and he was cheeky when told off. He took the bits of the stick and used them as a toy; he always, in his mind, made the best of a bad job, a theme he would revisit regularly to explain how a boy from a normal background made it good.

All this explains how he put up with, but still hated, the regular violent bullying at the mill. His master Richard Porter hit him repeatedly on the same place on his back and the point of his cane pierced an existing wound. Putrefaction set in and even his father was alarmed. Young William was bathed in Kedleston water, local spa water that cured the gravel (kidney stones) when drunk and healed skin and ulcers when bathed in. 'A cure was effected, and I yet carry the scar,' said Hutton, and this was not a metaphor.

Accidents were common in all areas of life and the mill was no better, but not necessarily much worse. He had a near miss, almost losing a hand in an accident where the machine could not have been stopped in time if it had been more serious. Hutton resented the unnaturalness of it all; the lack of choice in personal relationships, and the inability to make lasting friends, learn a trade or make personal progress. After his seven years of servitude, his 'apprenticeship' had failed to find him a job, and he was not surprised at all.

On 29 March 1732, aged 9, Hutton attended his first execution. John Hewitt had poisoned his wife, with the assistance of his lover Rosamund Ollerenshaw, and the pair, walking to the gallows with a clergyman on either side and surrounded by a great crowd, were hanged in their shrouds. The crowds were so enthusiastic that he had the greatest trouble getting there, being pushed into the river at the stepping-stones.

Death, poverty and coarseness were everywhere. Hutton's mother died in 1733, after the birth of yet another child, Samuel. Her nurse was useless and Ann did the work herself; Hutton claimed it was rinsing sheets in cold water that hastened her death. Ann had a miserable life living with her drunken spendthrift husband; the days of involuntary fasting did her more damage than washing in cold water. Hutton recalled the Christmas of 1728, when the lack of food in the house was made worse by having no knives, and his father, who 'was never in the habit of buying except ale' sent out Hutton's sister to borrow one.

When he was told about his mother's death, Hutton burst into tears but immediately went back to work at the mill. He was told by a friend of his late mother that it was fruitless to cry for he, too, would be dead soon. In the 1817 edition of his book, he mentioned his grandfather's children who had also died early. 'They slept before their time; nor is it of much consequence whether a man sleeps at one or one hundred. When the candle is out, no matter how long it has burnt.'

Then Hutton's father lost the plot completely. He moved away, set up with a widow who had four children, forcing Hutton to fend for himself, aged 9. He lived on cheap hasty pudding, which was merely flour and water. He developed the rustic-sounding illness of 'chin cough' that is, in fact, whooping cough and he suffered this lung infection for three months. He also developed boils; and all this time his father was in the pub. On his tenth birthday, in a small rite of passage, his father gave him a quart of tuppenny beer. A quart is four pints, and it would have been much stronger than anything available in twenty-first century pubs – the equivalent of six pints today.

Hutton tried to look upon his father in a rational way. He marvelled at his success with women, despite being old (42), drunken, not very handsome and not very clean (due to his hot and greasy occupation). Hutton senior also only had one eye, having lost the other in a botched operation that involved it coming out of its socket; when the eye was returned, it no longer worked, and grew disproportionately bigger as he grew older; yet the women of the area 'were still much inclined to pull caps for him.'

In 1734 Hutton witnessed an outbreak of vicious lawlessness in Derby. There was 'drinking, fighting, cursing, injuring, animosity and murder were the result.' This was not civil war or insurrection, but an election to the House of Commons or, more precisely, a contested election. Most seats were two member constituencies, which would normally be divided up by the local influential families. The Tory candidate Lord George Cavendish was elected successfully, but a fight ensued between the Whig candidate and an interloper. A mob appeared outside County Hall, windows were broken and there was fighting in the street. One man who tried to stop the mob had a stick thrust into his eye and died the next day.

By 1737, Hutton's apprenticeship at the Silk Mill had finished, and it had achieved nothing. What was to be done now? His father dithered; he did not want his son to be a wool-comber like him, or a stocking-frame worker like his brother. Hutton chose to be a gardener, which his father agreed to, but did nothing to make happen. Another hasty U-turn was made. His father now allowed his son to move to Nottingham and be an apprentice frame-knitter to his Uncle George.

He was 15 and entering yet another seven-year period of servitude. There was no reason to believe that he and his two fellow apprentices would have any kind of secure future. It was no more a learning experience than the mill had been. He was expected to produce garments from the start; if he earned 5 shillings and 10 pence, he would get sixpence. There was no more bitter way of learning the exploitation of labour. If he earned less than this, then he owed them money. His aunt watched every mouthful he ate with resentment as well.

By 1739, Hutton was looking at girls, but they were not looking at him. The importance of clothing was great, perhaps even more than today. Clothes were 'a passport to the heart, a key to unlock the passions and guide them in our favour.' 'My resources were cut off, my sun was eclipsed,' Hutton complained. Paradoxically, as long as people like Hutton produced textiles by hand, people like him would not be able to afford nice clothes. Our mass-produced clothing can hide social status to some extent, but in the eighteenth century it was different.

Winter 1740 was freezing; snow fell on New Year's Day, and it was still around in March. Both of his fellow apprentices had gone away. Uncle George had problems recruiting, which confirmed Hutton's suspicions about the quality of the apprenticeship. By 1741 things were improving just a little; he hated his frame but persevered, his aunt was still watching every mouthful of food with resentment, but he had found some reasonable clothes and better company – 'the girls eyed me with some attention, nay I eyed myself as much as any of them.'

It all went wrong in the week of the Nottingham races. Work in domestic industries would stop during such traditional events. Hutton had been idle for five days – it hovered over him – and on the sixth day it did not leave him, despite being threatened with a thrashing if he did not do some work. His uncle produced a birch broom handle and attacked him with it. The locals heard the noise, correctly worked out that somebody was being thrashed, and did not care. His pride was hurt more anything:

> Standing by the palisades of the house in a gloomy posture a female acquaintance passed by and turning with a pointed sneer said 'You were licked last night.' The remark stung me to the quick I had rather she had broken my head.

Hutton was nearly 18, getting better known and popular with girls; and then this humiliation. The next day his uncle seemed a little contrite and offered him cherries, but there was to be no compromise. He decided to run away. Leaving the house, he found 10 shillings and took 2 for himself, leaving the rest. He left with one bag, a sixpenny loaf of coarse blencorn bread, some butter wrapped in the leaves of an old copybook, a new Bible (value 3 shillings), a shirt, a pair of stockings, a sun dial and his best wig carefully folded and laid to prevent crushing.

There was no plan. Perhaps he could go to Ireland? His conscience was clear, though. He was not a thief; he merely took enough for his journey. He walked home to Derby, but without any wish to go to his house. It was 10.00 pm and, as befits a society with no lighting and no evening entertainment, everybody was asleep. He bedded down in a nearby damp field full of cows and horses who kept him awake all night, the horses by jingling and the cows merely by breathing. 'I need not say that I was a boy, this rash action proves it,' he said from hindsight, but thought differently at the time.

The childish melodrama continued the next morning; Hutton woke up, 'starved, sore and stiff', and waited on Warburgh's Bridge for his brother Samuel on the way to the mill, announcing that he would go to Ireland and they would see him no more. He moved to Burton, and then Lichfield, where his bags were stolen after he left them unattended for 10 minutes. He ranted and raved at the theft, forgetting what he had done at his uncle's house. That night he slept on a butcher's block on the street.

The next day he hitched himself on a wagon of carrots and cherries – he may have remembered his petulance when his uncle tried to make peace – 'my wounds were too deep to be healed by cherries.' The plan was to gain casual labour at Walsall market. He was directed to the stocking-frames of Birmingham, the job he was running away from. On the way, he saw unusual female labour – women with smutty faces thundering at an anvil. These were nail-makers.

He was not going to get a respectable job without references; 'You are a runaway apprentice,' many people correctly guessed. He asked three masters in Birmingham: the first sent him away, the second bribed him with a penny to go away and the third was a family friend from Derby who asked about his brother. Hutton told a lie to appease him and more lies to protect his lame story. He was getting sick of the lying needed to prop up his pointless pride.

He was given charity in Birmingham and slept in an inn; the next day he was in dark and dank Coventry and he slept in the Star Inn, 'not as a chamber guest, but as hay chamber one'. The following day he walked to Nuneaton, where he claimed he could hear 'prentice' whispered as he walked, then to Hinckley. He was then directed to a Derby man called Mr Millward, who gave him work and a bed for the night and persuaded him to return to his father in Derby:

> I told him that I had no objection to the service of my uncle but that I not submit to any punishment and if I were not received upon equitable terms I would immediately return to my own liberty.

So by the age of 18, his hinterland was Nottingham, Derby, Burton, Lichfield, Walsall, Coventry and Birmingham; geographically limited compared to today's youth but what he actually did while visiting would make a modern young adult quake in their boots. He returned to Derby and was reconciled with his uncle, despite his silence when they asked him the reasonable question – 'are you not to blame?' Uncle George was not a bad man, albeit henpecked, and in his heart, Hutton really knew it.

The whole escapade did not live up to its name as he escaped from none of his problems. He was in debt, still in an apprenticeship that he regarded as servitude, was now plagued by ague (debilitating diseases struck earlier than they do today) and his courting of females was not going well. In 1743 a girl proposed to him with Valentines, 'accidental' meetings, and then talk of matrimony and worries that his apprenticeship had two years to go and marriage was not allowed. He was so indifferent, she eventually had to propose to him – 'she took a liberty totally forbidden to her sex.'

Another liberty was taken in 1745 by an 'old aunt' who looked after one of his love prospects, Miss Woolley, who accosted him drunkenly; 'I love thee, If I was but as young as thou I would have thee, if thou wouldst but marry me.' Had she tried it on, he would, 'for once have run away from the embraces of a woman.' Love eluded him, as he still had no money. Eventually somebody did fall in love with him; if he continued working with the frame, he would continue to be poor; the love of his life agreed to be poor with him, but he knew that it was impracticable.

Work was wobbly. In December 1744 his latest apprenticeship ('second servitude') ended, but he was unable to make a living as a frame-knitter. He proposed to his uncle that they set him up on the very lowest rung of the artisan ladder; hiring a frame. His uncle agreed, and then changed his mind – 'I would rather eat hay with a horse' he said, under pressure from his domineering wife, thought Hutton.

Family life was not perfect either; his sister and her husband separated, and the feud with his uncle bubbled under. His brother Samuel ran away and was not heard of for five years. Hutton visited his father in Derby who, for the first and only time, kissed him. Hutton noted that his father was drunk. In 1746, his uncle threw up a quart of blood, had some touching pre-mortem conversations with his friends and family, took to his bed and died there five days later. This was Hutton's fifth deathbed scene – mother, aunt, brother and friend; it did not make it any easier, as people today seem to think, and he realised that he actually loved his uncle a lot. 'I was ignorant how much I loved him till my sorrow for his death informed me.'

He bought an expensive watch as an outward sign of prosperity, and the watch broke. He tried and failed to learn how to ride; not everybody in the eighteenth century casually leapt on a fine horse when they wanted to move about. He was literally going nowhere and marking (or, in his case, not marking) time until mediocrity embraced him for a lifetime.

However, the young man who had left home in a huff was now changing. He was becoming a better, more educated and more resilient person, while having no money, as he is always quick to remind us in his biography. He bought a bell harp, but had no money to buy advice on how to play it, so he taught himself. He borrowed a dulcimer, learnt to play that – 'for if a man can play upon one instrument, he may learn upon any' – and made one of his own (by breaking up a wooden trunk, a family heirloom) using tools from his stocking-frame. He sold the dulcimer for 16 shillings, bought a coat and made a new dulcimer.

The hatred of books that had been instilled in him by the sadistic school teacher was receding, but money remained a problem. He bought shabby books and learnt to repair them; it turned out that he was as good a bookbinder as he was a musician. He triumphed over the mean and nasty bookseller who tried to sell him a binding press that did not work.

> I considered the nature of its construction; bought it and paid the two shillings. I then asked him to favour me with a hammer and a pin which he brought me with half a conquering smile and half a sneer. I drove out the garter pin which, being galled, prevented the

press from working and turned another square which perfectly cured the press. He said in anger 'if I had known you not have had it.'

He used that binding press for the next forty-two years; it was a symbol, a victory for the clever and resilient against the bad and lazy. As he progressed in life, the tone of his biography becomes more self-regarding, verging on the hubristic. His own 'conquering smile' was seen more and more. He was the boy with no prospects made good. He was the prototype man made good by self-help. No wonder the Victorians saw him as one of their own.

So Hutton became a bookbinder and, in 1749, he went to London. His sister gave him the money; he sewed 3 guineas in coins into his clothes and put 11 shillings in his pocket as a sop to footpads, because he was walking to London, having neither coach fare, horse or riding skills. Londoners were not friendly to the people who lived there, and were even less so to the penniless tramp who had come to buy materials for his new trade. He was impressed by the tourist sites, but upset by the poor reception caused by his voice, appearance and implied inability to tip:

> I joined a youth who had business in the Tower, in hopes of admission. But the warders, hearing the northern voice, came out of their lodge and, seeing dust upon my shoes, reasonably concluded I had nothing to give, and with an air of authority ordered me back.

The new resilient, multi-talented entrepreneur still had one more low point in his life – the opening of his stationery shop in Southwell, while living with his sister in Nottingham. Once again, he walked to work; there and back, six days a week, often carrying books, starving and freezing in a cold shop for about 6 shillings a day on a permanent diet of beer and cheese. On one early morning journey, he met poachers coming from Sherwood Forest with four deer, and he was surprised that he wasn't 'knocked on the head to keep silence.' He assumed that they had not seen him; he was told later that they had.

One day he got lost in Sherwood Forest and was befriended by a poor family living in a two-room hovel. He was both repelled by and attracted to them; he sat round their meagre fire and they had nothing to offer him to eat other than pease porridge. This was perfectly acceptable to Hutton, a man who had lived on furmity (thick porridge) and drunk from horse troughs in London and on his escapade. His host was a widow who had married somebody younger to avoid debt, and had had two children that he could clearly not afford. Hutton, careful in his own courtship, was not impressed; 'this I considered an excuse for misconduct.'

When the gruel arrived, it was not by the light of a candle, but a screwed-up piece of paper from a book. Hutton did not have time to consider the metaphor for, in the light, he saw the hair shorn lip of the host's sister-in-law, and was too repulsed to eat. When he saw them the next morning, he was further repulsed by the scabby filth of the man; caused by idleness, he thought, hardly surprising for a man who spent 10 hours a day commuting to his work. This was the undeserving poor, and his Victorian audience would have agreed.

1750 was a key year. Hutton's own commercial life began to improve and he opened his first stationery shop in Birmingham. He was still poor, but now had a few trusted friends and reliable customers. It was all about connections, and Hutton was starting to get some. An employer of his sister, a dissenting minister called Ambrose Rudsall, sold him unwanted books on the basis of a promise: 'I promise to pay Ambrose Rudsall one pound seven shillings, when I am able.' Hutton was so poor that he had to walk to Gainsborough to see him, and had no overcoat, but now he had credit with some key people. He was respectable and could be lent money safely; he was worthy of credit in both senses of the word.

By the end of 1750 he had saved £20, spending five shillings a week on food, washing, rent and lodging. He was hounded by the poor law overseers who wanted him to go back to Derby in case he became a burden on the parish. He spent two years in dispute with them, offering to pay his contribution to the poor rate, while at the same time buying new clothes from one of the overseers who was bothering him.

In 1751 Hutton rented a house at £8 per year. He now wore clothes that allowed him to make respectable acquaintances. He was moving towards prosperity and local importance that was the mark of a minor gentleman. He had the house so he needed a housekeeper – the first sold his books and drank away the money; the second burnt his dumplings. In 1753 he was doing well. One of his new habits was to put 50 shiny guinea pieces in a row so he could admire them. A new friend enquired whether he had a will after a health scare. He was only 30 years old; intimations of mortality visited people early.

Then there was marriage and courtship. This had hitherto been abortive. Hutton had been too poor and perhaps his bar was too high. Now he was better off, the bar was still high, but more appropriate. The patriarch of the local Tilt family of Bromsgrove assured Hutton that 'he was welcome to either of his daughters'. He was now marriage material, but it did not work with the Tilts. He approached one of them 'which I liked best, though she was not the handsomest' but her hesitancy put him off.

The future love of his life was there, in plain view; not only had he known Sally Cock for some time, but they had been truly antagonistic. Their courtship was unusual, possibly non-existent – 'nor did we ever spend one evening together past ten, or that without company.' It was a 'daylight courtship', he reassured.

Hutton clearly believed this was another in an increasing string of correct, successful decisions. Marriage was still all about money, and Sally's minor farming family absolutely strained themselves to raise a dowry of £100. The businessman Hutton knew this was not enough; but his romantic side knew that it did not matter as this would be long and enduring love. He took only what they could give; he did not want to be a 'spunger'.

On 23 June 1755, he woke up with a determination to marry and the conviction that a date in the future was 'a shackle on love'. He and Sally were married by special licence and were together in a love match that lasted for forty-one years. Their daughter Catherine was born four and a half months later; she lived to be 91 and the editor of her father's papers.

Suffering and death did not go away:

> It is not possible to be connected with the world and not taste its bitters; but sometimes they are administered in large draughts, which overcome and cast down the individual.

Sally's uncle, who had introduced them (and required evidence that he was solvent before he gave his consent) became short of breath, and the quack solution was to open a vein 'as wide as a weather cock', which led to a fainting fit and dropsy. Whatever the disease was, it was certainly the cure that killed him.

Family, Friends and Society: William Hutton 1723–1782   13

After her uncle died, Sally noticed a lump in her left breast which they feared was cancer. She was also pregnant, so surgery had to wait until after the child was born. Their son, Thomas, survived but it was a great trauma for Sally. Her afflicted breast festered, broke, and underwent many surgical operations. It recovered but neither 'the flesh nor the milk returned to their pristine state.' Then his father died, but Hutton was, unsurprisingly, a little less concerned:

> After a miserable life, pressed down by affliction, he departed, December 13th, 1758, at the age of sixty-seven. Five feet seven, corpulent, weighing about sixteen stone.

Sally, pregnant again, had life-threatening jaundice. During her pregnancy, William, born in 1758, died. The next day, their baby was born and he was called William as well; it was common to re-use names in this way. Then Thomas contracted smallpox and measles, then Catherine did and Hutton developed jaundice as well. These were killer diseases. In 1762, the Huttons had a stillborn son. Sally wished to go to her parents' home – quickly due to the distress she was in. The physical pain lasted a lifetime, as a reminder of the tragic event:

> We went in a chaise, at sixpence a mile, the first time we either of us rode in one. She ever after complained of a pain in her left side.

Hutton was extremely prosperous in business, but it was up and down. He had mistakenly tried to build a paper mill, lost £250 and, like a good businessman, worked out that he lost another £750, money he would have made elsewhere had he not wasted his time on the mill. The years after 1763 were much better in all aspects:

> I, my dear wife, two dear sons, and one daughter, were in health, and acted to my wish. Trade was successful, we enjoyed our little pleasures, and lived happily. Dress, the tennis-court, and our excursions, came of course.

Sadly, their son William died in 1767, due to the incompetence of the doctor's servant. One of the great myths is that people in the past developed a studied indifference to premature death; their reaction feels very 'modern':

> We were inconsolable at the loss of this lovely child, which was followed by daily tears. I could observe thousands of faces pass by, which carried every mark of serenity; while our inward oppression was beyond bearing. Every article which had been his was prudently kept from my sight; nor durst my dear wife or I ever mention him during more than ten years, though he was not one day out of either of our thoughts.

In 1768, with a satisfaction he failed to hide, Hutton became an Overseer of the Poor; appointed by the same people who persecuted him for poverty nearly twenty years earlier. He claimed to be much loved by the dependent classes. He opposed the Lamp Act, which would have involved knocking down houses in the centre of Birmingham to improve public health. His concern for the poor was qualified, precisely because he had been poor himself but had pulled himself out of it.

Hutton became obsessed with business and buying land – the ultimate route to respectability. By 1769 he had £10,000 and, until his story stops in 1782, he had little but rich people's problems. His problems of affluence sound familiar to the modern ear. Builders would exploit you if they knew more about a project than you; the best way to encourage tradesmen to work hard was always to be present. He discovered that firm friendships could end over property disputes, but that rule did not apply to lawyers as they were never your friend anyway.

He discovered social snobbery as he rose up the ladder. When buying some waste land away from home, he found it was robbed and vandalised. What right had a tradesman to come among them, said the locals, while protesting their innocence He discovered the real but frankly not very interesting problem of being rich in assets but poor in hard cash; so much property and investment in the eighteenth century was financed by debt, which was in turn supported by reputation.

1779 was a bad year; he had been defrauded by a carpenter and a brickmaker. More importantly, his wife started a seventeen-year slow but steady decline in her health; she died of asthma, immobile in a chair, unable to walk or even stand, with William holding her head up. His daughter Catherine had a nervous complaint and suffered for years – mental health challenges are not modern. Hutton himself suffered a catastrophic health emergency that started with a tooth, chipped by a stone in a salad. Two days later, an orange eaten while watching a play infected the hole and caused inflammation of the gums. Then some teeth fell out, an abscess formed in his throat and his body broke out in boils. Life could become death in a blink.

When we leave Hutton in 1782, he was at a high point in his life. He had published his *History of Birmingham* and is regarded today as an antiquary, as well as a writer and entrepreneur. There were still important battles ahead, including being burnt out of his house by rioters in 1791 and being the first person to walk the whole length of Hadrian's Wall; but he won the war for self-respect, respectability and wealth.[3] And didn't he know it?

Chapter 2

A Picture of England from the Road
Karl Moritz 1782

The next Georgian witness is the Prussian intellectual Karl Phillip Moritz, who travelled through England in June and July 1782. He recorded his travels in the form of letters to his friend Friedrich Gedike.[1] Moritz was a convinced Anglophile; he loved English literature and the countryside, and was enormously impressed by London. He arrived on 31 May for his first visit. He was 25 and had only travelled 'in my reveries', as he put it, and through literature. His fluent English had been learnt in Germany; he was not quite as 'foreign' as we might regard a German today. He had lived in Hanover and King George III, as elector of Hanover, was his sovereign.

Despite his desire to visit and his connections, he did not leave his critical faculties at home. The first things he noted were dangers – the perilous sandbanks of Goodwin Sands and the masts of two sunken ships in the distance. It was not going to be an easy journey.

Moritz could not help admiring the country. It was politically free and prosperous with enterprising trade and agriculture, neat houses and villages. He tended to give England the benefit of the doubt, and his comparisons to Germany are normally unfavourable. The Thames was better than the Elbe, and he was pleased by the prospect of Gravesend as it was such a cleverly arranged town. He had not, of course, met the people or encountered the weather yet. He wrote about the joys of Gravesend from his cabin as the rain and wind were appalling. It was 1 June 1782 and the height of summer.

The Thames was choked with ships and trade, so much so that he disembarked at Dartford because the captain could not guarantee how long the rest of the journey would take. He walked to the centre of the town and was already being stared at; this was a watered-down version of what was to come. He also saw poor people living in brick houses, a remarkable improvement on the hovels of his home country's poor peasants, he thought.

In Dartford, Moritz saw his first soldier; in this era, soldiers walked the streets in full uniform. He also witnessed his first boxing match on the street. Yet he was still impressed by everything; the post-chaise that took him from Dartford, the excellent roads that allowed the driver to go dangerously fast, and the large beams that crossed the road at the entry to villages where the inns were.

From Greenwich, he could see a prospect of London. Moritz loved a prospect, and had good things to say about nearly all of the landscapes he encountered. This urban prospect was enveloped in a thick smoke but he continued to be impressed; the number of people wearing spectacles; their robust good health; the lamp-posts lighting the excellent houses, and, of course, the famous buildings. Yes, it was inconvenient to be stopped at toll gates, and the streets of London were gloomy, but he forgave them by saying that the shadows were cast by the magnificent tall buildings. He had not yet worked out that Europe's biggest city was powered and heated by the burning of sea coal. Later, when he sat in his lodging trying to keep safe from influenza, he speculated that the locals wore spectacles because they spent the evenings peering at their coal fire. The coal was better than the coal in Berlin, of course.

Finding his lodging taught him another lesson about the English. Not only did the locals judge people on appearances, but the poor judged their betters as well. As a foreigner whose belongings were still on the ship, he discovered that he would not have found any lodgings without the help of the two companions in the post-chaise acting as character references. Eventually, he rented two large rooms from a tailor's widow, with a lock-up cupboard for his tea, coffee, bread and butter at a reasonable 16 shillings a week. Moritz befriended the widow's son Jacky, a 12-year-old who told Moritz off for singing a song on a Sunday, but they got on well and proposed a visit to the renowned St James's Park. On this occasion, Moritz was not impressed:

> The park is nothing more than a semicircle, formed of an alley of trees, which enclose a large green area in the middle of which is a marshy pond.

It did have cows grazing on it, and you could buy the raw milk on the spot; but it was nothing special. Similarly, the houses of the Royal Family, like St James's Palace, were equally modest. Nothing pleased him more than the amiable mixing of the classes, and he was to do a lot of that himself over the subsequent weeks.

Another disappointment, seen first in London and then repeated in the provinces, was the standard of the food and hospitality. His travelling companions took him to a pub with food; it was uninspiring and expensive and Moritz learnt that tipping was essential, even to achieve a mediocre service. He decided to self-cater and sat in front of his coal fire (remember, it was June) and ate his bread and cheese and pickled salmon from his lock-up cupboard. He seems to have been on half-board in his lodgings, and the food did not improve:

> For an English dinner, to such lodgers as I am, generally consists of a piece of half-boiled, or half-roasted meat; and a few cabbage leaves boiled in plain water; on which they pour a sauce made of flour and butter. This, I assure you, is the usual method of dressing vegetables in England.

He hated the coffee – it was brown water. He did, however, discover toast – simple and economical because English food was primitive, and he was poor. On his later travels, he discovered cheese on toast, which he regarded as abominable.

His first task was to bribe the customs officials. Import regulations were excessively complicated. Simplification was only five years away, but when Moritz arrived there was no such thing as tariff-free trade. His trunk should have been sent to the Customs House and money paid; instead, he offered a *doucer* to the officer who had come aboard his ship. He was surprised and disappointed to have to repeat the bribe twice more, but the calculations still held up; it was cheaper than doing things properly.

Foreign exchange was the next practical task. In the absence of central banks and fixed exchange rates, you had to exchange foreign coins of known and agreed value for sterling. Moritz was carrying Friedrich D'ors – gold coins – but eventually relied on a credit note from a German friend to avoid poor exchange rates. He had already exchanged some Dutch dollars and was aggrieved that he had only received 8 shillings.

There was a lot to like in London after the tiresome bureaucratic tasks were completed. He liked the pavements and the politeness; people stepped aside for ladies or those to whom you wished to show respect; men walked on the outside. London was large and impersonal, so when a funeral procession struggled its way through the street, nobody noticed or cared, but he liked two more things; that people of all classes mixed together, and even the poor were relatively clean.

Moritz liked the shops in The Strand and their colourful signs but he worried that the most common was 'dealer in foreign spirituous liquors'. The English were reckless with alcohol. It was only two years since the Gordon riots of 1780 where more people were found dead near brandy barrels than were killed by soldiers. He also lamented the amount of brandy and gin consumed as part of normal life; at this point, he did not know how much he would be reliant on alcohol to make friends and influence people.

Coach transport was cheaper and better than Berlin, but Moritz walked everywhere, even at night. The streets were brightly illuminated, so much so that he told a story about an unnamed German prince 'who came to London for the first time, once, they say, actually took it, and seriously believed it to have been particularly ordered on account of his arrival.' This was German princely pomposity compared with English progress.

Moritz spent an evening at Vauxhall Gardens, the premier summer centre of festivity and entertainment. He crossed the river, paid his shilling at the entrance, and was entranced. It was a pleasing mix of society, but it was rough and rowdy. There were also pickpockets and prostitutes He had found company with some German gentlemen but they were 'importuned by women of great boldness who asked for wine for themselves and their followers in such a way as the gentlemen found hard to refuse.'

He liked the woods and the walks, while some of the locals would have liked the areas for romance and other activities. He appreciated the socialising and the chance to chat in German. He liked the music and the singing, and admired the statues of Shakespeare, Milton and Dryden, being particularly pleased with the statute of Handel as an example of a German who could be welcomed in England. He felt that all this showed a connection between the ordinary people and their most distinguished intellectual figures.

Moritz loved his Milton; he would have had his slim volume of poetry in his pocket in the Vauxhall Gardens and he was to meet humble people on the road who knew their great poets and authors. His landlady also knew her Milton. Like other subjects, all the classes were able to have a view: 'there is hardly any argument or dispute in conversation, in the higher ranks, about which the lower cannot also converse or give their opinion.' Cheap books and circulating libraries were part of democracy. He bought a copy of the *Vicar of Wakefield* for a bargain sixpence; the kind of money that you would need to bribe a waiter to bring your boiled or roasted supper.

Moritz then visited the competition to Vauxhall, the Ranelagh. He liked it very much for the same reasons. At first, the much higher price and the cheek of the prostitutes who grabbed his arm and asked him if he was on his own shocked him, but he noted that it was more select, food was included in the inflated price and he was told that even the modest citizens such as his landlady saved up and came to the Ranelagh once a year, which is what he wanted to hear.

He then went to the Strangers' Gallery of the House of Commons, his second attempt to gain entry; on the first day, the usher on the door said that he needed a 'personal recommendation'. He took this at face value, and walked away with the words 'bottle of wine' ringing in his ears. The price of a bottle of wine was the sweetener, bribe or motivation that allowed you in. The following day, he gained admittance for 2 shillings. He described his experience:

> thus I now, for the first time, saw the whole of the British nation assembled in its representatives, in rather a mean-looking building, that not a little resembles a chapel.

It *was* a chapel; this was not the Palace of Westminster that we see today, but the old Commons meeting place in St Stephen's. It was cramped, Moritz noted. There was no dress code; some wore overcoats and boots, others ate nuts or peeled oranges, 'or whatever else is in season'. As well as being informal, it was disordered. Members of Parliament stood up and took off their hats if they wished to speak, and directed themselves to the speaker. If speakers were boring or indistinct, members would chat among themselves or shout across the room. It sometimes sank to low farce:

A Picture of England from the Road: Karl Moritz 1782

It is quite laughable to see, as one sometimes does, one member speaking, and another accompanying the speech with his action.

Moritz was amazed by the chaotic and inefficient voting system:

Those who are for the question are to say aye, and those who are against it no. You then hear a confused cry of 'aye' and 'no' but at length the Speaker says, "I think there are more ayes than noes, or more noes than ayes. The ayes have it; or the noes have it," as the case may be.

When inspiring people were speaking, MPs shouted, 'Hear him! Hear him!' This is the derivation of 'hear! hear!' that is heard today, but originally it was an order to those who were inattentive. Moritz listened to a two-hour speech by the Whig politician Charles James Fox and this was his reaction:

I have since been almost every day at the parliament house, and prefer the entertainment I there meet with to most other amusements.

It was gloomy, cramped, chaotic, rude and often tedious and farcical; Moritz loved it, was deeply impressed and thought that this experience alone was worth the journey to London. As far as he was concerned, this *was* democracy; this was the political nation debating without fear and favour in the most egalitarian system in the world. We may not think so today. The Commons were elected by just over 200,000 people, no more than 6 per cent of the adult male population; but Moritz was not making a comparison with today, but with his own country of Prussia where the electorate was one person; Frederick the Great.

By 17 June, he had grown tired of London. He had seen what he wanted, was sick of the smog and wished to breathe sweeter air. He had done so in the villages of Paddington and Highgate. Previously, he had boasted of walking the streets at night; now he noted with concern the amount of crime. There were other disappointments; the schools were clearly second-rate, despite their grand names; the theatre was expensive and noisy, and being June, Covent Garden and Drury Lane were closed. His own visit to the theatre was traumatic. He was in the pit because he was poor, he sat on his bench but somebody took it, and he was hit by flying orange peel. The crowd was rowdy, but democratic; they also flung fruit at their betters.

He left London on 21 June; 'before you well know that you are out of London you are already in Kensington and Hammersmith.' Unlike the time of Elizabeth Chivers, footpads and highwayman were still feared, but sunset was past 8 o'clock on this longest day, which would have been a reassurance. He liked the English stagecoach, at this point of his travels at least, and Moritz repeated one of the myths of the time – that the highwayman was a romantic, gentle figure who looked after ladies and took their money with regret and, unlike the plebeian footpad, did not murder their victims.

The immediate danger to the passengers was the lack of regulation; this was not the era of health and safety. There were six people on the top of the coach, severely overcrowding it. Moritz was surprised that it was legal; it would remain so for another six years and then the new law would be ignored.

A Jew boarded the stagecoach at Kensington. Georgian anti-Semitism was real, but of the relatively mild variety. There was no question of him being refused a place, but when he himself refused to be yet another person on the outside, the other passengers were outraged; why this level of entitlement when he was nothing more than a Jew? Who did he think he was?

After a day's travelling, Moritz arrived in Richmond where another shilling was demanded by the driver. This doubled the fare, but it was still better value than Berlin. Richmond both cheered him up and upset him. He now felt 'chagrin and sorrow for the days and hours I had wasted in London.' The capital was a dungeon compared to this paradise. The houses were not blackened by smoke, and people were just sitting out in the street, chatting and doing nothing. Besides, some of his favourite English poets came from Richmond. He devoted pages to the landscape that inspired the famous Alexander Pope and the now obscure James Thompson.

Moritz was so entranced by the scenery that the name of his inn went right out of his head. When he found it, the plan was to go to bed early and get up to enjoy another morning in Elysium. The reality of the English inn spoilt his plans, for the first, but not the last time. He was kept awake by the landlady talking loudly to her servants. He wanted to rise at 3.00 am; sunrise was 3.40 am and he was looking forward to another day of sighing and sightseeing. But the servants opened the locked doors at 6.00 am ('the great inconveniences they sustain in England by their bad custom of rising so late') and the fact that it poured down with rain and he could not see anything at all in an overcast sky. The erratic summer weather had spoilt his prospects, in both senses of the word.

His only companion was a staff – a large stick. He had planned to walk most of the way to Windsor. It didn't go down well. His landlord at Richmond was amazed at his decision. As he planned his journey, he was reconsidering; 'A traveller on foot in this country seems to be considered as a sort of wild man or out-of-the way being, who is stared at, pitied, suspected, and shunned by everybody that meets him.' On his journey, he asked if the road was correct for Oxford; he was told it was, but that he would need a carriage; the helpful stranger looked at him significantly and shook his head.

It was summer and the road was dusty; dust is a road problem that the modern age has forgotten about. Moritz sat in the shade of a hedge and read his pocket Milton. People passing on transport made strange gestures and shook their heads, so much so that he felt the need to hide. He was offered lifts 'on top' by coach drivers who would 'shoulder' his fare (put it straight in their pockets); women said 'Good God!' when he passed; poor farmers on shabby horses (literally) looked down on him. Only the desperate walked at 4 miles an hour, but being demonstrably poor did not reduce the prices he paid at the inn; 'for a little wine and water, I was obliged to pay sixpence.' His nationality was noted, but it was no particular concern or surprise and was less foreign to most observers than his mode of transport. He made it to Windsor by noon, and in the castle the whole Royal Family would have been speaking his native language, not English.

Moritz loved these long, difficult walks. They represented the English freedom to go about your business. It was, once again, better than Germany – no walls, no gates, no sentries, no garrisons. 'No stern examiner comes here to search and inspect us or our baggage; no imperious guard here demands a sight of our passports.' He rejoiced at his right to walk the streets in freedom dressed as a tramp. The students of Eton College stared at him impudently; not because he was German or on foot, but because he could be plausibly seen as a plebeian, and they treated all members of that class with the same disdain.

The servants at the local inn also looked down on him – 'no doubt this was the first time this pert, bepowdered puppy had ever been called on to wait on a poor devil who entered their place on foot' – but they still charged him an extortionate 2 shillings for dinner and coffee. When he asked for something better than a prison cell for a room, he was told that there might be something more suitable for his sort in Slough. Instead, he went out to view the prospects of Windsor, which he was beginning to like more than the people.

Guides were available in Georgian tourist hotspots but Moritz was not impressed. They were 'venal praters, who ten times a day, parrot-wise, repeat over the same dull lesson they have got by heart.' He did fall for it at Windsor where a local charged him a shilling for views of St George's Chapel, and he regretted it afterwards. He saw the king for nothing, passing in a very plain, two-wheeled open carriage; locals raised their hats and both parties got on with their day. This was the type of relationship between ruler and ruled that he approved of.

Moritz found a new inn where the landlord was more welcoming but the inverted snobbery came from the servers – this happened again and again on his tour. He was given a reasonable room and a gentle hint to adjust his dress; he was advised to go down to the Thames for a cold wash, watching the naked bathing on what had been a very hot day. Then a long solitary walk cheered him up, but the reverie was broken when he went back to the inn and the staff were rude to him again. It seemed that he had not tipped enough; Moritz had not learnt that tipping came before good service and not after it. The angry maid had 'accidentally' given his room to somebody else and now the inn was full, apart from a room with two beds, which would mean sleeping in the same room as a stranger.

He retired early, but he was above the tap room where the low people were drinking and singing songs as crude as those in Germany; the bed next to him was empty, and he feared that the space belonged to one of the vulgar party. He was correct; eventually, the stranger stumbled in drunk, just about managed to find the empty bed and fell into it fully clothed.

When the morning came, Moritz again opted for the English countryside rather than its people, but his view of English freedom is dented by the 'Take Care!' signs in the fields. There were steel traps and

A Picture of England from the Road: Karl Moritz 1782   25

spring guns there to deter and punish poachers. English freedom did not extend to free rabbits for the poor without the danger of death or mutilation, and Moritz became rightfully afraid.

The staff at the inn still hated him and told him that he could not stay there any longer. He saw two Germans in the coffee house. He knew that they were from Hanover, subjects of George III, but he did not explain how he knew. He did know that they would not talk to a pedestrian.

His humiliation continued. As he left, the waiter obstructed the stairs with his hand out and asked him to 'remember the waiter sir.' This was the man who had reluctantly served him an old chicken for supper and charged him 6 shillings. Moritz gave him three-halfpence, about a third of what would be expected (guidebooks advised people to carry lots of sixpences so that you would never have to give anybody a shilling) and he was loudly cursed for it; his persistent chambermaid got nothing, and he left Windsor to the sound of loud abuse.

It got worse; when he walked through Maidenhead, he was robbed. A man with huge hands and a stick so large that it was clearly not for walking came up to him and asked for a halfpenny. Moritz had not eaten all day, but he had given away all his small coins to annoy the waiter, so he asked to be forgiven as he had nothing smaller than a shilling. The man waved his huge brawny fists about and Moritz gave him the shilling. 'Whether this was a footpad or not, I will not pretend to say, but he had every appearance of it.'

Moritz marvelled at the woods, fields and hills, regularly consulting his English guidebook, but the hospitality was still horrible. He sought out the most modest inn he could find but they would not have him. He stayed in Nettlebed and was placed in the kitchen with the lowest of the low: militia soldiers 'dancing, singing, and making merry.' He thought himself in a novel by Henry Fielding 'which certainly give one, on the whole, a very accurate idea of English manners.' He also noted that, despite being poor, they were the English poor and had lots of food: 'sugar-loaves, black-puddings, hams, sausages, flitches of bacon' but, being English, they only boiled and roasted it.

While he was there, he encountered guests getting much better treatment. They had entered the inn in a hurry, ordered a few beers and then left; everybody stopped what they were doing and watched at a respectful distance. The only difference was that they had arrived by post-chaise; this was all that the lower orders knew about them, but it was sufficient.

Moritz's room had a decent bed and carpet for a change. He put on new linen for the Sabbath and, because the landlord had been listening to the quality of his conversation, he was upgraded from 'master' to 'sir' and from kitchen to parlour. He attended his first service at Nettlebed Church, borrowing his landlord's prayer book. Moritz gave the details of the service, comparing and contrasting with Germany, but mostly praising. He liked the centrepiece for the Ten Commandments, the local musicians and the fine dress of the local farmers.

The clothes were fine, but their manners were coarse. On his way to Dorchester,[2] he walked, read his Milton and saw a lovely hill with an exciting prospect of a prospect. He was seen by people in a house as he climbed up, and again when he climbed down as there was nothing to see. They were laughing at him. Dorchester and later Nuneham were beautiful but the welcome was cold. He could get neither bread nor a bench to sleep on, even at full inn prices. This was the nadir of his journey, but improvement and some excitement was around the corner.

It was a warm June night so Moritz decided to sleep under a tree; he heard somebody follow him in the dark. 'At first I was alarmed, but my fears were soon dispelled by his calling after me, and asking if I would accept of company.' It is hard to imagine today that this added information would make you less alarmed, but if murder and/or robbery were the aim, they could have been achieved without needing to speak at all.

They walked, and Moritz told him that he was poor, in case robbery was on his new friend's mind. He need not have worried. His acquaintance was a curate who had delivered a sermon in Dorchester and was returning to Oxford. Now he was able to drop the persona as a reluctant pedestrian because of poverty, and become better acquainted with men and manners. They spoke in Latin and his new friend condemned the religious views of the Unitarian Dr Joseph Priestly. Moritz did not disagree and offered his admiration for the Church of England and its clergy. This seemed to gain a good opinion; flattery worked in the parlour of a pub, and it did so here. Moritz probably thought he had met his soulmate… but he hadn't.

The pair arrived in Oxford High Street. It was too dark to discover this beautiful street, said Maud, his new friend, offering up the opportunity of them meeting again. Maud readied himself to leave; Moritz performatively started to look for a stone bench to sleep on. Instead, they both ended up in a public house, the Mitre, full of clergymen, at midnight. The serious-minded Moritz paraphrased his welcome without realising that it was meant to be light-hearted:

> My travelling companion introduced me to them, as a German clergyman, whom he could not sufficiently praise for my correct pronunciation of the Latin, my orthodoxy, and my good walking.

Moritz spent the morning drinking and chatting with these apparently very respectable men and comparing the amount of student violence in their respective universities. The talk was getting louder and more inebriated, and no subject was out of bounds. There was a row about whether God liked wine, solved by throwing a Bible amongst jugs of beer – 'Waiter! Fetch a Bible!' Somebody found Judges, Chapter 9, Verse 23; 'Should I leave my wine, which cheereth God and man?' Yet he was still surprised when his new friend Maud greeted the new dawn with a blasphemy; 'D-n me, I must read prayers this morning at All-Souls!'

Moritz was now drunk; strong English ale stupefied him but he wanted people's approbation more, so kept on drinking. The tip debacle at Windsor still rankled, so he overcompensated. He told the waiter 'that he must not think, because I came on foot, that therefore I should give him less than others gave…it was probably not a little owing to this assurance that I had so much attention shown to me.' He found a room easily because he had spent four hours drinking with the clergymen (and tipped extensively) so was now 'respectable'.

He promised to meet Maud the next morning but he woke with an almighty hangover and could not meet his new friend for a trip around the town. He decided to get his linen cleaned. He knew by now that the English judged by appearances because he had heard two women judge him already:

> Look at the gentleman there! a fine gentleman, indeed, who cannot afford even a clean shirt!

He enjoyed the hospitality of his new acquaintances, but they cheerfully told him that he would not have seen the inside of their house if not for the introduction of the drunken cleric who accosted him under the tree. He came to a reluctant criticism – 'a poor peripatetic is hardly allowed even the humble merit of being honest.'

When he eventually got the tourist visit from Maud of Corpus Christi, Hutton's attitude had cooled a little since their midnight walk.

> Mr Maud also showed me, over the altar here, a fine painting of Anton Raphael Mengs, at the sight of which he showed far more sensibility than I thought him possessed of.

Maud also chortled about earning 6 guineas per sermon as a substitute lecturer; Moritz seemed to think that the Church of England was a little superficial and secular-minded, and the praise was faint [author's italics]: 'Mr Maud seemed *upon the whole* to be a most worthy and philanthropic man.'

Oxford did not impress him much. Despite a lingering alcohol-induced headache, he climbed a hill for a prospect of the city, but found it over-Gothic and grimy and the students just a slightly older and more sober version of the ones he saw at Eton.

He left Oxford by the public stagecoach and noticed the class differences. On the outside, in the cheap seats, were soldiers and their wives. All the women wore hats, and the level of fineness was an indicator of class in the same way as where people sat, but he noted that all women were interested in fashion. It was all more ambitious and egalitarian than he was used to. There was a class system, but it was fluid and therefore democratic.

He *still* had his Oxford headache. Somebody talked to him but he did not reply at first – a great British tradition. He was perplexed by 'how do you do.' He learnt that the only acceptable answer was 'pretty well, I thank you; how do you do?' When he thawed out, he asked a fellow passenger why the liberal Englishman, capable of seeing many points of view, would not walk, and was told that 'we are too rich, too lazy, and too proud.'

In the Midlands, Shakespeare replaced Milton. Moritz was a little weak-kneed and rhapsodic when he reached Stratford-on-Avon. He visited the Bard's house, which seemed to be a rustic operation run by two old people who did little more than let people in. He chipped a bit of the poet's chair as a souvenir, and then lost it; and these were the people who were actually interested in the past. The final stop was Birmingham – 'Brummidgeham' as the common people called it' and he learnt that his contact, Mr Fothergill, had died eight days earlier, so he decided to start walking again.

Moritz was told at Oxford that the further north you went, the friendlier the people were – a view that exists today. Burton-on-Trent proved this to be wrong. It looked grand, a little like London, and it was then (as now) famous for its beer. The locals may or may not have been friendlier to each other, but they were obnoxiously insular when it came to strangers. They were rustic and rude and pointed at him from their houses as he ran the gauntlet through their streets. He did not understand; here he was, walking through England out of love and respect, and people were hissing at him. He did not bother to enquire at the inn; he started on the road to Derby although he was never going to make it without being exhausted. He stopped at a toll house on the road, hoping to stay with the turnpike-keeper.

Instead, he met a farmer on a horse who offered to take him to the nearest inn, and he accepted. Moritz, and people at the time, did not seem to believe in 'stranger danger', although if the farmer wanted to kill or rob the tired and lonely vicar on a dark empty road, he did not have to give him a lift first. When Richard Warner, our other pedestrian (Chapter Seven), turned up at a North Wales cottage seeking directions, the owners lent him their 12-year-old daughter as a guide. This was not the first or last time Moritz or Warner came upon a rough and rustic person who offered to guide them up a mountain, through a ruin or over a river. They almost always said yes.

Moritz's next inn, The Bear, was disappointing at first but then he remembered the trick of drinking the landlord's health, chatting with him and establishing himself as a gentleman, thus earning a separate table and the appellation of 'sir'. Despite having already had a dozen horrible experiences in pubs, he claimed to have learnt this trick from Goldsmith's *Vicar of Wakefield*; turning 'vicarious experience' into less of a figure of speech.

They talked about the relative merits of George II and George III; the landlord favoured the latter, and it was an example of how freely, in both senses of the word, the English could talk about politics, a fact that pleased our liberty-loving vicar. It was a reminder than Britain was more closely linked with German-speaking Europe than it is today. Later in Duffield, where he did not quite reach the gentleman level and was placed in a poor parlour with the cold meat cuts, he saw pictures of the King of Prussia. Later in his journey, he noted that inn walls often had motivational slogans like 'make no comparisons'.

The bill, as random as ever, was very good value for a change, and like John Byng in Chapter Four, Moritz realised that a good two-way egalitarian chat with the landlord could push down the final bill. He moved on to Derby, which did not impress him, but at least the children were pleasant and the grown-ups did not stare at him.

The next inn, before Matlock, broke his recent string of good luck. His Goldsmithian tactic of flattering the landlord with gentry-level chat and drinking to his health was thwarted by his inability to distinguish the landlord from a group of rustic farmers. Moritz became so nervous that he forgot to salute anybody and was humiliated by the landlord who, despite not being recognisable himself, could recognise a foreigner who was too proud. The whole evening was uncomfortable. He sat, by hostile invitation, in a corner to be ignored. He was becoming homesick (although not a word that was in use at the time); he was a long way from home that night.

For only the second time on his journey, he met some Englishmen who offered to walk with him. This was not Mr Maud, walking to the pub in Oxford, but two artisans who started to speak of Homer, Horace and Virgil. This was democracy in action; the middling sort was able to hold the same conversations as the affluent because books were cheap in England. One of them, a saddler, who was working away from home and tramping, told of his family life:

> He never quarrelled with his wife, nor had ever once threatened her with his fist, much less, ever lifted it against her. For his own sake, he said, he never called her names, nor gave her the lie.

If the fact that you never hit your wife was a conversational gambit that made you better than most tells you a lot about the Georgian era. During this conversation, Moritz also reminded himself that 'liar' was fighting talk amongst English. He had used the word in London as a joke, and found himself in serious trouble with his lodging family.

In the next night's inn, he discovered toasted cheese, which was regarded as good eating. Like many travellers who fundamentally liked their host country, both small and big things delighted him. The morning after, he joined the throng to be shaved for a penny (despite it being a Sunday). When people took him for a gentleman, he believed that it was his one-guinea London hat that had impressed them; 'I considered this as a proof that pomp and finery had not yet become general thus far from London.'

Moritz continued to be a critical and reflective friend of a country he loved. He did not always find the behaviour of English people to his taste, but he was able to produce an insightful picture of the country, its people and the wide variation in its topography and traditions, sometimes with disappointment, occasionally with anger, but mostly with affection.

Chapter 3

Man of Feeling
William Windham 1784–1810

On a warm July evening in 1809, William Windham MP (1750–1810), was walking along Conduit Street when he saw a fire that was about to engulf the house of his friend, Lord Frederick North. North was travelling in the Mediterranean and his library was about to go up in flames. Windham did not hesitate. This was not like him; he normally felt the need to reflect deeply, painfully and continually on events, large and small, but this was different. Books and learning mattered *a lot*. He acted without thought of the consequence, and the consequence was his own death.

He used his famous face to recruit three volunteers to help him empty the library of its treasures. It took four hours and he did not stop until the flames lapped around him. He fell and hurt his hip, but persevered. Later the next year, the hip developed a tumour and after taking seven medical opinions, Windham opted for an operation. This procrastination was more his style.

The operation went well, but subsequent complications fatally weakened him. He was administered the sacraments and modified his will. His wife was in the country, and he did not inform her of his deteriorating health, which was seen at the time as the height of sensibility and good manners in not burdening a woman with bad news. The king had sent his own surgeon Henry Halford and his best wishes to 'a real patriot and a truly honest man'.

A rumour went round that his reason for the rescue was more embarrassment than bravery. His friend and hagiographer Edward Malone, explained:

An idle story has been propagated that the Hon Frederick North... left his books and manuscripts to the care of Mr Windham and had requested him to remove them to his own house; that he had neglected this charge and thence had the stronger inducement to exert himself to save them.

The story cut through because it fitted with Windham's reputation as a procrastinator.

He was mourned extravagantly in the Commons, a little less so in the newspapers, where the word that often came to editors' minds was 'eccentric'.[1] MPs were more interested in his integrity, generosity and determination. Earl Grey compared him in importance to Fox and Pitt, which has not been the verdict of history.

Windham is now obscure and only remembered because of his agonised diary showing him to be a man of great intellect, great feeling, constant misery, introspection and self-doubt. His diary is unique as it lists his faults, weaknesses and peccadilloes, regularly and in great detail, while most diaries – of this or any age – are just designed to agree with the writer.

His diary runs from 1784 to 1810.[2] At first glance it depicts an enviable life. He had a base in London and a country house in Norfolk, and split his time between the two. He had fashionable friends; he drank and chatted with Charles James Fox, Richard Sheridan and Joshua Reynolds. He was on friendly terms with both the famous actress Sarah Siddons (he visited her in her dressing room) and the Bishop of Exeter (they chatted about theology).

Windham had mainly sporting hobbies – he liked skating, rowing, boxing and ballooning, and spent his evenings at fashionable parties, theatre and routs. He was never at home; he slept at Brookes Club for the company and the convenience. On the first page of his diary, he had already attended the opening of Parliament and visited his friend Samuel Johnson.

He was a mathematician of note, a linguist, a book collector, a great polymath and had a voracious appetite for knowledge of all kinds. He was a rich, intelligent, popular man, a member of the landed gentry. It was the best life that could be had in late Georgian England. Externally, everything was perfect, but internally his mind was a seething cauldron of anxiety; having nobody in his life to criticise him, he took up the role himself. Although he burnt the candle at both ends, he hated himself for wasting time:

7th February 1784; Did not rise till past nine from that time till eleven did little more than indulge in idle reveries about balloon. About twelve went out called on Mrs Siddons.

His life was blighted by the belief that time was passing, and he was wasting it:

From the commencement of this account, January 1 to the present day February 8, a space of five weeks and four days it appears that excepting one morning viz 2nd, and that for about an hour not an attempt made to resume mathematics, no Latin written, little read, no Greek even looked into, no translation, no progress made in any author nothing but a little odd information collected of history physiology and biography.

Windham's chronophobia meant that he could not be happy unless he was busy and productive, and he set himself standards so high that he was bound to be unhappy. Later in the month, he berated himself for reading something in Latin that could have been achieved quicker and as profitably in English, allowing himself more time to do mathematics. His idea of a pleasant Sunday in June 1784 was church, writing letters and 'working on a logarithm or two.' Writing letters was more than an intellectual exercise for him. He would occasionally write at length to somebody he knew he would meet very soon. Working on logarithms was not a matter of looking them up in a book or a slide rule. It was a long mathematical calculation, something he enjoyed.

All his intelligence did not lead to much independence of mind or consistency. People noticed at the time, and later. In 1839, Lord Brougham looked back on his life:

he was too often the dupe of his own ingenuity; which made him doubt and balance... His nature... was to be a follower, if not a worshipper, rather than an original thinker or actor... Accordingly, first Johnson in private and afterwards Burke on political matters were the deities whom he adored.[3]

It was true; Samuel Johnson and Edmund Burke were his mentors. We may even owe the existence of the diary to the advice that Samuel

Johnson gave to all his friends – to record their state of mind, and make judgements later.

Windham's personal comments on people he knew were few but, in February 1784, he was counting the days since he had seen Johnson; it was nineteen, and too many. The first year of the diary was the last year of Johnson's life; Windham notes Johnson's thoughts on every subject and notes the hour of his death in his diary.

From his friend Burke, he developed his political opinions and seemed unable to keep a consistent course. Windham's nickname in politics was 'weathercock Windham'. Artist Joseph Farington (Chapter Five) noticed that he was also called the 'Apostate' and the reason was the same – he started off as a Whig, but served in the governments of the Tory William Pitt, and became one of the fiercest critics of Napoleon after initially welcoming the events of 1789. This is what the obituary writers meant when they said he was 'eccentric'.

Windham was a politician, our only Georgian witness who served in the British cabinet. We can guess that most of the conversation on his nights out was not political – 'Conversation more pleasant than usual till at last we got to politics which I have enough of elsewhere.'

His diary reads like a whirl of activity, but it is really an internal dialogue. It is an act of self-discipline and control. With the exception of one long and famous description of Johnson, Windham never tells us anything about the conversations he had. On the occasions he does, it does not sound promising; one evening concerned an argument with his half-brother George Lukin about the bankruptcy laws. He did not do small talk either; it was a waste of effort and people noticed, especially women, and he sometimes found himself staying longer at social events because he had upset them with his 'asperity'.

Windham's fear of wasting time stemmed from an undiagnosed illness in 1780. It was some form of fever from which he never fully recovered, which he mentions when it flared up. After a six-week tour of Scotland and Northern England with his friend Burke in 1785, he reminds himself of this:

> I should do well to recollect how ill I was or how much at least my illness such as it was rendered me incapable of employment that I may learn to improve with diligence the advantages of health and neglect no reasonable means by which those advantages may be preserved.

Sleep was the ultimate in wasted time, so he was preoccupied with the time he got out of bed. When he wrote in his diary that he did not rise until 9, this was a confession not a boast; his aim, he said, was to get up in the morning the very first time he woke up.

Sleep annoyed him; not sleeping annoyed him. On one evening in June 1786, he went to the Duke of Bolton's and Lady Howe's, and did not come home till near 4; 'the light let in at Lady Howe's windows and the sight of Hyde Park destroyed all the inebriation of a midnight amusement'. Time had been wasted again.

One constant theme is that he could not do his mathematics and reading when in London. His main dilemma – one that perhaps garners little sympathy today – was that he enjoyed both the company of celebrities *and* intense intellectual activity on his own. People at the time thought he was good at both and hailed him as a polymath; he thought the opposite, as he confided to his diary in 1790:

> I am now a little of two characters and good in neither: a politician among scholars and a scholar among politicians.

Windham did much of his reading and studying on transport; he was driven to and from his home at Felbrigg Hall near Cromer, Norfolk in a private chaise, and he tried not to look out of the window, sleep or have idle thoughts:

> Returned to Norwich. My thoughts on the drive were employed in settling the question to the pressure of fluids.

On 1 March 1784, he travelled home from London, which took two nights. He did a lot of very laborious travelling on the notoriously bad roads of Norfolk. On some occasions, progress was so slow that Windham could get out, stretch his legs and still be in sight of his vehicle. At his country seat, he could carry out the mathematical, scientific and literary work that he could not do in London, although he would often chastise himself for thinking too fondly about the place and the surroundings. He produced elaborate plans to stop wasting his time, and then despaired that he had spent valuable time doing this and wasted more time not applying it.

Windham was fascinated by balloons and ballooning. He would tell himself off for dreaming about balloons, or seeking out balloon news and gossip from his friends, or putting down a classical or theological text to dream about balloons. Both idleness and study led him to balloons. In a non-rational moment, for which he hated himself, he dreamt of them when he was reading the poetry of the second-century Greek poet Oppian's poem *Halieutica* (in the original Greek, of course) This was a philosophical work mediated through the lives of fish, but it still reminded him of balloons.

On 19 September 1784, Windham was one of about 150,000 who witnessed Vincent Lunardi make the first free flight in a hydrogen balloon accompanied by his companions, a dog, a cat and a pigeon (which, unlike humans, could be jettisoned if the flight went wrong, especially the pigeon) and drifted for 24 miles before landing safely in Hertfordshire. Windham's comment was short, and the date incorrect:

15th Lunardi ascended Dined at Sir Joshua Reynolds's with Burke, Lord Inchiquin Dr Burney etc.

On 5 May 1785, he went up in a balloon himself. He allowed himself some brief joy – 'much satisfied with myself' – but then produced a tightly argued paragraph of wrist-slapping self-questioning. Why had he been so fearful? Why had he underestimated how easily fear could be overcome? What had he missed in his life because of this?

It was his interest in balloons that led him to realise that he did not know why the Tropics of Capricorn and Cancer were so named. He was ashamed of himself. This knowledge was so easily got that it was an absolute disgrace he did not know it. The bar was always too high, no matter how great he was at jumping.

His other interest was boxing, which may seem strange for a sensitive man of letters, but for him it was an art form that built character. He was 'Fighting William', removed from Eton College for doing it to excess, which, given Eton's reputation, must have been pretty violent conduct. Windham could watch a bloody confrontation by the lower orders and then have dinner with William Wilberforce and the Duke of Devonshire. He would leave the House of Commons early in order to see a boxing match (or, indeed, to row, swim or hunt or any form of gambling on sports).

Despite being a man of feeling, the era of sensitivity about cruelty passed him by. In 1788, at Brighton, a boxing match led to the death of one of the fighters and the Prince of Wales declared that he would attend no more; Windham wrote to the *Morning Post* defending it.

In June 1788, he travelled down to the small Surrey village of Croydon to watch three boxing matches; the second was the best because it was evenly matched, showed nobility and skill and, in the end, Watson the young butcher from Bristol beat 'the Jew' Crabbe. Jews were always identified in much eighteenth-century writing, even when there was no context that made it necessary. In June 1795, he got wind of a semi-legal fight; he wanted to go with his friend Elliot but when he showed no interest, Windham lost his own motivation. He did go, tortured himself unnecessarily that he would miss it, or that his information would be wrong. He catastrophised endlessly about life. Simple joy was beyond him.

He was prone to sudden and unexplained 'strong paroxysm of mental malady' and he monitored this in his diary. In some of the most glittering company, he pretended – 'talked, rather than felt, gaily.' One phrase that he used regularly was 'the feel'. It described a state of mind that could last for hours and needed to be avoided because it was so debilitating. It was sometimes phrased as 'more of a feel than of late' and similarly 'more of a feel than I am acquainted with.'

Windham was anxious when he could not make his mind up, or felt unable to perform any task. To him, all failure was caused by lack of preparation and hard work. If he anticipated enjoyment, but it was not quite as good as anticipated, this would stress him – 'feeling enjoyment, but not as much as I thought.' The 'feel' hit him when his relative George Lukin brought his own son to their shared breakfast and spent time with him, rather than in conversation. He thought it was folly on Lukin's part; the child was 'stuffed full of chocolate at the expense of our conversation.' At times he sounded like a child himself.

He agonised about marginal decisions, especially in social situations – 'I might have done better by staying, and I might not.' If an event that he had been reluctant to attend turned out to be excellent, he would berate himself. If he did something enjoyable for the first time, he would criticise himself for not doing it earlier. He was haunted by the Latin translations not completed or the mathematics not studied.

When riding to Oxford in July 1786, his horse threw him off. He blamed himself. Did he need to fall, or did he want to? How afraid was he? If he had been boxing, would this amount of fear have made him give in so quickly? There then followed 150 words of analysis, and the final conclusion – 'it destroyed the pleasure of arriving at Oxford.'

The process of seeking happiness was self-defeating. In the spring of 1789, in a particularly good mood, having got up two days successively at 7.00 am, he rode his horse around Cromer and visited his friend Greville Wyndham. His spirits were so good that he started to sing, fluently in Italian, one of his languages. His singing voice was terrible and, in any case, it was a distraction. He tried again and was a bit better, and resolved not to use singing to keep up his spirits but to practise his voice only.

What about his personal life? Well, there was little agonising about that because it was hardly mentioned. During the busy summer of 1790, he did find time to say this:

> I felt that strong sense of the unhappiness of my own celibacy – that lively conception of pleasure I had lost – that gloomy apprehension of the conviction which I should feel of this hereafter, clouding all my prospects, relaxing all my motives and in an especial manner destroying all enjoyment that I might ever [have].

He was 40, unmarried and had no heirs. This is what he meant by 'celibate'. This was another imagining that was ruining his life. He was a rational man, and said this:

> It is indeed sufficiently plain that wisdom must condemn the thinking on uneasiness which thinking cannot mend.

As ever, he did not take his own advice. Later, he did marry; his diary entry of 10 July 1798 records that he got up between 6 and 7, wrote letters, then went to Binfield and was married to Cecilia Forest. He said he hoped he would remember it forever; a rational wish rather than an emotion. Present at the wedding was Cecilia's brother-in-law John Byng, who was married to her sister Bridget. Windham had already been friends with the whole Byng family for quite a time. In January 1785, he broke off an evening with Plato to visit Mrs Byng and his future wife. He 'found the satisfactoriness of my visit a sufficient compensation for my absence from home.' They saw *Othello* together (two days earlier, he had seen *Macbeth*).

There was no honeymoon. By this point, he was in the government as the Secretary of War and he spent the next week involved in naval procurement in the Red Sea and the Mediterranean. When the happy couple got round to entertaining, Cecy singed her feathers and there was 'slight ill humour'. There were to be no children and no more entries about her in the diary. He had bigger things to do. He had a reputation as a womaniser, and some commentators suggest a too close relationship with Bridget Byng; this was, of course, not in his diary.

This was an era of Whigs and Tories, and it will come as no surprise to the reader that Windham was not really either of these. He started as a Foxite Whig, a friend of Charles James Fox and was first elected for the constituency of Norwich in 1784. His diary entry about his election is scanty, but it would have been politically difficult, expensive and stressful. He does not even make it very clear that he actually won, although he does say that he set off to town in order to vote for Fox at Westminster, as a reminder that elections took place over weeks in the eighteenth century.[4]

This was an unreformed parliament, where most men and no women were unenfranchised, constituencies were small (Norwich was much larger than average) and squires from Norfolk could hope to be elected by virtue of their connections. Most of his friends, like Fox, favoured reform, but he did not. He did not mind people buying parliamentary seats – it seems that in the late 1770s, he did not become the member for Sudbury because he did not have enough cash to pay for the seat; and he was in favour of the old system.

He spoke for the first time in the House of Commons in February 1785, and did so only three more times in the next three years. He hated it and, like most anxious people faced with a daunting task, it dominated his mind for days beforehand. Many of his speeches were later published, and they probably read better than they sounded. His voice was odd, often high-pitched, sometimes low and depressed, and the content was always painfully detailed and sometimes convoluted. His second speech had some admirers but he dismissed them as 'being so good as to be cheaply pleased.' On 18 April 1785, he made a particularly poor speech about Parliamentary Reform, or at least he said so himself, and he was probably not far from the mark. One supportive observer said that, on one occasion, he was the colour of a lemon.⁵

The later part of Windham's diary has more emphasis on his work in the Commons, and when he joined the centre of government, his diary becomes less revealing about his own opinions and feelings. Sometimes, it is a practical problem; diary writers do not make a record of the obvious and unarguable. Slavery, or more precisely, the slave trade, was a good example. On many occasions, up to abolition in 1807, Windham prepared his speeches on the subject of the slave trade; it is impossible to work out his view from his own notes as he knew his conclusions and felt no need to write them down. He was, in fact, one of the strongest opponents, as he said elsewhere:

> Those who argued for it seemed to be sensible that it was possible they might be West India planters, but they did not allow themselves to think of being African slaves.⁶

This empathy for slaves was a common view of much of the establishment, but it is not to be confused with the belief that black lives were equally valuable. The remarkable thing was Windham was able to show any empathy at all, as it was generally believed that, despite all his intelligence, he did not know people or understand them.

The artist Joseph Farington, mostly a purveyor of gossip (see Chapter Five) understood why he had trouble relating to people:

> Windham [Secretary for War] is not a comfortable companion, he cannot confine himself to his seat in company and has a wildness or eccentricity of thought always prevailing.

Edward Malone, known to both men and sympathetic to Windham, understood why he found political life hard. He did too much thinking – 'he has too much sensibility for a public situation,' said Malone.

Windham was clear about the consequences of the French Revolution, following Burke's lead. His support for the war against France became fanatical, and he did a lot to organise conspiracies of French royalists to assassinate Napoleon, as his later diary shows. There was also talk of secret assassination, but there are, of course, no details in the dairy. It does contain references to money and help given to French royalists and there is no doubt that Windham was working night and day to defeat the French.

In 1799 he realised that he would find it hard to keep his seat in Norwich; it was a large constituency by unreformed standards, and contained voters who did not share his fanatical support for the war at all costs and complete hatred of Napoleon. In anticipation of defeat, and after using the dubious methods that the parliamentary reformers wished to outlaw, he moved to the rotten borough of St Mawes (electorate of 20 people) and was told all he had to do was to pretend to like the Cornish pilchard and that would be enough; he did not have to eat one.[7] Once again, there are no details in the diary.

Windham was briefly in government again in 1806–7, in the same post, but his career had stalled and there was no prospect of him returning when he died tragically in 1810. He had changed his mind too many times, did not have the charisma to build up a set of supporters, and despite his hard work, was not always seen as reliable.

His house, Felbrigg Hall, still survives as a major National Trust attraction, and William has been spotted there. He is a poltergeist who moves tables and chairs about in the library, but only in order to read books rather than cause a commotion.[8] Staff and volunteers report seeing William sitting at the table or relaxing in a chair amongst his 5,000 books. The rational Windham who rated fact and knowledge above imagination would have hated the whole idea, but the concept of a man still unsettled after death is grimly appropriate to his character.

Chapter 4

The British Grand Tour
John Byng May–June 1789

Our next witness is the inveterate traveller, the Honourable John Byng, younger brother of the fourth Viscount Torrington, George Byng. He was brother-in-law of William Windham and nephew to the infamous John Byng, the first (and the last) Admiral of the Royal Navy to be executed for failure to carry out orders in battle in 1757. John's brother George had three sons who all predeceased him. When George died, John became the fifth Viscount Torrington for a mere twenty-three days before dying himself in 1813, and never making an appearance in the House of Lords.

Byng is a reminder that not everybody in the Georgian era looked forward to the future, or cultivated new habits of thought. He looked to the past and found it far, far better than the present. One (of many) things that got his goat was the Grand Tour. Although it was a century-old tradition for people of his class, he thought it was now snobbery, no more than the rich and privileged favouring Europe over England to prove their cultural superiority.

He had fifteen sightseeing holidays in England and Wales between 1781 and 1794, never earlier than May and never later than mid-September. He rode his horse from place to place, sending his servant ahead as an 'avant courier' to secure accommodation and stabling, and spent his days researching and sightseeing. Byng travelled in his home country only and not the continent, and this was unconnected with the French Revolution; for much of this time he could have gone to France, but he genuinely believed that his native land was interesting, that much foreign travel was vacuous sightseeing, and all the young gentlemen brought back was frightful architectural and artistic pretensions:

> Talk not, therefore, gentlemen, of foreign parts, till you have seen and learnt something of your own country: – ye, who drive by

Canterbury Cathedral, without deigning a look, and return boasting of rialtos, eclipsed by the work of the most ordinary Welsh masons.

He had no time for the rich on their Grand Tour. Their only interest was in money and the revenues from their estates when at home but they turned into swooning culture vultures when they were abroad, and returned home superficial and affected and 'fatigued their listeners with their hackneyed account of ROME.'

He was not talking from direct experience; there is no evidence that he ever did the Grand Tour himself. He was very much content with England and had little time for the Scots or Scotland, a common view at the time. Unlike some of our other travellers, he held no real interest in windswept, picturesque and romantic scenery, but he appreciated well-made roads, country houses, old buildings, neat villages, healthy horses, well-kept fields and happy peasants. 'I do not know a road of more beauty that the one from Biggleswade to Huntingdon,' he said, both wishing to provoke a reaction but also believing it to be true.

We will follow him briefly through his travels in the Midlands in 1789.[1] At the beginning, he issues a warning; he is full of uncommon opinions and he is not going to change his mind:

My habits and thoughts are now fixed like rusty weather cocks, or like matrimony, for better or worse.

The only way Byng could be liberated from stupidity, selfishness and superficiality was to be on his own or with a very select group of friends, or at the very least to have the option of being on his own when he needed to. He did have a close friend, one that understood him, and with whom he had no disagreements at all; that was his horse Poney – 'I found that I liked him, and that he understood me. That's the best rule for society.'

Poney had belonged to John Howard, the famous penal reformer and fellow Bedfordshire resident, and a man with a track record of kindness to horses; Byng could not stand cruelty to horses, not because he hated cruelty but because he loved horses. Byng did not hate all humanity, but preferred them as an abstract mass rather than individuals. There were powerful exceptions; his children certainly, his wife not so much.

The British Grand Tour: John Byng May–June 1789   45

He was always early to rise; he left his son Frederick on Friday, 29 May 1789 and walked from his home in Bedford to commence his trip in Barnet:

Up at five, kissed my Lamb Frederick left in my Place in Bed, When, encumbered by a loose Great Coat (for it was a dripping morning) stuffed Pockets, and a new pair of Boots, I made my Departure for this grand Tour.

The lack of capitalisation at the end of the sentence is not an accident.

He was walking to Barnet because that was where Poney was. It was a five-hour walk on a beautiful day, and no stagecoach came along the road to tempt him into a ride. Poney was waiting for him; there was time for some breakfast of tea and dry toast at the Red Lion at Barnet, and the first of many warnings about the state of food in the inns; 'never get anything buttered, or you get stale butter.' He had strong views on food, drink and hospitality in English inns like our witnesses Moritz, Chapman and Warner.

Byng liked traditions, even semi-defunct ones. That day, 29 May, was Oak Apple Day, an annual celebration of the Restoration of Charles II in 1660 – 'Every horse, carriage, and carter, were adorned with oaken boughs, and apples, in memory of this once-famous day.' He looked back, not forward and mostly saw the present as problematic. He was an early version of William Cobbett, riding the countryside in his *Rural Rides* and mostly finding fault.

A common thread through his travels is that he tried *not* to see people, even his friends, as an inconvenience. He was not, strictly speaking, a misanthrope. He got to like some people and did have friends, but his views were severe, even with people he liked – 'My old friend Tray, quartered at Barnet, was not at home; that's wrong, as I said I should call; but right, as I wish not to be delayed.'

He left Barnet to the sound of blackbirds; he preferred birdsong to the music in London soirées, the smell of hawthorn to the musk perfume of a metropolitan ball. Summer anywhere was better than summer in London. Most travellers, like Warner (Chapter Six) started their British tours in August; Byng started in June, as that was when London became intolerable to him. He hated the expenditure, the insecurity and the superficiality of the London season, which he viewed as no more than a grubby marriage market.

He was certainly capable of *Schadenfreude* and admitted it openly. He found it amusing when his friends had accidents; this was the case with Mr T, who came from Biggleswade and ran the Sun Inn, where Byng stayed when he was in town rather than the mansion of his elder brother. The accident was hilarious; a stagecoach broke down outside the inn where Mr T was recuperating; five women fell on top of him, then the roof collapsed and the luggage also fell on him. People tended to take stagecoach accidents with a hint of melancholic resignation, but it was uncommon to actually find them funny.

Byng moved to a pub in Welwyn and added two warnings to his earlier musings about rancid butter; choose something cold over something heated and covered in sauce, and always open the crust of a dessert pie and look at the fruit before buying it. It was hard to reject a pie if you had already taken a bite.

It was also easier to reject the fruit pie than to stop total strangers talking to you. He was forced to talk to three 'sons of the angle'. One of them 'related to me every minute circumstance (as sportsmen will do) of his morning's diversions' and he was bored, not because he found fishing tedious, indeed he loved it; but because he hated other people's stories, especially around dinner time. He liked to eat at the point of appetite; woe betide any eating companion who opted for something that took a long time to prepare. He often scanned the local newspaper while waiting to be fed. He briefly noted that the Welwyn Assemblies were still being held, not as often as formerly, 'when all the world danced not in London.'

When he passed Stevenage, he issued another warning about modern commerce. If there were inns on the same road, do not assume that they are competing with each other and so the quality will rise; they might just be owned by the same person. He intended to stay the night at Baldock, but the inn was too noisy as 'there was a cargo of wild beasts, and much drumming and trumpeting to a puppet-show.' He did not leave London every summer to endure this level of triviality, so he pushed on to his beloved Biggleswade.

Like many apparent misanthropes, he changed his behaviour when meeting people he liked. He knew Mrs Knight, the landlady of the Sun Inn; and the staff; 'my old friend, the waiter, and I are very familiar and we hold conversation without contradiction; and it was not in the least "improving"'. Both he (chicken) and Poney (corn) were well fed, he had time to visit an old church and get to bed in a quiet inn. This was all he wanted.

He hadn't started his tour yet, but the landlord of the pub, Mr Knight, knew exactly what Byng liked – ruins, history and antiquity. Landlords were often tourist guides, and more; in this case, he showed some copper coins from the Roman camp at Sandy. They were forgeries, Byng thought, as there had been a steady supply of them for years. Producing fake coins was a common crime in late Georgian Britain, and antiquities were no different.

Byng liked churches, especially ones with historic inscriptions about ancient families. He liked the church at Flitton[2] and admired the memorials to the Kent family, except the most recent burial; those of a later date were abominable; 'a son of the last duke, a lad, in a wig, and shirt!' He liked the vault and gave it the best possible compliment; it was dry; the coffin covers had not deteriorated, so presumably the bodies had not either, avoiding the sweet smell of decay common in Georgian churches. He then saw a boy who looked just like his son Frederick and for that reason alone, he gave him a halfpenny.

Lunch was at the George in Silsoe. It was empty, they treated Poney well, the hawthorn and briar smelt nice, which worked in its favour when the fried beef steak turned out to be poor, but he had his own sauce. This was one of the many things that a prudent and picky traveller would carry around from place to place; the other items were bedsheets.

Byng revealed his political views for the first time; although not a Tory, he was conservative, but could not be content because the land-owning classes were letting down the poor. The nobility, with their affectations and foreign travel, were not helping either. There were none in the area, noted Byng, so at least money was not being wasted on pretentious travel. Modern agricultural improvement did not impress him. On many occasions, he saw sheep where crops used to grow and enclosed land that used to belong to the poor, and disapproved:

> The cottagers, everywhere, look wretchedly, like their cows; and slowly recovering from their wintry distress: Deserted by the gentry, they lack assistance, protection, and amusement.

He may well have spoken the last word verbatim to the landlord, as he told Byng that every May they had morris dancers, fools, a man in women's clothes and music. However, this was very much *not* what Byng meant by amusement; he was looking back into the past and something less crude and shallow, although he was sometimes at a loss to give concrete examples.

King George III had been ill for some time but had recovered, and there were national celebrations; Byng describes one in Stamford that could have been anywhere in the country. It was led by the munificent local gentry. There were prayers and sermons; illuminations in windows and treats for the poor; fireworks, flags, bells, toasts and dancing. Most people approved, but not Byng ('they are my opinions, and I cannot restrain them'). This contrived and institutional hospitality was no replacement for the day-to-day responsibility that the rich had for the poor, most of whom were women and children who would have been at home when the beer flowed and the beef was roasted. The sturdy and wicked were doing the consuming, and the calculated acts of charity would be written up extravagantly by stooge journalists, leading to a few people being pleased with themselves without any permanent material improvement for the poor.

Byng's own supper was port wine, pigeon and splendid isolation; there was nobody else in the inn. The only noise was the crickets outside, who neither talked about trifles nor held up his meals. He then wondered why the insects were so loud, which was a bit much for a man who could so easily denounce other peoples' conversations as trivial.

Sunday, 31 May was a busy day; his stomach was in spasms all night and he woke up to the bad news that neither of his two companions would be arriving: 'the former is prevented by business, the latter by idleness,' he commented, unforgivingly. His wife had sent a letter telling Byng to expect her the next day; she was clearly confident that it would arrive on time to make such time-sensitive news worth passing on. His morning started with letter-writing and a call for the apothecary, who arrived with the day's newspapers – very much possible so close to London by the 1790s. Mr Gall ('good name') promised a treatment later for his stomach; despite his constant complaints throughout the dairies about the quality of the food and its preparation, this type of malady was a very rare occurrence in the diaries.

Mr Knight was one of the few landlords he actually liked; when crickets outnumbered customers the night before, he was even able to squeeze out some empathy for his business. The next morning, the two went riding and Mr Knight searched for some famous medicinal water in the meadows; Byng was cynical and unconvinced as ever by the 'well water in the meadows, which assuredly ought to be fenced, described, etc., etc.' They visited a farm owned by the landlord – many Georgian innkeepers were substantial business people – and Byng took an instant dislike to a conceited tenant and his ugly daughter. He pulled no punches and fools were not suffered gladly. He worried about ordinary people in the mass, but drew the line at sympathising with actual human beings; he loathed the system, but hated the oppressor much more than he loved the oppressed.

Byng much preferred the tench in the moat, the two birds' nests that he found in the garden ('a circumstance of consequence to a cockney'). Mr Knight went home but his hunting spaniel stayed to entertain. It was a nice day, and the mass of the people were having a good time:

> A lovely, growing day! Such a show of plenty upon the ground, with the lasses in their best bibs and tuckers, exhilarated my heart; and I thought I was passing my time very rationally.

Lunchtime was spent in the bar with the German doctor – 'drinking, without expense, his port' and Dr Gall expressing an interest in the same antiquities as Byng, who could not tell if he was really interested or merely singing for his supper.

He was never wont to come to a generous conclusion, but he was moderate when it came to religion. He was not particularly devout, unlike many who put pen to paper in the Georgian age, and religious difference (at least amongst Protestants) was idle banter to him:

> The waiter tells me, that the Doctor is a Lutherian, aye, says I, a Lutheran; No Sr. a Lutherian – Perhaps you mean A Moravian? There you have hit it, sir, it is a Moravian.

Certainly, Byng was not resting on the Sabbath. They rode out after their port to visit the doctor's horses and saw a crowd dispersing from a sermon of the local Methodist minister, the Reverend John Berridge, friend of John Wesley. Byng did not share the suspicions of many of his class towards the Methodists – they were committed and sincere. The movement, on the whole, was part of the solution even if he did not embrace its principles:

> If these preachers do restore attention, and congregations within the churches, and do preach the word of God, They appear to me as men most commendable; they are like military martinets, who are scoffed at by the ignorant, and indolent, but who preserve the army from ruin.

He later went out to see the moon and surveyed the poor enjoying themselves outside as best they could in 'our half warmed climate'. This was the way to live; riding, hunting, and thinking about fishing, and watching honest young men and women courting and frolicking; the mirror image of London. One thing was absent. Byng seemed to be missing the human company that makes good experiences even better. Despite being a good day 'this I hope will be the last that I shall pass alone, upon this tour.'

The next day, 1 June, started well. He had a buttermilk drink and went for a walk. It was common for both rich and poor in the Georgian era to do something first before having their breakfast. On the road, he met the first aristocrat of the tour, Lord Ancaster, riding alone to his country seat in Grimsthorpe. His Grace the Duke was an acquaintance and they were of the same opinion about the London season. The Duke's wife and daughter were taking part and he did not want to be there, hence inviting Byng to his house to enjoy what he rather passive-aggressively called his 'bachelor's fare'.

Byng launched another attack on London. 'Countess, or Courtezan, all alike lost in confusion of dress and perfume of the marriage market.' It was the cost of carousing in London that made the aristocracy either ignore their local estates or squeeze it for every last penny, but once again the reader is left with the impression that he resented the spending of the rich more than he worried about the suffering of the poor.

On that day he saw strawberries and peas growing for the first time and, once again, thought of eating them with his son Frederick, who always seemed the child who came to mind, despite having twelve children at the time of writing. He then visited the fair that he had seen the preparations for. He thought the entertainment – drinking and dancing, the sleight of hand man and the learned pig – were contrived and trivial. The crowds, the jostling and the stink were not for him; neither was the chasing of women (by the men under 30) or the chasing of beer (men over 30). Neither set of men could steer a straight route home. This wasn't rational, uplifting recreation.

Up to then, the day had been more to his liking – a long ride, a visit to an old house, a grave with inscriptions about family history, some lovely marble and granite, a priest hole and some scenery. He visited a church but had to have it unlocked first – many churches were locked on his travels. There was a crime wave in Georgian England, the worst of which was still to come.

Byng visited the neat village of Cardington. 'Neat' was one of his favourite words, as it implied the two things he valued most – the honest prosperity of the masses, and the good order imposed on them by their betters. The village was also the home of the prison reformer John Howard. Howard, like Byng, had done a lot of travelling, while doing a lot of good. Howard himself calculated that he had travelled 42,000 miles visiting prisons. In June 1789, he was about to plan a journey to Ukraine, where he was to fatally contract typhus after a prison visit. Byng wished him all the best when he saw his house, but it was not to be.

In Cardington he met some children on a roundabout, which Byng thought unjoyfully as just a way of making them sick after gorging on gingerbread. He also saw some well-dressed children in the uniform of a local charity school with their grateful mother. That was more of the things he liked; charity schools provided by the good conscience of the rich to provide a basic education for the poor.

At lunch he chatted with his landlord about elections and county matters, partly because he enjoyed it (this was his county, and the conversation would have been two-way) and partly to keep his costs down – 'now it is always right to converse sociably with landlords, both for information and cheapness.' He then reported in triumph the low prices he had paid, and it was a reasonable boast because everybody knew that the Georgian innkeeper was in total control of what was charged.

So after a day of pleasure with houses, horses and history, he retired to bed – he had had his normal pint of brandy – but he was still human and a bit lonely:

> A close for this day: and this I hope will be the last that I shall pass alone, upon this Tour.

The next day, Tuesday, 2 June, there was to be no companionship as neither of his friends had arrived. He had planned pigeons, asparagus and good beds – it 'galls me having no letters' so he could not go anywhere in case he missed them. Mrs B would come in the evening; he assumed it would be 10.00 pm, past his desired bedtime. It was going to be a dragging day.

He tried fishing, wished to do it alone and stomped off when this was not possible. He visited his friend who had the coach accident. Then his anger was compounded when a note arrived from one of his friend's servants; his master would dine with him; but no time was given and Byng overflowed with frustration; 'how easy is the writing six words on a slip of paper, to be sent by either your servant or the post!' Byng made no compromises with uncertainty; he dined at two, as normal – cold beef, tarts and custards and then waited for hours. 'No W. W. at 5 o'clock: Here did I sit, like a lady waiting for her company; and in such kind of twitter.'

He went angling again until 8.00 pm; and then rode up and down for an hour. Why no communication by servant or post? Was there not a penny post in London? Anger turned to worry as the hours passed, as it does with people today:

> Till a certain hour one is vexed, but after that alarmed: Some accident may have happened upon the road, or some sickness in London!

They didn't arrive until 11.00 pm, both companions and his wife; he ate again, was late to his bed and his stomach was full of spasms once more.

On Wednesday, 3 June, Byng took charge of the itinerary, which was, as usual, neat villages, churches, mausoleums and some tourist trophies. He saw the famous bed where the supporters of William II accused the Stuarts of smuggling a supposed heir to James II into the bedchamber, and a picture of Oliver Cromwell by Peter Lely. He also liked an emotional inscription, even if it was about premature death; and it feels like something favoured by our sentimental age as well:

> Here our Children lies, with their pretty Eyes
> Whom God seem'd fit to close
> He tane them home while they were young
> To take a sweet Repose.

The next day, 4 June, was the birthday of King George III, and he put on a new shirt, but did nothing else. He was matter-of-fact about the monarchy, which is fair enough as the execution of Admiral Byng was widely seen as a severe injustice, but he was still a king and constitution man, and had been a page boy at the wedding of George II. Byng held an easy job at the government Stamp Office that allowed him his extended summer holidays.

It was tourism day again, despite the pouring rain that had started the evening before. First it was a Cesar camp at Sandy Hills, without the women, who they met at the church at Eton Bray. He liked the thirteenth-century font there; and worried that it would be replaced by some modern bauble, carved by a greedy stonemason, who would also, by happy coincidence, be the local church warden. He disliked modern ostentation. Byng would be pleased to know that the thirteenth-century font is still there today.[3]

He liked the army, and never failed to comment when he saw the regulars or the militia. He saw the Scots Greys and praised them. He had been a colonel before he retired and loved to see a well-turned-out troop, but was always ready to make a negative comment too, unsurprisingly.

The poor weather was spoiling the day, so they took shelter at a public house called the Creamer's Hut. Byng approved of such places; he was without the snobbery that some of his class would have had. The parlour was neat, the bread and cheese were adequate, and they ate it in 'the finest dress that could be borne at the same hour in St James's Palace'. Byng enjoyed that paradox; the whole event was honest, appropriate and without ostentation, and he enjoyed mixing with the poor. The Georgian elite thought nothing of this kind of fraternisation; it was the uptight respectable Victorians who split themselves off from the poor and their drinking places.

Later, the Wheatsheaf Inn was less good. Dinner, ordered for 3.00 pm was not ready. The half-hour before dinner was always a snappish time for Byng even when the food was on time, but the inn was cold, miserable and the prices were akin to London – for tench 'in a brown sauce' they were charged 7 shillings. The atmosphere was not helped by his friend's oilskin and apron, made stinky by the constant rain, and the pet dog Wowsky, who was equally wet and smelly. His evening meal was acceptable; there were no new peas, despite seeing them being harvested that very morning; he was still worried that he would have spasms again so he ate hardly anything.

He need not have worried; he slept well and undisturbed, as did his horse. His companions slept too well, as they were 90 minutes late for breakfast so there were no more post-chaises to rent out. They went fishing, and Byng was sardonic about their excuse: 'the two late and sick risers now betook themselves to fishing, from damp grass, and in a north wind to improve their health.' Then there was a local walk to a pretty village called Thornhaugh, with the usual church, churchyard and inscription. Tench was available for lunch (he had, of course, had one only the day before), but he was afraid to eat, not because his stomach was worse, but because it was better.

After the meal, or lack of it, they went to Peterborough by chaise to have tea and look at the cathedral. The two anglers had returned, after catching nothing, and Byng could not quite contain his glee. He could see nothing nice about Peterborough but was looking forward to the racing and mentioned the cock fight – 'the Main of Cocks that would take place between Gentlemen of Leicester and those of Peterborough.' In the 1790s, cruelty to poultry was still a classless occupation, enjoyed both by Liverpool lowlife like Vaux and the gentlemen of the East Midlands, although that was changing; some cruelty – mostly lower-class iterations like cock fighting were becoming less acceptable to ruling class sensibilities.

There were two tourist possibilities on the way home; the famous Burghley House and the much less visited Milton House of Lord Fitzwilliam. One of his landlord's had told him that 'the entire world' went to see Burghley so they set off for Milton House, without an invitation. It was pure contrariness. Byng was annoyed that they could not gain entry into the house, and he had to content himself with peering through the lower ground windows. He wasn't being entitled; it was reasonable for even the common people to be shown around a grand house by a servant without a prior invitation. 'A refusal of the sight of any house known commonly to be seen, is very unpolite, and cruel upon the tourist', claimed Byng, correctly.

After a busy day, he was content; the anglers had still caught nothing and he was very pleased with the inn they had chosen for a second night. The two things he liked most were the food and the state of the beds; this was a universal feeling in the Georgian era.

So Saturday, 6 June was the start of the main tour; his fellow travellers managed to get up at a reasonable hour, and they packed their trunks that were moved in advance by the stagecoach. They were not travelling light; it was fresh air and history during the day, but their own bedlinen and clothes in the inn. Byng's wife Bridget left for town. It was not a long visit and there was a clear feeling that it was not a relationship overbrimming with either love or much enthusiasm.

The tourists passed Burghley House again – far too popular with the masses, it was hinted, and he saw the South Lincolnshire Militia at Stamford. These were part-time volunteers and Colonel Byng always had reservations; in this case, reservation became criticism – 'a set of as awkward, unsightly, ill dressed men as could be drawn together'. They were volunteers who had been dragged from their work to assembly monthly from their more important work on the farms, as they would have been yeoman farmers.

Byng could not see the point of the militia. If there was a fear of invasion, he said, then there would be enough time to recruit some gentlemen to lead these common folk and be trained without these assemblies, which he describes as 'debauched and corrupting', as well as taking up the time that should be devoted to honest agricultural labour. Militia service was demoralising them, both as husbandmen and husbands. The vices learnt in the town were taken home to the 'cottage quiets'; and it cost the nation a fortune. He didn't like Stamford either – it was ill-built and had no industry, and his main preoccupation was to find a stomatic medicine, while watching what he sarcastically called 'The Troops!', meaning his own companions.

Next in view was Grimsthorpe Park. The Duke had invited him to a poor bachelor's fare a few days earlier, and he had not been joking. 'My cook is in town, and I am unprepared,' said the Duke as they met again. Byng wished that he had failed to get in, but was obliged to act on his acquaintance's invitation. The house, already unimpressive, was made worse by being uninhabited. The Duke's taste was condemned, although some of it was clearly subjective. The New Front Hall was built by Sir J. Vanbrugh 'in all his clumsy taste', said Byng, a view that is not generally held today.[4] There were too many bad pictures of horses and men, and of dogs and bears, and faded pictures by Sir J Reynolds and some original Hogarths 'that might be valued by some'; his Van Dyck was a copy, and Byng implied the Duke did not know this. The criticism continued. His chapel was devotionless, his lawns were unimaginative and his rooms cold. And he had not been fed, which would not have helped. He left the cold house, bowing as he made his escape.

His journey proceeded, and Byng continued to be the weary judge of man and morals. Some of the same themes reoccur, but Byng retained the ability to shock and amuse. His diaries are still available as a lavish Folio Society edition. That's because he can still be read for enjoyment, albeit of the cynical and world-weary kind.

Chapter 5

The London Bubble
Joseph Farington 1793–1802

Our next witness is Joseph Farington, who kept a diary from July 1793 until his death on 30 December 1821. The focus will be on the first volume, covering the period July 1793–August 1802. He was a prominent, but by no means pre-eminent, landscape painter, but was important because of the hold he had on the Royal Academy, so much so that he was known as 'the dictator'. Farington's life and diary revolved around his work and art, and it is an unparalleled source for the machinations of the art world in the late Georgian era. If that sounds a little niche and possibly dull, the good news is that Farington was also a gossip.

Apart from art, his other interests were scandal, money and death. He did not discriminate – it could be about celebrities, friends, acquaintances, strangers or the utterly obscure. It could be first-hand, second-hand, factual or incorrect – it just kept coming. His diary is peppered with short and long pen-pictures; they are not usually character assassinations because Farington was not very judgemental. He knew a lot of famous people well and was acquainted with many more within the small artistic and political circle of London. Much of his information was second- or third-hand, picked up at polite social gatherings. He drank a lot of tea, went to a lot of dinners and was hardly ever at home.

His machinations at the Royal Academy had no historic consequences so after his death, he was soon forgotten. His reputation as a first-rate Georgian artist has not survived either; yet his work is still sold at auction houses for respectable amounts of money – expect to spend £10,000 at Christie's for one of his more substantial works.

Farington knew the Royal Academy founder James Christie, and gossiped about him. Christie, he said, had married four times and had four children by a servant. Christie's father was a feather-bed beater.

Farington liked salacious stuff, and he was regularly wrong, as he seems to have been about Christie, which acts as a warning caveat for the rest of his revelations. He never checked his sources if the story appealed to him.

His obscurity ended when his diary was rediscovered in a mahogany case in a lumber attic, a century after his death. He died in 1821 and left his diary to his brother Richard Atherton Farington (1755–1822), but as his dates suggest, Richard was short of time to read them. The diary passed to Richard's nephew and then to his son, forgotten until the *Morning Post* published extracts in the 1920s. The reviews understood the limitations of the diary. Farington was an 'industrious chronicler of trifles' said one[2]; 'a notable man in an era of great men,' said another.[3] It was not the place to go for comments about the state of the nation at that very turbulent time, said another reviewer, but this was a little unfair. The war with France loomed large, Farington knew about events at court and at Westminster, the state of the economy and business, and he was fully aware of the rising social tensions of the 1790s, although to be frank, he didn't care very much or worry at all.

The diary is not the personal confessional of an unconfident man, like Windham. Indeed, it is not personal at all. On 24 February 1800, Farington's wife died. This came as a great shock to him; she had been weak for years, winter was about to pass and he hoped that 'the most affectionate, the most amiable of women, my beloved wife' would survive. This was the only reference to Susan Farington, née Hammond, in the diary. In fact, there is no domestic element in the diary at all, but it would be wrong to draw the conclusion that he was unfeeling. For six weeks after Susan's death, he wrote nothing and could neither draw nor paint. By April he was being gently encouraged by his friends to entertain and divert himself or his excessive grieving would cause mental and physical problems. His wife's death was God's will, and failure to accept that was impertinence.

Much more typical of the diary is the materialistic and gossipy pen-picture:

> Banks will be able to make a profitable job of the Statue of Lord Cornwallis. The marble, including the Pedestal, will not cost him more than 200. He may clear 12 or 1300 by the Statue. Banks returned from Italy well stored with just Ideas of his art, and was well

qualified for great works, but was not encouraged. I observed that his conduct with regard to Politicks had done him harm. Flaxman thought his indiscretion in that respect both in Italy and in England had hurt his interest, added to which the bluntness of his manners had disgusted many.

Farington found it impossible to mention a work of art without commenting on how much was paid for it, or how much profit it would make. Here, he has been gossiping with the sculptor John Flaxman, and this was not the first time he was to do so. They discussed the onerous customs duties on art; Flaxman told him that 1,500 a year were murdered in Rome; like all gossips, he also talked behind the backs of people he gossips with. His friend John Hoppner had demeaning things to say about Flaxman – 'I cannot draw, but I can draw better than Flaxman can.' There are hundreds of examples; John Opie is a better painter than Hoppner; Hoppner was too much like Sir Joshua Reynolds. Henry Fuseli thinks that Thomas Lawrence is deeper in mind than Hoppner. These were some of the great artistic names of the time. The diary is full of it – chit-chat disguised as artistic discussion. It was backbiting if he knew them and gossip if he didn't.

Farington encountered a lot of upper-class gambling. It was an equal opportunity, yet ruinous occupation. Farington heard about some terrible stories; aristocrats who would 'weep and lose', but there is no moral condemnation, only near glee.

> Lord & Lady Besborough; it is expected must go abroad on account of extravagance. He stays at Brookes' till 3 or 4 in a morning gaming and she goes out at one in the morning to her friend Lady Ann Hatton.

Women were particularly keen on playing 'faro', a card game that was essentially a game of chance. He reported that when Sir Joshua Reynolds came into a house with a faro table, he would put his money out of reach.

Farington held grudges tenaciously. He had a particular aversion to the now-forgotten Chichester poet William Hayley (1745–1820). There were a few reasons for this; Hayley was adjudged to be hostile to the Royal Academy and Farington believed that he had been gossiping about it to Joseph Wright of Derby. The dairy is littered with micro-aggressive comments; he was Hayley [the poet], as if he needed to remind himself; or 'Hayley the versifier'. Farington wrote that Southey had said that 'everything about that man is good except his poetry.' His poems 'were popular in his day'. Hoppner said his verses were indifferent. Hayley was also a 'violent republican'. He had written a book about John Milton that was 'dangerously democratic'. Farington, unsurprisingly, was a firm king and constitution man.

The references to Hayley were brief until early 1799 when illness piqued Farington's interest. Hayley's natural (illegitimate) son Thomas Alphonso was struck down by unknown diseases that left him bedridden, shrunken in size by several inches, disfigured by curvature of the spine and immobilised by softening of the bones. This was reported to him by Flaxman, who was teaching him sculpture. It was all a bit of a shame; he was a promising student, said Flaxman, ignoring the obvious reason for concern. There was more. Hayley had married Eliza Ball, daughter of the Dean of Chichester, after Thomas's birth. Thomas's natural mother, Mary Cockerell, had moved into the household; Eliza could have no children, according to Farington, and she invited Mary to bring up her child in a *ménage à trois*. Eliza suffered a mental breakdown and they separated, but Farington was equally interested in the amount of money in the separation settlement.

Modern research seems to suggest that there was more to the story than Farington's account, but the same pattern reoccurs throughout the diary.[4] Farington does not judge morals, only art. He shows no empathy in people's suffering (Thomas Alphonso lingered for two painful bedridden years), but also shows no *Schadenfreude*. The story had art, scandal, money and death, so it very much ticked all of the boxes.

Illegitimate sons of the aristocracy who ran off and married pastry cooks would be granted a gleeful mention. Lord Egremont lived with Mrs Wyndham, reported Farington; Mrs Wyndham visited with an attractive 2-year-old – who was (his emphasis) *very like Lord Egremont*. Lady Abercorn had eloped with Captain Copley of the Guards, said the newspapers. Lord Andover accidentally shot himself in the loins as a servant passed him a gun; he lingered and died, being able to exculpate the servant. Lady Andover was a widow at 22; where would the money go?

Farington liked to repeat gossip others had told him; Boswell told him that Doctor Johnson was a two-bottle man only; in the context of Georgian drinking habits of the upper classes, this was nothing. In 1794 he took an interest in the trial of Warren Hastings and the investigation into the Mutiny on the Bounty which cleared Captain Bligh. He particularly liked gossip when it had figures. In 1794 he was told by a disgruntled architect that he had still not been paid for his work at the Theatre Royal, Drury Lane, despite the fact the box office receipts for the eight days of performance in the year was £30,000. When Boswell died, he was behaving so badly that Farington thought he was mad. Joshua Reynolds took two boxes of snuff a night, and any more he could cadge.

Much of the tittle-tattle was personal. Goldsmith's poem was fine, but the central idea that commerce destroys villages was wrong. Fanny Burney's new novel showed that she had run out of ideas; later in the year, he was angry that she had made over £2000. 'The novel is so indifferent; it renders the genuineness of her former works suspected.' He also spread poison amongst his friends. Sarah Siddons, he had heard, was a poor actress and relied on her looks and deportment. The sculptor Ann Damer wore men's hats, shoes and jackets and had passionate relationships with women, especially the author Mary Berry. When they had recently parted, the servants described the separation as if it had been a parting before death. This was a second-hand innuendo but Farington thought it was worth repeating.

He knew a lot of people in his own artistic circle before they were famous. Mr Burns the Scottish Poet who knows no Latin and whose 'general appearance (is) that of a tradesman or mechanic.' This does not mean he did not buy his poetry. He knew, or knew of, Stubbs ('animal painter') and Blake ('the engraver') and accepted the opinion of others that he was a genius, not a word he used very often. He knew about the affair between Emma Hamilton and Lord Nelson, although you did not need to be inside the London bubble to know this; as he reported 'his attachment to her is very great, to the injury of that to Lady Nelson.' All three were constantly at the same social occasions, including on 13 April 1801 at Beckford's House at Fonthill. 'She is bold & unguarded in her manner, is grown fat, & drinks freely,' Farington judged. In August 1802, when the couple finally separated, Farington knew this was common knowledge but added that Lady Nelson was given £1,800; it was all about the money again.

Sometimes, he passed on stereotypes so broad, or information so insubstantial, that they are hardly even gossip. Napoleon, when thinking hard, used to pull his mouth or squeeze his cheek with his right hand. Lisbon stinks; people threw their rubbish out of the window. The Portuguese were proud, and the upper classes were morally loose. Irishmen made terrible sailors but better soldiers, says Captain Cheshire of the HMS *Plover*. Tiny fragments interested him – Lady St Asaph was cut by Lady Jersey, he had heard; but of course, social humiliation only works if somebody notices. Minorca was taken in November 1800; General Sir Charles Stuart wore the same clothes for sixteen days. The Duke of Württemberg was fat, but not in the traditional way. He was both very fat and, at nearly 7 feet, very tall – 'in him it looked like a deformity.'

Much of this was neither new nor news, but Farington must have got a kick from simply writing it down. Some stories had a point. His colleagues Johann Zoffany and William Daniel visited a gypsy encampment in Norwood Common, and found that forty of their key words were similar to the natives of Bengal, and twenty-six were identical. Farington did appreciate intellectual endeavour, but it was not very high up his list of interests.

His other obsession was money; not merely money due to himself, or even the value of the art produced by his friends and rivals, but money for its own sake; the price of random things, and the wealth of people he did not know. Whether it was an artwork or a bar bill, Farington jotted it down. The hull of a man-of-war cost £30,000. He could not look at a ship without commenting on cost and tonnage; in the same way, he could not comment on people without mentioning how much money they had or what they spent it on. Eton cost £200 a year. The Leeds subscription library cost £3 to join and then 7/6 per year. A knighthood would be more likely with a £100 donation. A boxing match Jackson between and Mendoza prize fund was £200.

Income was an interest. The Duke of Marlborough's rent roll was £57,000 and he paid £25,000 income tax, which sounds too much. Income tax was introduced by Pitt to pay for the war, but Farington's figure seems wrong. Dr William Vincent, the head of Westminster School, had £1,200 a year. The eccentric William Beckford, builder of Fonthill and a customer, had an income £155,000 per year; he earned money from his Jamaican plantations. This made Beckford an excellent customer.

The burning issue of black slavery in the Caribbean did not move him. In July 1796 he reported (without comment) that in Jamaica seventy dogs were being employed to hunt down the maroons – escaped slaves – and that they would be very dangerous to the women and children. When he was told that the slavery in Demerara was much crueller than elsewhere, there was no condemnation. Instead, there were more facts; enslaved people cost £50 per head on average, a single man cost double that. He also maintained his interest in death; yellow fever starts with headache, pains in bones and delirium and kills in two and a half days.

One particular piece of navy gossip intrigued him; on one occasion the prize money for a captured French ship was £2,000 for the captain and £4 for the ordinary sailor, with £10,000 going to the agent, which explains why the crook James Vaux (Chapter Six) was so happy when he fell into the business. The potter Josiah Wedgwood died with £400,000. Farington liked wills, where death and money coincided with the added spice of the gossip around its distribution.

The 1790s were a terrible time for the poor of London, and there was a lot of working-class agitation that worried the ruling classes (in 1794, Farington noted the inhabitants of Norwich were becoming violent and democratic). Poverty was of no interest or concern to him; his interest was not the poor, but the previously well-off who now had nothing.

The price of bread *was* a problem for the poor. Farington was occasionally aware that the poor filled their stomachs with bread in order to survive. On 9 July, he noted that the price had been increased to 1 shilling per quarter loaf, an unusual entry for a man not usually interested in such mundane things. 1795 was a particularly bad year for food harvests; it was a third lower than usual and Farington noted a House of Commons resolution to add inferior quality flour to their own family's bread to encourage the poor who insisted on using bread made with better flour than necessary to survive. Lord Hawkesbury observed that in Scotland, their bread was made of oats, at Newcastle, of rye, and in Cornwall, of barley; and yet these people were as robust as any in the southern parts of the kingdom. Who needs wheaten bread, thought Farington, in the same way that some modern conservative commentators remind the poor that porridge is cheap.

For a man like Farington, bread was something student artists used to rub out drawing mistakes. In 1795 it was decided to save 16 shillings a week at the Royal Academy by banning bread, to encourage the young gentlemen to get their outlines correct first time and desist from throwing the bread at each other.

Fine wines were a different matter. The disrupted trade with Europe caused high food prices, mass unemployment and, more importantly for Farington, a shortage of champagne. His friend was rationing it:

> Champagne is become very dear and scarce since the French troubles began, but as it has been customary we ordered it should be served once round.

Later he was triumphant when an acceptable substitute to French art paper was manufactured at home. He lived in a different world.

As his comment about the citizens of Norwich shows, he was no democrat, but did not join in the panics that many of his class had about the radicals of the 1790s. He was mostly phlegmatic about the influence of the London reformers at that time although he suffered a little from the mob when it was being populist and patriotic. Ironically, the only time he was bothered by the power of the mob was when they forced him to illuminate his house in celebration of a military victory.

Farington hated the reign of terror of Robespierre and told the story regularly in his diary. He gave as much time to debates about who had produced the best history of Greece or how often the Academicians should award themselves a gold medal, but this did not mean that he cared nothing about current affairs; he listened to many influential people, was up to date with politics and finance, and made many sound predictions. In mid-1802 he predicted that Napoleon wished to become Emperor, an event that happened two years later.

In late 1796 there was a real nationwide fear of a French invasion, which led to a shortage of specie – hard currency – at the banks, making his artistic buying and selling much more difficult; he was more concerned by the looting of Rome by French soldiers than any sufferings at home. In 1797, when sailors mutinied at the Spithead and Nore, he put their rebellion down not to poor working conditions but by the damage done to deference and obedience by Sunday schools and increasing literacy.

Not only was he not a democrat, he was an elitist even amongst the elites. On 4 January 1800, addressing the Royal Academy dinner, he told the audience that too many people of no real note or distinction were being invited; the audience agreed, but for his speech to have any meaning, some of them must have been the nonentities he was complaining about.

Farington was also very interested in how people died, and would record stories told to him, probably in confidence, by friends and family of the deceased. Severe illness was common and death was not the taboo that it is today; it was a legitimate topic of conversation, not to be shied away from.

He talked about James Boswell's death with Boswell's daughter while visiting Edinburgh. Boswell took six weeks to expire, Farington noted; but his interest was not salacious or morbid; he was just interested in routines, and when things happened, especially their meals. For example, His Majesty was woken by a page that does not knock on the door but gently scratches on a piece of wood that makes gentle rattling sounds. His Majesty dined at 4.30 pm and then dealt with state papers. The Inniskilling dragoons ate at 5.00 pm. His friend Garvey told him that he had met somebody in Bath who was previously a maître d'hôtel. Pitt had his breakfast at nine, but worked so hard that he had not eaten anything by ten.

He also took a special interest in how people died if they were members of the Royal Academy. When Edward Gibbon died in January 1794, Farington noted that he died of mortification, occasioned by a hydrocele of sixteen years' growth. This was an enlarged left testicle and tumour that went down to his knee; it was the size of his head before anything was done and it was cut into twice. It seems that he had had problems since 1761 and by 1790, he was looking for expert help in the form of Henry Cline, a famous surgeon. Lord Sheffield and Joseph Banks knew about it and gossiped to Farington.

He learnt from Gainsborough's nephew that the great painter had died of a cancerous tumour on the neck – 'six years, nothing done' – and it had not been recognised by two eminent doctors; 'my lieutenant colonel grows bigger I think', Farington reported, partly amused by it all.

There was more. The Duke of Leeds died through mortification of the bladder, not a surprise as he was a great drinker, consuming three pints of claret quite quickly in the evening, rather than spreading it over the whole day. Dr Letson of Bath died of putrid fever, according to the newspapers. He recognised the symptoms and bled himself. His father, also a doctor, said that he might as well have shot himself.

In January 1795, painter Robert Smirke called and told him that 'Hickey the sculptor died yesterday after an illness of three or four days owing to having lain in a damp bed.' This was regarded as a very plausible explanation for death in the eighteenth century. When Edmund Burke died in 1797, there were details; he spat blood and wasted away without pain, was able to sit up and read and say something horrible about William Pitt – 'he had great parts but little soul.' Even the merest hint of mortality deserved a mention; eleven months before Burke died, when most of his friends, like William Windham, had not given up hope, Farington was reporting that permanent decline was feared. When Burke died, Farington speculated about his money.

He was always in the market for gossip about William Pitt, who was the Prime Minister for much of this period; despite Farington's severe reservations, or perhaps because of them. He acknowledged Pitt's enormous work rate, and it was a toss-up whether it was the work or the constant drinking that killed him. In 1800, when Pitt was recuperating from illness, his physician put him on a draconian alcohol-light diet of only half a bottle of port in the afternoon.

Farington's interest in how people died, and where their money went reached an apex with the death of Horace Walpole, Lord Orford in March 1797. He paid Orford a visit just before he died, with a matter-of-fact attitude to death that jars a little today – the sulky Swiss attendant told Farington that his master was dying. He then listed the details of the will and was not happy with it; the wrong people were rewarded. Anne Damer the sculptor was bequeathed his famous home, Strawberry Hill; Farington had an opinion here too – she was famous only due to her connection with Walpole, then described her as his 'pet' but also called her a 'female genius', with the emphasis on the first word. The postmortem was regurgitated. An abscess of the throat killed him; he died in pain; he starved to death.

Farington was only one step away from the Royal Family, nearer than Rees Gronow (Chapter Seventeen) but not on regular speaking terms like Ellis Knight (Chapter Sixteen). He narrates rather than judges, but conclusions can be drawn. In July 1796, he recounts the story of his friend

Robert Smirke about the sculptor John Rossi who had an appointment with the Prince Regent to model a small head sculpture of the Prince as Colonel of the 10th Light Dragoons. Smirke had to wait for two shoemakers, one of which gave the Prince forty sets of shoes to try on in an hour. He waited three hours and had waited five hours the day before. These stories are presented without negative comment, but with the implication no better could be expected and this rudeness was normal for a prince.

Farington liked a good royal 'money' story, as ever. He tells the story of Charles Dumergue, the royal dentist who tried to charge the Royal Family £3,000 for services at Windsor Castle over an eighteen-month period, and received £1,500. Lots of people made up bills to see whether the rich would pay them, and Farington never criticised. It was the way that he and his companions made a living. He knew, for example, that the Prince of Wales was a spendthrift, but when Pitt reduced all his creditors' bills by 30 per cent, he was aghast only because of the financial damage done to his artistic friends.

He was aware of the permanent rift between the Prince of Wales and his wife, Caroline of Brunswick. When it proved impossible for Caroline's portrait by Thomas Lawrence to be shown in the 1801 RA Exhibition, Farington reported that the Princess said there was an 'outdoor influence' that prevented it. He also knew that the young Princess Charlotte was being kept away from her mother. 'Lady Elgin has the entire care of her and Princess sees her only twice a week', he reports. It was more like once a week at the time of Ellis Knight (Chapter Sixteen).

Farington told a story of the Princess seeing a picture of her husband and asking when it was painted. When she was told it was five years ago, she suggested that it was more like twenty years since he looked that slim and healthy. For balance, Farington reported that Hoppner had said Caroline was short, full-chested and with jutting hips. Other people at the time said much worse.

Farington travelled outside of London, but mostly took his London bubble with him. In August 1801, he went travelling to Scotland, in more style than any of our other Georgian witnesses. He had his own coachman and groom, and travelled in a landaulet. Just as in England, he was prone to generalisation; Scottish children are beautiful; the adults less so, perhaps because the women do not wear hats. Their houses and inns smell; which seems rather surprising when they have so long had the example of their English neighbours. He also tells us the cost of everything.

There was kindness and respect from the locals, but they were not clean; even when their inn rooms were clean, the kitchens would put you off your food. The only standards they had were those imposed on them by English patronage. The Welsh were worse; the innkeepers were rude, and the peasants pretended not to speak English to avoid being cooperative. At least the scenery was worth painting.

He was absolutely unimpressed by the anvil marriages of Gretna Green, often treated in the English newspapers as either romantic or comical, or both. In fact, it was a grubby trade, often scarcely hiding the fact that it supported child abduction or exploitation of women, and it was performed by men held in great disrepute in Scotland. There were three of them – a 70-year-old drunk and tobacconist called Paisley; a man called Lang who transported women over by coach from Carlisle; and another man called Lekel who was in cahoots with local stagecoach drivers. They charged what they could, up to 50 guineas and had no education or religious qualifications. Farington had data, of course; there were about forty to fifty marriages a year at Gretna Green.

Only two of our witnesses experienced mass factory production; Hutton worked in the Derby Silk Mill and Farington visited Arkwright's famous manufactory at Cromford.[5] He met some children leaving after a twelve-hour shift (with 40 minutes for lunch at noon). Hutton hated his factory for personal reasons, but Farington shared the common view of the time that children must work, and this was an excellent option:

> I was glad to see them look in general very healthy and many with fine, rosy, complexions-. a Boy of 10 or 11 years of age, told me His wages were 3 6d a week, & a little girl said Her wages were 2s 3d a week.

A little education and religious instruction were provided, creating an excellent bargain for parents and children, but especially for Richard Arkwright who became one of the richest commoners in Britain. Farington approved, like most people.

He knew both Turner and Constable, recognised their talent and helped them with advice and introductions. His link with them was the reason that his diaries were deemed worthwhile in the 1920s. He met 'Mr J Constable of Ipswich' on 25 February 1795 and acted as mentor and artistic adviser from that point: 'Constable I called on. I told him his picture has a great deal of merit but is rather too cold.'

He also suggested at one point that he 'unite firmness with freedom, and avoid flimsiness', which we can only assume meant something to him. Farington visited Constable in a melancholy state of mind in March 1801; hurt by criticism of the now-unremembered artist Reinagel.[6] Farington supported Constable against his father, who thought him chasing a shadow and wished him to get a job. He also helped him price his work; suggesting 10 rather than 5 guineas on one occasion, doubling his income and giving him a sense of self-worth.

J.M.W. Turner, like everybody else at this time who wanted to be associated with the Royal Academy, came to Farington to canvas his support. When Turner told him of his domestic situation, still living at home, Farington paid him a visit, later advising him to move into cheap lodgings rather than encumber himself with the costs of a house. Farington was pleased when Turner told him that he would stop giving lessons at a mere 5 shillings a time to concentrate on his work. It was Farington who guided Turner into Associate and Full Membership of the Royal Academy. When, in 1802, he was elected a full member; Farington records the names of those who voted for and against him.

The diary continues beyond 1802 for the rest of his life, and is a worthwhile read throughout. His morbid interest in unusual death had a slightly ironic twist. Wearing galoshes and holding a hat and prayer book (he was at church in Didsbury on a wet and damp day in 1821) he fell downstairs, smashed his head and died. The young Farington would just have found it interesting and certainly worth writing down, but on this occasion, he wasn't able to. His niece did it for him, though – 'mark the uncertainty of life!!' God was praised for his mercy, taking him away before his declining health got worse. Perhaps it was the end he would have wanted.

Chapter 6

Plausible Villain

James Hardy Vaux 1782–1801

Most Georgian criminals were desperate, illiterate opportunists who left no impression on history until they were apprehended. We only hear their voices when they were facing the noose or transportation, and then, of necessity, they were lying. James Hardy Vaux (1782–c.1841) was one of the very few who defied this stereotype. He was an accomplished liar and confidence trickster who wrote a highly literate memoir entitled *James Hardy Vaux – A Swindler and a Thief*.[1] The preface was written by Barron Field, a judge of the Supreme Court of New South Wales, and although he seems highly suspicious of Vaux, he was prepared to help him write his book. This was his second spell of transportation to Australia. He had been transported for the first time in 1801, aged 19, and was pardoned but sent back in 1808. Vaux was not just determined and clever; he seems to have been able to charm people who should have known better.

Why did people buy his book? Probably for the same reason that 'true crime' became popular in the twentieth century, except that in 1819 it was rare to have a book by a criminal – buy this, and gain an insight into a man with no conscience! Yet remember that he was also a vain liar! This was Field's *caveat lector;* but the stories and anecdotes are very interesting, and ring true until blame was being apportioned.

Vaux's own introduction keeps up the theme – yes, he is a miserable wretch! He was writing at the age of about 30, and he saw himself as a soul lost to normality and good society, and while he tried to blame himself, he does not do a convincing job. He was as much sinned against than sinning, he said, and the special pleading starts immediately: 'I DID NOT REALLY KNOW MY FAMILY!'

He was born on 20 May 1782 in the village of East Clandon, Surrey, and came from a respectable family with respectable antecedents. His father was a gentleman's butler and his grandfather was a lawyer, but he was unable to give the traditional family history expected in memoirs:

> I should give some account of my ancestors. This I can but imperfectly do for the volatility of my disposition and the early age at which I left my friends prevented me from ever making pointed inquiries on the subject.

In 1785, he moved to Shifnal to live with his grandfather, for reasons not stated but unconnected with family harmony. He was an appealing child, even if he said so himself. He was spoilt but not vicious and did very well at school. He spent his pocket money in the circulating library and all his spare time in the bookshop, being bookish and artistic. Despite living in Shropshire, he loved the navy and had to be dissuaded from running away to sea, aged 12. For the rest of his life, his primary instinct was to escape from problems rather than face them.

He needed his childhood stories to explain his later bad behaviour. His grandparents, with whom he lived, were virtuous, but Vaux inherited his 'disposition to instability' from his parents. He was introduced to his surviving sisters very late (he was the firstborn and had clearly not been back to see his parents in six years). When he *did* see his father, he proved his son's point by opening a hat and hosiery shop in Great Turnstile Street, a business for which he was completely unsuitable.

His genteel education continued in Stockwell – at a boarding school paid for by his grandparents. Vaux liked French, the extensive library and drama, and he planned to run away with some strolling players. Family pressures moved him from place to place (London, Shifnal, Wisbech, London and Shifnal again), which is why he did exactly the same when he was an adult.

Vaux wanted to join the army or navy, but his parents refused to allow it; 'the dangers attending these honourable professions were however insuperable bars to consent of my fond parents', he announced, wordily. Like William Hutton's father, the family had no connections that could have helped their son in any profession; but Vaux was able to charm his way into the affections of a gentry family, the Moultries of Aston Hall. He became a friend of their son, Austin, and was loved by Austin's mother for his intellect and charm, reading to her son and, even if he said so himself, helping to educate the youngster to her delight. The whole truth is unknown, but it does seem that he found it easy to make people like him. Mr Moultrie liked him so much that he offered to pay for his admission to Oxford. Or so he said.

However, he refused to go to university. He wanted to be free of his parents, who prevented him getting the 'gratifications of mind and body'. He needed to 'debut on the stage of life' – an appropriate figure of speech, as he would spend most of his life pretending to be somebody he was not.

He was censured but still got his way, not for the first time and not for the last. He was, like William Hutton, to be an apprentice, in his case at a Liverpool linen draper's at the typical age of 14. Somebody – his grandfather, probably – had invested a lot of money in this apprenticeship as a premium of 100 guineas would be expected. Swan and Parker, his new employer was a large outward-looking organisation that offered their employees well-paid and interesting jobs, but none of these were available to the lowest apprentice. Vaux polished counters, trimmed lamps and carried parcels. He was meant to be there for seven years, so there was no hurry; the food, pay and accommodation were all reasonable and his employers had growing faith in him. He started well in his job, lived comfortably and was treated with respect. Almost every 14-year-old in Liverpool would have envied him.

He liked Liverpool. It was a fast-growing town, making money from trade rather than manufacture, and his favourite part was the docks, the ships and the sea, and implicit in them, the chance to roam and to be anonymous. He would always run away from responsibility, and was tempted to do so even before he had any. He loved the slave ships, called the Guineamen, in an era when slavery was legal but not universally liked. Nowhere in his diary does he have a strong moral conscience about slavery, or indeed anything.

And then somebody corrupted him. It was a young man called King, similar to himself in many ways but a much livelier, interesting chap with the same theoretical income as Vaux but considerably more money from somewhere. Vaux fell in with a bad lot, and was influenced by them, although few delinquents throughout history ever seem to have fallen in with a good lot. He began drinking and visiting houses of the vilest repute: 'scarcely a night passing without our visiting one or other of those houses consecrated to the Cyprian goddess with which the town of

Liverpool abounds' – a wordy way of saying that, turning 15 years of age, he was visiting prostitutes in brothels.

A night with Venus leads to a lifetime with Mercury, as the saying goes. He ended up with some form of venereal disease, being obliged to visit the 'Æsculapius of Gilead house'. Vaux had a smattering of a gentleman's education here with his reference to the Greco-Roman god of medicine, but he still had the clap, and probably bought some dodgy medicine from the side door of a quack doctor.

Another downward step was his interest in cockfighting. He fancied himself an expert, it having been yet another of his childhood hobbies that he had kept secret from his relatives. While carrying a parcel for his employers, and having the money in his pocket, he 'accidentally' came across a cock-pit. He then deliberately started to gamble on the outcomes of the fights and was about to win big, as a cock was about to kill his opponent, and then his luck changed:

> but in a moment the scene was changed. The fallen cock in the agonies of death made a desperate effort and rising for a moment cut the throat of his antagonist who was standing over him in the act of crowing with exultation on his victory. The latter immediately fell choked with the effusion of blood nor did the victor survive him many moments.

Vaux had lost everything; it reads like it was the animal's fault. Like his lack of concern about stinking slave ships at the port, any concept of animal cruelty would have been incomprehensible to him. He was now surrounded by lowlife to whom he owned money, so he handed over the cash received for the customers' packages in order to save himself from cruelty to humans, which he did understand.

He went home, got drunk (to 'drown his chagrin', he said, a reminder about how clever he was) and vowed to steal a little each day to repay the money he had taken; his cure for stealing was more stealing. It would take him two months, and then he would reform. Instead, he chased his losses in the cock-pit; stole the cash straight from the till and continued to get away with it because there was so much money in circulation; it was tinged with an excuse 'what I abstracted was a trifle compared to the gross receipts of the day.'

Vaux was eventually rumbled by Mr Parker and sent back home to his grandfather, but not in disgrace. He still seemed to have the confidence trickster's knack of extracting the benefit of the doubt from everybody. Parker, notwithstanding Vaux's clear criminality, said he was wonderful and active; all of his relatives at home believed his excuses. His grandfather gave him letters of recommendations to friends in law offices in the capital; from Liverpool to London was a leap further into urban depravity. He was genuinely interested in the law; he liked its pleasing complexity and, for the moment, was happy to be a copying clerk at Lincoln's Inn.

He was also happy to lead the rational lifestyle of other modest bureaucrats; a neat room as a lodger and dining out cheaply at the modest chop-house, with nothing more exciting in his life than the coffee shop and the occasional half-price theatre ticket. He did well at work once again, like the conman making a good initial impression, and he learnt enough law to defend the guilty; later, he used this skill to help himself. After three months, he tired of respectability and the 'Liverpool' pattern repeated itself; drinking and whoring and spending his grandfather's money: 'Several young persons of both sexes which unavoidably engaged me in a course of expensive dissipation to which my means were inadequate.'

He was gently sacked, again. He blushed at his unworthiness, but nobody was prepared to be horrible to him; perhaps it would have helped if they had been, but it was too late. He could no longer be reclaimed by advice.

Armed with a forged 'character' (a reference), he found a post as a clerk in a wholesale stationer's in Lombard Street at twice the salary, but with none of the prospects. This was not a career, but a downward step, although he did not stay there long enough to get bored with it. It was too far from Covent Garden and Drury Lane, where his dissolute friends were and where the action was. This was a turning point; the career ambition was now gone forever.

Vaux became a confidence trickster. He invested in one expensive set of clothes, and like William Hutton, used them to inspire others; but in this case it was shopkeepers, who were convinced to give him credit for other purchases. This was 'maceing' in the criminal cant of the time.[2] He also moved house when money was demanded for rent 'for which I had so many other uses.' He would sneak out his belongings first and flit during the night. He assuaged his guilt by no longer asking his grandfather for money, as flitting and maceing was now providing his funds guilt-free.

He moved easily from job to job. He copied legal documents by day and spent time in the Blue Lion in Greys Inn by night, with the law his companion by day and grubby criminality his best friend at night.[3] It was a double life; he was fooling his grandfather, his employer and himself. Hundreds dated their ruin from this pub, said Vaux. It was full of 'thieves, sharpers and other desperate characters with their doxies'. He sat in the corner smoking a pipe and listened to their increasingly understandable criminal conversation, but not interacting with them. Later he wrote a book based on his interactions with criminals; the fact that we know the criminal slang of the late Georgian era is down to him.

It was at the Blue Lion that he fell in with another person slightly older than himself. This was D-------, who wanted to resume his naval career, and Vaux decided to go with him. He sold his excess clothing, still unpaid for, and accompanied his new friend to Portsmouth, his third den of iniquity. He left his lodging without paying, spent the whole evening drinking and set off to Portsmouth in the morning. They planned to walk and sleep in a field to save money but 12 miles into the 72, they had spent half their money in a pub in Kingston. The time between the pious good intention and failure to live up to it was now down to hours, rather than months.

Another evening and morning drinking at the Eight Bells, and a failure to sleep in fields like they said they would, led to a crisis. Their food and accommodation bill was 4 shillings more than they had; bilking was impossible, not for moral reasons but because the landlady had taken all their belongings before offering them any credit.

Vaux's literary skills came to the rescue in the form of the 'letter racket'. Criminals would buy a forged letter of recommendation in their own name, recounting their blameless calamities and asking strangers for charity and to sign their letter in support. Vaux wrote his own highly literate list of lies. It needed subscribers and when the Mayor of Kingston refused to sign up and pay, Vaux added his name anyway. He used his charm to encourage others to actually sign and pay up. Thus, Vaux was able to make the move from passive to active theft. An imaginary 5 shillings got the ball rolling. He was 15 but a student of human nature:

(people) without a grain of Christian benevolence in their composition will give liberally from motives of ostentation when they see that their neighbours have already contributed and that their own names and donations will also be made public.

His confidence was staggering. His success was easy to understand; he looked the part in his stolen clothes, invested in a road map to seek out the houses of the rich, and could tell a good story. He found himself outside the window of Lady W-------- while she was having a party. He told his sob story, read out his petition, got £5 from the guests and a slap-up supper in the servants' quarters (including a pint of port). For a strange man who had tapped on her French windows late at night, in a society that was on guard for charity hoaxes and begging, it was a remarkable achievement, and he knew it.

He returned to the Eight Bells in triumph and decided to go out again and levy further contributions from the gullible of Kingston. It worked; he took sixpences of the poor and crowns from the rich and was compelled to take potatoes from poor farmers, but he gave these away to 'more needy beggars'. In a typical act of doublethink, he claimed that he invented the letter racket *and* that his corruption was coming from external sources.

His joy was cut short when he returned to the inn; his friend had fled and the constables were looking for him. It was useful that he understood the law, so he knew when to panic and when not to. His landlady suggested that he flee; but he decided to stay as they had nothing on him. He ordered tea when his friend returned and they got their story straight (difficult when the charge was unknown). When the forces of law and order arrived, they were not very formidable and the pair were allowed to finish eating before going to the Town Hall.

The magistrate was one of Lady W--------'s guests, which was bad news as he was present on the first evening of the 'letter racket', but the good news was that Vaux was accused of trespass and criminal damage, when he had been wandering about the garden prior to his sting. They gave their story separately, with Vaux cheerfully admitting later that he could not remember it because it was all lies. His friend was told to leave town and Vaux split the money that he alone had made; there was some honour among thieves. Vaux was banished from town with half a crown in his pocket from the magistrate in order to return to London. As ever, he was given another chance and punishment was postponed into the future. He neither left immediately nor went to London. He walked and conned his way to Portsmouth and extracted money en route. It was a profitable fortnight.

He was soon reunited with his friend, hired a room in St Mary's Street, Portsmouth, ready to 'enjoy such amusements as the town afforded, as long as my money lasted.' He did not care where he lived; he had money from crime and when that ran out, he was literate enough to get a reasonable job and glib enough to charm people into employing him. He found a post as a legal clerk with Judge Moses Greetham, who dealt with naval prizes and their distribution. The pattern returned; he liked his job and was good at it, and he liked his employer. He particularly liked the free celebration dinners at the Crown Inn in Portsmouth. Had he stayed, he would have prospered mightily. He said so himself and it was probably true.

He eventually lost his job in a fit of incomprehensible childishness; another employee tried to sit down with a cup of hot coffee and Vaux kicked the chair away. This was part of a low-level bullying campaign. His sacking was, of course, not his fault. It was just a joke; he was sacked for something that was not even a crime. He was given a guinea, bilked his landlord and spent a week drinking wine at the Blue Posts. He had, of course, not paid his rent, and was attempting to do the same at the Blue Posts, but people became suspicious. It took real skill to build up debt in a rough public house but still know when to cut his losses and leave.

He escaped in the direction of Petersfield. He still had his letter to raise funds, and £10 in his pocket, as he never, ever, paid cash when credit was available.

Later, in London, he used all the methods at his disposal to live, except being honest and hard-working. He maced the shopkeepers, pawned goods, ate cheaply but kept himself neat and tidy so he could trick the gullible. One night in the Saracen's Head, Snow Hill, he ordered a glass of Negus (an up-market choice) and a newspaper, and fell into conversation with a Mr Kennedy, a naval surgeon on the *Astraea*. Vaux's ability to lie and a genuine interest in the navy persuaded Kennedy into giving a letter of recommendation to a man he had met hours earlier. It was 'running away' time again and he went to Sheerness to visit another ship, the *Carolina*.

This was Vaux's perfect wooden world. There were girls, dancing and grog was the order of the day, and Vaux was an honoured guest. He had also reconciled with his grandfather and had been recalled to Shifnal to say goodbye to friends and family, and to be given more money to start his new career as a midshipman.

But the pattern returned. He was good at his job. He was both more intelligent and worldly-wise than his eight other colleagues. He learnt dead reckoning easily. The banter was good and there was a Welsh person that they could all make fun of. His maturity had a downside; going to sea early in life made you immune to sea-sickness and heights. Vaux hated both and he hated work too. He was not used to starting work when others said so, and certainly not at 4 in the morning. He fell asleep during his watch, despite the punishments for this:

> We were sometimes sentenced to sit on the main top mast head for two four and sometimes eight hours at other times to sit on the weather cat head exposed to a cutting wind and other similar punishments depending on the humour or severity of the officer of the watch:

He claimed that his health was damaged, but he never had the discipline in him. It was made worse by the fact that they were sailing the North Sea and could see land most of the time. It had gone wrong and it had disappointed him. When unable to run away or deflect any blame, he sounded like a prig:

> However I continued to weather the gale as well as I could and conscious of the rectitude of my intentions suffered patiently those little mortifications I had not power to avert.

He fell upwards once more. His love of books earned the ridicule of his comrades, and he was told he should have been a clerk, or, a worse insult, a parson. Then a clerk job became available. He had his own individual cabin, and now that he had his own way, his ambitions revived – to be a purser and live without manual work.

It was going well, again. He had three days' leave in London, had prize money and pay in his pocket, visited a prostitute ('Cyprian'), but this was not to be a one-night stand. She took all his money, partly because he spent all three days with her, and partly because he did not mind her; 'she had a generosity of mind seldom met with in females of her description,' Vaux said, speaking from experience.

He returned to his ship but could not live without her. He deserted and took a coach to London only as far as the obelisk at St George's Fields, changing to a chaise to make it harder for the authorities to find him. He even left all his valuable belongings in his chest; however, they had been bought by friends and family in Shifnal, and it was easy come, easy go. His sixteen months in the navy were over. However, no one needed to judge him, as he could do it himself; 'It is impossible however for my reader to condemn my folly or rather wickedness in stronger terms than my own conscience has ever since done.' Luckily, he was able to forgive himself.

His new friend Sarah K---e agreed that they could live together. She thought he could support her indefinitely and Vaux did not contradict her assumption. He knew that the money would run out in about six weeks, which was further ahead than he usually looked. His temporary lover had a back story, which sounds like a cliché but was possibly true. An officer in the Brigade of guards seduced, and then deserted her, and she was too embarrassed to go home; being 16 in London, she became a prostitute and made money, or in the wordiness of Vaux, 'the pecuniary emoluments she thence derived had enabled her to live elegantly.'

The money dwindled; he pawned his watch, but the inevitable was interrupted by a raid on their room in the early hours by her father and a couple of constables; as Vaux was not the original seducer, he was not apprehended. He could not trace her as he did not know her real surname, and he did not care.

He was back to square one, making an inventory of his clothes and begging his grandfather for money, lying that he had returned to the legal profession. As it turned out he did not need to resort to defrauding landlords and shopkeepers. Instead, he developed the criminal skills of sharping. Parting people from their money, either in a game or from the audience's side bets, was an immense intellectual and psychological effort in persuasion. It was a skill Vaux already possessed, so all he had to do was to pick a game.

He invested time in improving his billiards, working a morning shift when the more ruthless gangs of sharpers were still in bed, and parting the gullible from their money. In the evening, the professional sharpers were suspicious of him, but later, by Vaux's strategic sycophancy to one of their leaders and his obvious talent, he was allowed to join them. This scam did not last as the sharpers moved away to summer cons at races and fairs, and at cockfights, and real money could only be made by working to a script in an established team. He had neither people's trust nor friendship to do this.

Vaux got a job as a legal clerk in cheap, respectable and rustic Bury St Edmunds. For a month, he did a good job, copying deeds. He then grew bored, bought clothes and books on tick from gullible tradesmen, including an 8-guinea watch from a local maker, Lumley and Gudgeon. Mr Gudgeon believed that he was brilliantly 'selling up' to a simple yet honest clerk who would struggle to pay half a guinea a week in repayments in his desire to be a respectable member of Suffolk society but, in reality, Vaux was just going to run away with it and give him nothing. Faced with a 17-year-old boy, Mr Gudgeon thought that he could exploit Vaux's naivety, but he had none:

> I began to examine others of a cheaper kind but still letting him see that I had a strong inclination for the one he had recommended. This induced him to repeat his praises of the latter and to press me with greater energy to fix upon it I at length with a shew of much reluctance suffered myself to be persuaded.

He left suddenly one morning with the watch 'on approval', leaving a trunk weighted with stones to delay the search for him, and made his way back to London. There, he picked up a portmanteau of clothes that he knew his boss was shipping to London because he had opened his mail. He convinced the booking clerk to hand it over without full authorisation, sold the trunk to a pawnbroker, and bought a new one to conceal his stolen goods. He pawned the goods stolen as he did not know any fences, or receivers of stolen goods, and lived for six weeks on the proceeds. He had a gentlemen's life of leisure – books, tea, theatre and exhibitions but without, he hastened to add, the intoxication and debauchery that caused so many problems in London, Liverpool and Portsmouth.

When he was obliged to do paid work again, he found one transcribing legal documents, but it was in the same building as Mr Dalton, his employer in Bury St Edmunds, used when in London. He gave the area a 'wide berth, as the sailors term it', but one day as he went into his office, the door was locked behind him, and Mr Dalton was sitting there. He had done his research about Vaux's thieving; Vaux was even wearing the bilked watch. Dalton threatened him with transportation or worse. His room was searched and some of the clothes and paperwork found. He was detained by the constable. Dalton tracked down the man he had used for his reference for the lodging, and informed him about Vaux's behaviour. It seemed all over for flash Jim – but it wasn't.

The referee, Mr Presland, agreed to lend him the money to buy back everything that he had stolen, on the basis that his family were honourable and would pay him back. The family that he blamed for all of his problems was saving him again. It cost £30 to restore Dalton's property, who agreed not to prosecute. Presland gave Vaux another £5 and told him to return to Staffordshire. He promised to go home, but he lied; his disgrace in the navy was too well known there. He moved house and tried to get a job, not in a clerk's office but in a retail shop, where he could steal money a lot more easily.

How was he going to get a reference? Once again, he used his charm, psychological skills with people and utter fearlessness to get what was called a 'character'. Firstly, he selected and targeted somebody – this was Mr Giffard, who 'kept a large masquerade and habit warehouse in Tavistock street', essentially a fancy dress/sporting clothing shop, employing forty tailors. Giffard was clearly no fool, but Vaux had the better of him. He told him a plausible sob story 'with becoming modesty and propriety'. He had worked for a Mr Drake of Portsmouth, a town he knew well enough to lie plausibly about, but his job was terminated through a family tragedy with gruesome details that would have been laid on with a trowel. Mr Giffard liked his appearance – the con man needed to invest in clothes, as Vaux knew – and offered to write to the non-existent Mr Drake to confirm the details.

Vaux needed to get the letter and answer it himself, but it had already gone to the post office. Lesser or perhaps more moral people would have given up, but Vaux sought the driver of the Portsmouth to London mail coach, befriended him as he seemed able to do with all different social classes, and introduced himself as Mr Drake from Portsmouth. He asked his new friend to search for any letters for him in the Portsmouth Post Office, which, of course, would have been undeliverable as the address was imaginary. As always, Vaux's stratagems were usually more onerous than honest work would have been, but he enjoyed the challenge and reward of criminality much more than having a job.

The plan worked. He took delivery of the letter, replied with a warm recommendation for 'John Smith' and bribed a different coach official to take it to Portsmouth and post it there. Mr Giffard was about to retire and offered Vaux a post in the shop, working with his partner James Pettit. Vaux was disappointed that the business ran on credit and there was no regular money he could skim off, so he robbed the valuable textiles daily, smuggling them out in his overcoat and being careful not to take too much of the same item. He sold them to a Jewish fence rather than a pawnbroker. Vaux worked out that it would take about two months for his fraud to be uncovered.

The escape plan was the same. Fill a trunk full of stones, rent somewhere else, move his valuables slowly and unobtrusively to the new address and then flit. One of his last jobs was to deliver a ladies' riding habit to a coaching inn for onward delivery, but he decided to steal it – 'it occurred to me that I might as well embezzle the article.' His fence did not want it, so he sold it to a pawnbroker in Drury Lane for a pound more. This was a mistake; the shop was a mile from his employer's factory, and it was the first place that people looked for their stolen property. Often, they did not need to look as the pawnbrokers themselves would give up the information in exchange for a reward. The whole operation, like his other stings, lasted just less than ten weeks, but this one was not over.

Vaux gave up work once more with £60 in his pocket and lots of items to pawn. Two weeks later, he went back to the Drury Lane pawnshop where he was kept waiting by the owner long enough to summon Mr Pettit and a Bow Street runner. Vaux was detained in Cold Bath Fields prison, awaiting trial, the first time he had been caught.

He was unhappy in prison, but made the best of it. He was in a single cell, 9 foot by 6 with a bedstead, bed, blanket and rug, so he declined the offer to pay a bribe to get something better, as he believed he would only be there a few days. The next morning, breakfast was either a small stale loaf or whatever he wanted to pay for, and he opted for the latter, paying for all of his meals after that. He had £30 on his person and managed to get it past the guards, who may not have been looking very carefully. He was bored, but could hear conversations in the other cells of people also on remand:

> From their discourse, I acquired a more extensive knowledge of the various modes of fraud and robbery, which I now found were reduced a regular system, than I should have done in seven years had I continued at large.

Single cells were pointless if people could hear conversations and speak to each other. It meant that already bad people could train to become more efficient criminals. After a week, he was moved to New Prison in Clerkenwell while still awaiting trial. Life had its ups and downs. His home was robbed by a youth who he had employed to look after his valuables. He took it philosophically, as a thief would really be obliged to do. He and his new criminal mates chatted, drank and smoked, and swapped tips, while the prisoners with no money were confined to a large yard. He met toby-gils, buz-gloaks and cracksmen (highwaymen, pickpockets and housebreakers), who told him that there was no chance of him getting off, so he made no plans and lived in the moment.

Vaux's luck continued and he was acquitted. A year later, he was convicted for a crime he did not commit. It was the theft of handkerchief worth 2 shillings that got him the first of his transportations to Australia; he claims that he did not do it, which was believable considering what he shamelessly owned up to, but it *was* a little ironic.

Lack of space means this villain's tale must end here, but the rest of his adventure is a fantastic and fascinating read. He was a clever rogue, calculating and callous and full of cant; and the diary would be a brilliant, entertaining screenplay in the right hands. Hollywood has missed a trick with flash Jim Vaux.

Chapter 7

Walking in Wales
Richard Warner 1797

Our next witness is the Church of England clergyman Richard Warner. After a series of posts as a curate, he arrived in Bath in 1794. He started late in his career; he was strictly speaking a non-graduate as he never finished his studies at Oxford. He worked briefly at All Saints, a new proprietary chapel that was built for the increased population of Bath, where the congregation tended to be lower down the social scale. Within a few months, the fortuitous death of a curate allowed him to gain a position at St James, which was socially a cut or two above.

Warner was a man of strong opinions. He opposed the incipient movement for women's rights, and opposed more political rights for Catholics; unusually, he also opposed militarism and war, believing them to be incompatible with Christianity. His life was a constant round of provocations and responses. His sermons were popular, despite focusing on sin and hellfire rather than reassurance. His name was regularly in the *Bath Chronicle*. He was a big clever fish in his small pond, proud and preening, but in the end, quite likeable.

His interests were wide-ranging; he liked walking, scenery, topography, history and antiquities. He also did a lot of writing – history, fiction and travel writing, including about his travels through Wales. He walked through the Principality in August 1797 and in August and September 1798, taking with him both his intellectual interests and his English prejudices about Wales. To be fair, these prejudices were mild and not particularly directed at the Welsh, though he did prefer the Wales of the past. Like Moritz, he was enthralled by a prospect and advocated pedestrianism even when it led to social embarrassment, a perfect example of his radical views, in some areas of life at least.

Warner's book was a guide to walking, with the strong implication that the reader should consider doing the walk themselves, which makes it different to other travelogues in this book.[1] It contained maps, routes and mileage and was specifically designed for the pedestrian 'whose independent mode of transport enables him to catch the beauties in his walk through an Alpine (mountainous) country.' Wales was attractive, and not just the prospects. It was the land of the ancient Britons and the place where the tribes stood up against the Romans. He liked standing up to authority, albeit from the pulpit of the established Church of England.

Just like his sermons and social disputations in Bath, Warner was offering a radical manifesto; even if you were rich and could afford not to walk, the carriage was an encumbrance and the horse was an indulgence. Walking was intellectually liberating and connected you to the earth. So he walked: 469 miles in eighteen days, including two Sundays. There were no servants going on ahead, no post-chaises carrying his own sauces and sheets like John Byng. Instead, Warner had a large overcoat called a Spencer, which he had modified with extra pockets for his maps and compasses. It was old and shabby, but in a telling phrase, it would 'still make a respectable figure in North Wales.' He carried a small drinking horn to use when offered milk, as the containers proffered in Wales were much dirtier than those in England.

He took a companion to the Principality. His modern-sounding belief in the importance of intelligent tourism also included the notion that it was barren and empty to visit inspiring places on your own; you needed to 'interchange sentiment and communicate observation', and quotes Cicero – 'a journey to the stars without company would be but a dull kind of expedition'.

What was he looking for? His immediate aim was to avoid Bristol. It was not 'the towered cities or the busy hum of men that he wanted' but the countryside; he wanted nature. It was a lovely morning and he was reminded of the work of Scottish poet James Beattie – the lowing herd; the pipes of shepherds; the hum of bees, the rustling of corn and cry of the lark; the content whistling ploughman going about his work; it was the exact opposite of the crowded streets of backbiting Bath or busy Bristol.

Like most Georgian travellers, he encountered the inns and was disappointed with them. Breakfast at the Goat in Westbury was thin milk, stale bread and tepid water, but they left the place as happy as if they had feasted on the buns at Sally Lunn's in Sydney Gardens. Bath, the place he was overjoyed to leave, was never far from his thoughts.

They were walking on the turnpike road to New Passage in Gloucestershire (foot passengers were not charged at turnpikes as they could evade payment easily) when a vehicle carrying two fashionable women passed them. The companions were reminded that their own mode of travel was seen as weird. They had already had this debate before they left; two gentlemen walking in shabby coats was false shame, they told themselves; but when they recognised the ladies from Bath and knew they had been seen, all their egalitarian bravado melted away.

They all met again at New Passage, the place where the ferry left for Wales. Warner had his apology ready but the ladies were equally embarrassed about being seen in such a modest vehicle. But it was more embarrassing for Warner. The elegant women were in a cart only because they could get nothing else; Warner was on foot because they were 'passionately fond of exercise'. They had the same problem as Moritz; walking when there was an alternative always needed to be explained. Later during the tour, the landlord of Tan y Bwlch Inn simply slammed the door closed on them; in another inn they were allowed entry, but the waitress was ordered to count the silver cutlery.

Warner and his companion had missed the boat; literally in this case, as he claimed the captain saw them in deep conversation with the ladies and deliberately left without them. The fact that the owner of the ferry also owned all the other smaller boats made it a rational decision. The ferry fare was 9d (9 pence) but hiring a small boat would be 6 shillings. They are 'as rude, turbulent and violent as the estuary they navigate', said Warner, angry that the plebeians had the upper hand. He condemned them by comparing them with the Stygian boatmen, backed up with a few lines from Virgil that he did not translate for his readers because he knew he did not have to. As he crossed the Severn, the adventure began, as did the history – 'Tacitus, as you know, speaks of the Sabrina', and then quotes Milton, a poet that could be found in many educated Englishmen's pockets.

Caldecote, on the other side of the Sabrina, was the first of many visits to historical sites, too many to mention individually, but the pattern was the same. The two men liked ruins that were striking or picturesque or dominated the landscape. Warner did have historical knowledge of Caldecote Castle, but it was sometimes a little bare and inexact. He thought it was eleventh-century but most of what he would have seen

The Weymouth of Chapman, Knight and the Royal Family. (*Wellcome, London*)

A prison hulk, the temporary home of Holden and Vaux. (*Public domain*)

Vauxhall Gardens, enjoyed by Moritz in 1782. (*Public domain*)

The Houses of Parliament by Joseph Farington, where Moritz and Bamford visited. (*Public domain*)

Joseph Farington, RA. (*Public domain*)

Students at the Royal Academy. (Public domain)

William Windham makes a point. (Public domain)

William Hutton with a book to make a point. (Public domain)

Jane Austen, novelist and letter writer. (Public domain)

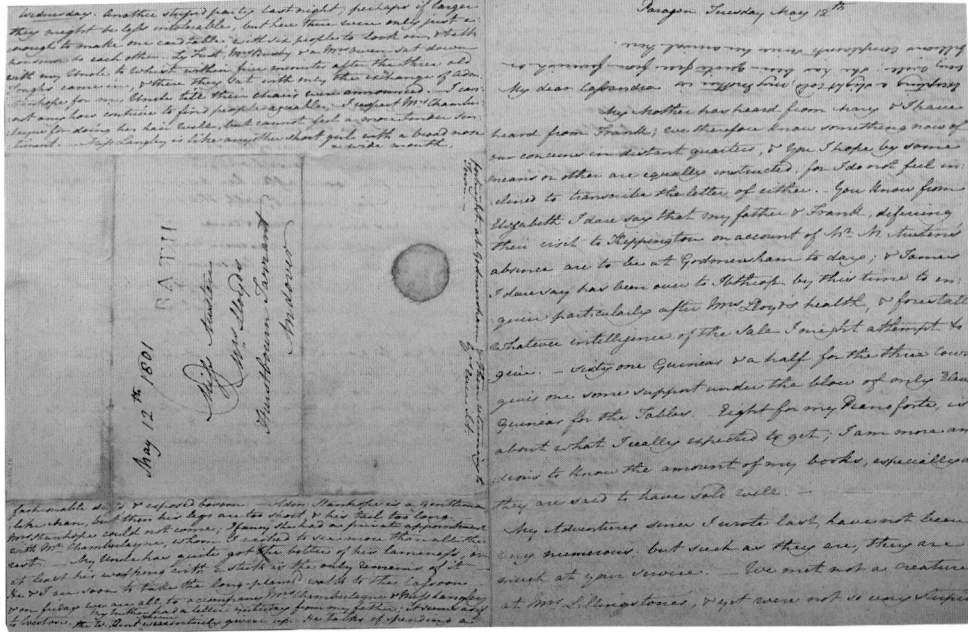

Jane Austen's letter to Cassandra. (*Public domain*)

Georgian Cruelty; the Body Snatchers and the Dissectors. (*Wellcome, London*)

Georgian Cruelty; the cock fight. (*Public domain*)

Carlton House, 1809, visited by Cornelia Knight. (*Public domain*)

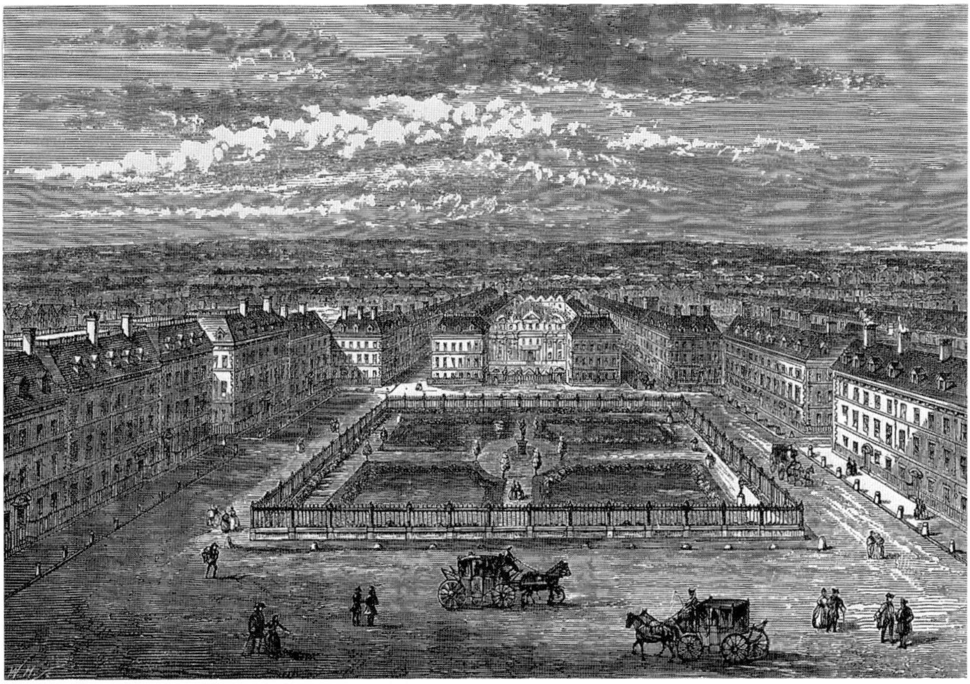

Soho Square, visited by Elizabeth Chivers. (*Wellcome, London*)

Handloom weaving, experienced by Bamford, Holden and Hutton. (Public domain)

Cold Bath Fields, a typical prison, also experienced by Bamford, Holden and Vaux. (Public domain)

The Gentry at play; gambling. (*Public domain*)

The Gentry at Play; dancing the quadrille. (*Public domain*)

A meeting of the rich; an assembly, 1820. (*Public domain*)

A meeting of the poor; a massacre, 1819. (*Public domain*)

was 200 years later; he knew it was connected with the conception of Henry VIII. Fact mattered, but so did imagination and emotion, and the latter was more of a subject for his book, which was meant to sell on its own terms as a book about travelling, not in itself a tourist guide.

Later in the day, they were disappointed with Caerwent; it was now a miserable village, unrecognisable from its Roman heyday. Warner and his companion sat and dreamt about its classical architecture, porticos, theatres and baths instead, using the ruins as a spark to the imagination, rather like modern tourists. And just like their modern counterparts, they became tired and wanted to replace history and ruins with food, drink and shelter. So they went to the Bull, stopped thinking about the classical world and tucked into beer, bacon and eggs instead.

Insider knowledge was needed for a walking holiday and this mostly came from the landlords of the local inns, who would have met the earnest traveller before and mastered the local detail. At the Bull, they requested a guide to the local ruins on which they had just exercised their imagination.

> After satisfying our appetite, we enquired for a ciceroni to conduct us round the ruins of Caerwent, and to point out a famous Roman tessellated pavement, which was discovered here in July 1777.

A 'ciceroni' was a direct reference to the Grand Tour, impossible in 1797. Naples had capitulated to the French, and Napoleon had conquered Italy, so the only available guides to culture were the landlords of Welsh inns or, in this case, his 18-year-old employee. The landlord was too busy drinking and smoking to be bothered, so he:

> committed us to the conduct of a fine lad about eighteen the ostler of the house who he assured us and I dare say with great truth would show the 'tiquities just as well as himself.

Warner noticed that the young man walked with a limp; three weeks earlier, his knee had swollen without an obvious cause, and the consensus in the village was that a local witch had taken ill to him. Warner was shocked – such superstitious beliefs and, more shockingly, only 30 miles from Bath! Later, the landlord of the Bull, who was no better a surgeon than he was a historical guide, lanced the knee and burnt it to the bone, making it worse. Warner feared for the old woman who was blamed, but was relieved when it transpired that she had given the lad practical advice and told him she was no threat. Civilisation had trounced superstition in Wales, but only just.

Warner's second visit to Caerwent involved describing and measuring the ruins and comparing them with what was said by John Leland in the 1530s.[2] He was very interested in the mosaic, 24 feet by 18, which had been found in a farmer's field two years earlier. It was surrounded by a wall low enough for people to steal the red, yellow, blue and white tesserae. It doesn't come as a surprise that many antiquities did not survive their discovery by the Georgians. Despite this outpouring of facts, the response to the ruins was still emotional and as they left, they sighed over the perishing remains and moralised on the transitory nature of human grandeur.

Their journey continued on the improved turnpike road. These were like modern motorways – convenient but tedious, and not what Warner was seeking on his travels; they diverted as soon as they could for the enthralling scenery en route to Usk, where they arrived at the Three Salmons Inn after walking 36 miles. The evening visit to Usk was pleasing, with the usual checklist of Roman remains, reformation ruins, parts of castles and a bit of reflective rumination – 'a melancholy monument of the nullity of human labours, of the vanity of man's attempting to make himself a lasting name by the works of his hands.' *Sic transit gloria mundi* – a moral that both the cleric and the antiquarian in him felt comfortable with.

They left the inn early at 5.00 am to enjoy the countryside and, as ever, with a poet to back up their plan. This time, it was James Thomson, a Scottish poet of medium importance who was also appreciated by Karl Moritz. Thomson died prematurely at the age of 47 by over enthusiastic bathing in cold water:

> For is there ought in sleep can charm the wise?
> Who would in such a gloomy state remain
> Longer than Nature craves?

It was 11 miles to Abergavenny and they had breakfast there at the Angel Inn. It was market day, so they went to do some people-watching at what Warner inevitably called the forum. This was the first time he had encountered Welsh, as most of the customers had come in from distant rural areas ('which have neither markets nor shops of their own'). Not speaking their language, Warner needed another way of judging them, so he chose the cleanliness of their vegetables and the neatness of their clothes. The judgement was favourable; everything was unsullied and neat, cleanliness was next to godliness, and the willingness to arrange one's vegetables was a reflection of how one's life was organised.

The verdict on the women was *mostly* favourable. They were attractive in a primitive way, but this rustic charm could not quite compensate for their guttural and inelegant language. He did not quite suggest that they were speaking their own tongue to exclude and alienate them, like Farington did, but this was because he knew that they spoke no other language. Warner did believe that such behaviour was appropriate from the simple and naïve descendants of the ancient Britons. After the bustle of the modern Welsh forum, they hurried off for more silence and desolation at the remains of Abergavenny Castle. They consulted Giraldus Cambrensis (Gerald of Wales), an author who was writing about Wales in the late twelfth century.

The theme of 'primitive Wales' occurred time and again. The less advanced economy of Wales had to export both raw materials and people. On their scenic walk, they encountered local black cattle going to pasture in Somerset and Wiltshire via Bristol; this could not be done in Wales because of the grass; which was literally greener in England. They also met hundreds of reapers crossing the channel to work in agriculture in the West Country.

They saw some Druidic stones; they were interesting but a superstition, thought Warner, presumably forgetting the history of early Rome. Crickhowell Castle was enjoyably ruined; then to the Beaufort Arms for their first ever Welsh beer. He called it *cwrrw*, but the actual word is *cwrw* and it means no more than 'beer', but he rebranded it as the drink of the ancient Briton. It was another hot day and soon they were looking for a farmer to provide them with 'new milk'; warm and straight from the cow. They succeeded at the second attempt and were not allowed to pay. The people were kind, rustic and straightforward, he concluded again, showing the same attitudes as modern first-world travellers who visit a poor country without understanding the language and culture.

At Brecon, Warner said directly something he had merely hinted at since crossing the Severn; 'Like most other towns in Wales, this place is interesting rather from what it has been, than on account of what it now is.' There was a castle, and a former religious abbey nearby, built by the Lords to deflect for all the acts of spoliation, rapine and misrule. We are reminded that he was no Tory.

Warner liked a good graveyard and, on this occasion, he noticed the inscriptions lacked pretension and were simple and sincere, which was his view of the Welsh above ground as well. The evening finished with Usk trout and Breconshire mutton at the inn.

The next day's hike was to be Rhaidr-Gwr. They started on the turnpike, diverted in a recently cut hay meadow, and got themselves lost. When asking directions, they were invited to a Welsh home by a labourer who spoke English and was very intelligent; these were two things rather than one. Such travel writing as this can take us where no other historical source can go – into the houses of the socially modest:

> On entering the tenement, which consisted only of a ground floor we found that it was divided into two apartments the inner one a bed and four chairs the outer displaying an infinite variety of heterogeneous articles, implements of destruction and books of divinity, culinary utensils and apothecary's drugs, tools and English classics, a cabinet and cupboard tables and stools chairs and benches. We were shaken by the hand and bidden to sit.

On the menu was beer, cheese, oatcakes and the uplifting life story of the tenant Robert Lewis. Warner liked a good story of resilience and moral rectitude among the poor-yet-honest, and listened respectfully as his own moral code was repeated back to him. Lewis was from one of the best families in Wales, but he must have been quite a distance from them as he was apprenticed to a tanner. He fell in love with a girl whose family thought him beneath them, and they were not only abusive and awkward but also attempted to kill him. When they failed, they destroyed his business; his wife died of a broken heart and he brought up their four children in the distressed but proud circumstances that they saw him in now.

Warner and his companion moved on to Bualt and came across the bridge where Llywelyn ap Gruffudd was defeated by the forces of

Edward I in 1240. Like many radicals at that time and since, Warner loved an exotic freedom fighter, and made this clear. The prince's body was received with savage joy by Edward at Conwy Castle; the people were worse, carrying the head through London on a silver spike, commiserated Warner. A few days later, he visited Machynlleth and the barn where Owain Glyndwr called the first parliament in Wales; he liked him, too, despite him being no friend to the English.

Towns held little interest; they marched through Builth Wells, but the River Wye was so beautiful that they lingered to admire it. Warner, like Moritz, loved a prospect that was beautiful, picturesque, awesome (in the sense of creating wonder) or panoramic. Like Byng, he preferred the cottages of the poor to be neat, as this implied that they were prosperous, being looked after by their betters and doing what they were told.

Their awe at the River Wye made them stay too long on this occasion. It was 16 miles to the next inn and there were only two hours of daylight left. They arrived at the Angel Inn at 9.30 pm and saw some stereotypical images: a groaning table of food full of beef, pork and fragments of geese, a vision compared to Hogarth and therefore 'English'; a group of Welsh rustics devouring the food; and a small huddled group of Scots pedlars with bread and rock-hard cheese, looking resentful and poor.

They themselves were not any type of cliché – English gentlemen, with no servants or carriage, completely covered in filth and having no reason to be there at all, but they were treated convivially. However, there was only one bed; it must have been small because males sharing a bed was common and had no connotations. A toss of a coin decided who walked the quarter of a mile to another cottage.

The next day was pure scenery in the direction of the Devils Bridge; a few hovels used by shepherds and were inhabited by 'the joyless beings who tended the widely-spread flocks that fed upon these mountains.' Warner was reminded that there was more to Wales than agriculture when he met a one-armed man fishing for trout and young salmon. His right arm had been crushed in an accident blasting rock.

When Warner showed an interest in how the accident happened, the stranger directed them to a lead mine, and gave a long description of what it was like to be a miner. It was, of course, tiring and dangerous. For a start, it was piecework – 5 pounds a ton, 'and for that he has to bore for the vein, blasts the rock, extract, cleans, and sorts the ore, and produces one ton of it fit for the furnace.' He had to pay for his own gunpowder. The dangers were the cold, damp and vapour, and the extreme physical effort; the wages were not related to the amount of work, but to the state of the market. The war had disrupted the industry, but only the workers suffered with a fall in wages and an increase in food prices. Money was borrowed from his employers to see him through lean times, so he was tied to his job by debt.

This miner-turned-fisherman was at the bottom of the heap. The real money was made by Mr Powell of Nanteos, who, by virtue of the ownership of God's earth, did nothing, while he and future generations of the family were made rich by the work of the poor. They were managed by Sir Thomas Bonsal, knighted a year earlier by George III and who eventually adopted a coat of arms with pickaxes on it. This story brought out the radical in Warner; he was briefly moved by local injustice and poverty, and, like the tourist, moved on.

There followed another 'only in Wales' anecdote. Warner took shelter in a gentleman's house when a visit to the inn was impossible because of the weather, and he got the painful proof that a Welsh gentleman did not live like an English one. The house was no more than a barn, despite the hospitality of the couple who lived there; his room had no shutters and curtains and the storm raged as he tried to sleep, so he had nightmares. He woke and saw a huge, black object glide softly into his room, followed by agonised screams in another room. He grabbed his stick, rushed to his friend's room for shelter, but as he left his room, he hit a rock-hard object that winded him and frightened him back into his room, where he locked the door and cowered all night. The huge object was a wandering sheep dog and the screams were a patient with horrible toothache.

Letter six (19 August 1797) starts with a piece of information that cheered all tourists; everything was much cheaper than at home. He had an excellently-priced meal in the Wynne Arms with London Porter rather than the usual brew, and the beer was nearly the price of the food, another modern touch. This was not because food was cheaper in the shops; indeed, the war was doing the same to prices in Wales as in England. He did not know why Wales was cheaper, but rejoiced at the fact.

The Welsh, or the 'Cambrians', as Warner called them as he became more whimsical, were flawed in so many ways, but most of them were endearing. A Mr David Pughe had a pompous manner and was pretentious about his family history, but that was deemed diverting and harmless. In winter, the locals chased the wild goats of Cader Idris with dogs. It was like hunting in England, but everything was just that little wilder and more rustic: 'The rocks and precipices re-echo the united sounds of huntsmen dogs and horns and a chorus is formed singular striking and indescribable.'

They walked and climbed themselves into a state of fatigue, and were therefore able to sleep well in their tiny, dirty flea-ridden hotel room. Their journeys continued with picturesque scenery, solemn ruins and more poor people telling Warner stories. He met Henry Roberts, an injured war veteran. Henry worked in the toll house, rent-free, sold provisions in his chandler's shops and helped tourists like Warner. He also had a daughter who was so lovely that she excelled her modest surroundings – tall, elegant, fair complexion, eyes beaming kindness, hair flowing in ringlets over her shoulders. Warner and companion listened intently to their story; as progressives, this is what they did, and in case the reader was unsure, then they were reminded:

> However as my companion and myself are not of the number of those who disdain to hear the 'simple annals of the poor' we neither hastened nor interrupted the detail but listened with all proper attention till he had concluded.

Like most of our witnesses, Warner saw non-conformity in religion as mostly a good thing.

He met a congregation of Presbyterians and it amused him that they were in the hamlet of Penstreet (although he does not explain the joke to his audience).[3] They were ordered and disciplined, and the appalling weather did not stop them worshipping; their religion and their morals were better than the similar lower order in England, who he called canaille – 'riff raff'. He may have been a radical, but he still preferred the poor when they were doing what they were told; he just wanted them to be treated fairly as reward for their obedience.

Warner and his companion were not too grand for some trophy tourism and, on 21 August, they attempted to climb Snowdon. They took a guide who told them that this was not the best place to start from, and prepared for the ordeal by drinking milk from a local farm and filling their 'leathern bottles'. They wished they had brandy, but their guide told them the mixture of alcohol and these altitudes would cause extreme intoxication. They reached the summit, but the clouds did not stay away for long to make it worthwhile.

The themes of the tour were repeating themselves by the time they reached North Wales. Accommodation was not great: 'if they could but boast good beds Wales be a paradise'; the Welsh were rustic today, but heroic freedom fighters yesterday. Caernarvon Castle had to be strong and extensive 'because of the fierce people ardently attached to liberty who wore the yoke of a foreign master with disgust and impatience.' The prospects around the Menai Straits area were a colourful joy: 'The mountains showed their grey heads the face of ocean smiled'; 'The white wave seen tumbling round the distant rock'; the locals played the harp beautifully, but then that is what they did, wasn't it?

Warner liked everything about Wales, and it showed. He also knew that it was a foreign country where things were done differently, and were done better in the past, but he mostly forgave them. Despite his weaknesses, this was a fresh perspective on Georgian Wales and, it has to be said, on the trendy clergy of Georgian Bath.

Chapter 8

Dancing and Travelling
Jane Austen 1796–1814

Jane Austen is our most famous Georgian for obvious reasons, but our focus will be on the 160 letters written to her sister, Cassandra, rather than her novels.¹ The real-life experiences narrated in the letters are inspirations for the novels in any case, but the letters are used as an unconscious witness to the late Georgian era for a clever middle-class woman with few prospects but many hours to fill.

What are the limits of the evidence? They were documents designed for the recipient and close family only, and not written for effect or an eye to the future, although the contents may have also been moderated by the fact that letters like this were often read aloud *en famille*. They are jokey and gossipy, and some have clearly been removed from the sequence when, or before, they were published in 1870.

The letters' *raison d'être* is to provide news about the family. In some, Cassandra was only 12 miles away as the crow flies; the letters read like chatty phone calls so scholars of Austen should be glad there was no telephone at the time as there would have been no need for newsletters like this. The documents show the minutiae of genteel provincial life and it is not surprising that *The Times* described them on first publication as 'not very interesting'. It added to the Victorian belief that Jane and Cassandra's life was more than a bit dull and insulated from reality.

However, this *was* their reality, their 'society' consisting of close family, extended family, friends, neighbours and connections – it was not *that* narrow an experience. The first letter Jane wrote to her sister, from the Austen home in Steventon on 9 January 1796, contained just over 900 words and namechecks thirty people.² Even those she did not know personally are mentioned, because of their relationship with somebody else she *did* know. They were part of her society, so their presence mattered.

There is too much detail in the letters for this book, so two subjects have been selected; both are about mobility of different sorts, and both imply that Jane's life was not quite as routine as some people have suggested. The first is a major interest of the sisters and similar women in their social situation – assemblies, dancing and the activities that went with it.

The headline news of the first letter was the recent ball that had taken place at the Harwood family residence at Deane Park, not far from their much more modest home in Steventon. The Harwood ball was a private affair with invited guests only, and a step above the assembly room affairs. Both public and private balls were a key part of Jane's social life, and the life of all unmarried people of her class. Balls took place either at somebody's home (you could expect ten days' notice of an invitation) or in a provincial assembly room. There would be at least one large rectangular room, with dancing from about 9.00 pm until early the next morning, with supper and some allied amusements like whist for the non-dancers, and normally another separate room. Jane often liked it when there was a separate anteroom for sitting and chatting. She makes it clear that chairs *and* dancers were needed for a good evening:

> There was the same kind of supper as last year, and the same want of chairs. There were more dancers than the room could conveniently hold, which is enough to constitute a good ball at any time.

Jane attended five balls in the winter of 1796, looked forward to the next one, reported back to her sister and expected reports from her. She was not an uncritical observer of balls or, indeed, of the people there, despite her fondness for them.

Today, we might assume that the ball was a good way of mingling freely with the opposite sex, but there was no mingling and nothing was free. Nothing about the activity was spontaneous. It was not the eighteenth-century equivalent of a discotheque, except perhaps in one respect. Whether private or public, it was a ruthless meat market, to use a phrase that Georgians would have understood even if they did not use. A single man at a ball was advertising his desire for a wife; a single woman was doing the same but with an asymmetry of power that made it much harder work for women, as Jane regularly noted.

In order to converse with men outside your family circle, you had to dance with them, so competent dancing skills were vital for both men and women. Books were published to guide would-be dancers. The steps and movements were complicated and could not be varied, and the social rules were as rigid as the dance itself. Only practice beforehand or a course of lessons would be enough.

Jane wanted some control over who she danced with, yet within the etiquette of a Regency ball. Dancing with people you did not like was 'a dance of mortification'.[3]

In the first letter, she managed to avoid 'to my inexpressible astonishment' the company of John Lyford. He did not ask her to dance but she had to actively try to avoid it – 'I was forced to work hard for it.' If she had refused Mr Lyford, a local surgeon, she would have been obliged to refuse everybody else and the evening would be ruined. Later in the evening, it was just about possible to claim tiredness as these balls were punishingly physically affairs and not the cool and sedate events shown in television dramas, but the rule generally held. The wrong man could spoil the evening:

> I had an odd set of partners: Mr Jenkins, Mr Street, Col. Jervoise, James Digweed, J. Lyford, and Mr Briggs, a friend of the latter. I had a very pleasant evening, however...

The 'however' is the key word here. There were two J. Lyfords, father and son, but this was probably the son, so Jane was probably unable to avoid him this time.

She would always have a chaperone. A mother would be ideal but at the Harwood ball, it was James Austen, Jane's elder brother. The fact that they spent some of the evening coaching James in dancing shows the importance of this social skill; but his most crucial role at the ball was to act as a social counterbalance for his sister, a single woman. He could not help her out by dancing with her to avoid unwanted contact. It was frowned upon to dance with close family – this was a mating game after all – but his presence was still vital. She did not resent it, despite 'modern' feelings on the restrictions on women. Indeed, she loved the presence of her brother at such events – 'a ball is nothing without him'.

She had six brothers; five are regulars in her letters. George Austen is never referred to. He had medical problems at birth that may have included epilepsy and he lived away from the family. While never forgotten, he is not mentioned, partly due to the stigma and partly because Jane's letters are news, and poor George was not doing anything.

Back to the Harwoods' ball; Jane listed her dance partners as she did in every letter about a ball she attended, but this one was much different to any other. She was 'flirting' with a young man, Tom Lefroy, who she had met the previous December. Tom almost got top billing with her beloved sister in the first letter, which begins with a birthday greeting for Cassandra:

> In the first place I hope you will live twenty three years longer. Mr Tom Lefroy's birthday was yesterday so that you are very near of an age.

There was actually a three-year gap between Tom and Cassandra; he was 20, the same age as Jane. She had taken the opportunity to talk with Tom, and not just between dances. Some dances, like minuets, involved watching other people dance and therefore they would have been able to talk while public attention was elsewhere. A dance could take up to 15 minutes.

There was some scope for touching as well; both parties wore gloves, which expanded opportunity by making it acceptable, but also dulled sensation. Jane and Tom may have spent slightly too much time in conversation and the room would have noticed, as Jane always recognised such behaviour in others. One advantage of rigid rules is that you can make your meaning clear with the tiniest infraction of them. Nobody was eloping to Gretna here and reputations would remain intact; indeed, this is how marriages began, and marriages were the ultimate point of the ball.

There was never going to be a marriage in this case. Jane met Tom Lefroy one more time – at another ball – and they never saw each other again. This is regarded as Jane's only serious romance and possibility of marriage (she briefly accepted a proposal from Harris Bigg-Wither but changed her mind the next morning; this is not mentioned in the surviving letters at all).

It is hard to work out how important this flirtation with Tom Lefroy was; Jane's light-hearted tone, which runs through the letters, does not help. But it seems that at the Horwoods' ball, Jane knew that her relationship with Tom would both develop and terminate at the Ashe ball. There was no meeting in any other social context. When she attempted to do more, it did not go down well:

> for he is so excessively laughed at about me at Ashe, that he is ashamed of coming to Steventon, and ran away when we called on Mrs Lefroy a few days ago.

There was a level of social embarrassment here. It is a truth universally acknowledged that an intelligent, accomplished 20-year-old member of the provincial gentry with no dowry was not a great marriage prospect. Jane was ultimately not good enough for Tom. She was an excellent dancer; on one later occasion, she opened up the evening's dancing, which was considered an honour. But dancing only led to marriage when the richer family was not marrying to make themselves poorer. Female accomplishments meant little without money.

Jane knew about these issues when meeting somebody through dancing. Although jokingly, social status was never far away when she told Cassandra about her dancing partners. On one occasion she danced:

> twice with a Mr South, a lad from Winchester, who, I suppose, is as far from being related to the bishop of that diocese as it is possible to be.

With Tom Lefroy, it was about the money as well. He was an eldest child, but still relied on others to pay for his expensive legal education. Jane's father was in financial difficulties. Tom, like Jane's brothers, had prospects and adventures. He would later become Ireland's Lord Chief Justice and would still have done so if they had married; however, she may well not have become Jane Austen the author. The work that was to become *Pride and Prejudice* was started in the same year, and it is very doubtful that a Mrs Thomas Lefroy would have ever finished it.

Jane continued to look forward to balls; it fitted in with her social life which consisted of being in 'company'. A lot of energy and time went into what was to be worn, especially caps. She made and altered clothes, turning a domestic time-killing activity into something that had a point. She also held clothes back for this special occasion – 'my china crepe is still kept for the ball' – because it was a place where you would be judged.

'Judged' is the key word here. People were on show. On 14 January 1801, Cassandra reported back on the Chilham ball, and was told off light-heartedly for dancing with Mr Kembler four times – 'why not rather dance two of them with some elegant brother officer who was struck with your appearance as you entered the room?'

What happened in the ballroom mostly stayed in the ballroom. Although you needed to have been formally introduced in order to dance at all, having danced with somebody gave you no more rights after the ball was over and certainly not on the next meeting. In December 1808, Jane describes meeting somebody who she had danced with:

> We have always kept up a bowing acquaintance since, and, being pleased with his black eyes, I spoke to him at the ball, which brought on me this civility; but I do not know his name, and he seems so little at home in the English language that I believe his black eyes may be the best of him.

Her decision to acknowledge him was within her power. Dancing did not imply a new relationship; this was impossible, considering the number of partners people had over a season. In her letters, she usually took care to list her partners to Cassandra, not because their names mattered, but because it was gossip.

Physical sacrifices were made in order to attend dances. Despite her eyes hurting, Jane attended a ball where she knew there was dust in the room and her need to keep her eyes open all night would exacerbate the condition. When she wrote to Cassandra, her eyes were still hurting but there was no question that it was worth it.

The number of dances, like the society, the room and the quality of the supper, varied. When there were more or fewer dances than usual, Jane commented on it:

> There were twenty dances, and I danced them all, and without any fatigue.

> There were only twelve dances, of which I danced nine, and was merely prevented from dancing the rest by the want of a partner. We began at ten, supped at one, and were at Deane before five. There were but fifty people in the room.

Dancing took youth and strength, two attributes that made you good marriage material.

> James, who does not dance well, finds it fatiguing.

The number of people and the gender ratio were vital for a good evening. On one occasion there were only eight couples and twenty-three people in the room. Jane was concerned that all women should have the opportunity to dance. The Miss Lances rarely had partners and were a particular concern of hers at times; perhaps she was a concern to others as well.

The Austen family was not quite rich enough to allow Jane much social mobility, and she often had the same problem with geographical mobility. In both cases, it would be important to be a member of the carriage company. Owning private transport was expensive. It required investment in vehicles, stabling, servants and taxes, and needed an income of about £1,000 per year in the 1790s. The Austens were on the cusp of carriage company; at times they had one and other times not, and it deeply affected Jane's lifestyle.

They owned a donkey cart, which could be used as transportation if there was nobody to see them leave or arrive. They did have a little carriage at Steventon and Jane used it to go to Deane. In her later life, she not only used this form of transportation but rode the donkey herself. When, in one of her last letters, she said she was using the donkey, her reasoning was that 'twill be more independent and less troublesome than the use of the carriage.'

How did you get to the ball, and get back at 4.00 am, without private transport? No eligible man or woman arrived at the ball on foot or donkey cart. Jane would regularly attend the Thursday assembly in Basingstoke, the nearest large town, but a carriage was needed to get there and they did not have one. By November 1798, she commented how pleased she was that the Basingstoke Assembly had declined, just as their ability to get there had been reduced:

> Our assemblies have very kindly declined ever since we laid down the carriage, so that disconvenience and disinclination to go have kept pace together.

This may have been a convenient excuse for what must have been a social blow, although favours from friends were possible. Jane often stayed with the Bigg-Wither family at Manydown Park after the Basingstoke ball, and sometimes they would be lent a chaise, but they were vaguely unsatisfactory options. In her novels, Austen identified the exact type of private transport as a way of pinpointing people's social status, so she knew exactly what her own was – fading gentry. [4]

When they were moving house again, in 1808, she took a different attitude:

> A larger circle of acquaintance, and an increase of amusement, is quite in character with our approaching removal. Yes, I mean to go to as many balls as possible, that I may have a good bargain.

Jane's social life largely consisted of visits by friends and relatives, and they would travel by private transport – either a private carriage or a private hired post-chaise. If you didn't marry somebody you danced with first, it would be someone who you initially had tea with and, in both cases, a private carriage would have transported them to your world.

In June 1808, Jane wrote a letter to Cassandra describing her journey from London to her brother's family at Godmersham Park in Kent. They did have their own transport when living in Bath, and Jane makes that obvious by adding a possessive pronoun to a word she used regularly without one:

> At half after seven yesterday morning Henry saw us into **our** own carriage, and we drove away from the Bath Hotel (in Piccadilly, London); which, by-the-bye, had been found most un-comfortable quarters — very dirty, very noisy, and very ill-provided.

The use of the word 'hotel' here is very unusual at this time. It denoted either prestige or pretension or both, and Jane may well have mentioned it as further evidence that their prospects were improving. Their brother

James took the public stagecoach, leaving two hours earlier. Then, as now, public transport was less convenient.

Jane did not spend her life at home writing letters or playing parlour games all evening. She did move about the south of England in a way that we would see as limited, but was average for her class and gender. For such a long-distance journey, there was no shame in not using your own private carriage. You could temporarily hire a private chaise, or you could go by public stagecoach, as Austen did later in life. When they went travelling in Kent in October 1798, they did so in a hired vehicle with room for three people and no space for strangers.

All Austen's trips away were family-related because there was little else they could be related to. She was in London in August 1796 – 'Here I am once more in this scene of dissipation and vice, and I begin already to find my morals corrupted,' she joked. She visited Bath in May 1799 with her mother, and listed the things that could have gone wrong but cheerfully announced that they had not:

> Our journey yesterday went off exceedingly well; nothing occurred to alarm or delay us. We found the roads in excellent order, had very good horses all the way, and reached Devizes with ease by four o'clock... At Devizes we had comfortable rooms and a good dinner, to which we sat down about five; amongst other things we had asparagus and a lobster, which made me wish for you, and some cheesecakes.

This was the best you could get, and, just like today, if it actually happened it was worth talking about.

Jane did not travel by public stagecoach until later in life when she was an established author – a right that would have been expected by her brothers since the age of 12. In 1799, she made the point that it was difficult for a single woman to travel on her own. Charles, her brother, wanted to meet his ship at Deal and planned to take a stagecoach. There was no space and he had to return home. Not only could men use coaches, they could stand out on a January evening and wait for one that might be full. He then considered a night coach, even more out of the question for women. Jane wanted to go with him – 'but the un-pleasantness of returning by myself deters me.' Ships, coaches and roads were available to her brothers because they had careers, prospects and agency.

Austen famously said in 1796 that she wanted to go by stagecoach into London but her brother Frank would not let her. Historians have always taken the quote seriously, despite the fact that the letters are filled with light-hearted remarks, but everybody knew how awful public transport could be. Her letters to Cassandra tell of one stagecoach journey on her own in August 1814; Jane was able to report good news:

> I had a very good journey, not crowded, two of the three taken up at Bentley being children, the others of a reasonable size; and they were all very quiet and civil.

Austen sums up the potential problems brilliantly and briefly: the loss of personal space; the danger of bad behaviour; and the irksome obligation to chat trivialities to strangers. Her brother Henry met her at the London terminus; she had travelled without a chaperone, also unusual, and they used a nice, large, cool, dirty hackney coach to get to his house. When arriving in London, she mentions her rides in her brother's barouche, a high-class carriage where the passengers were meant to be seen. She knew that this mattered. She may never have had the marriage, but she occasionally had the carriage.

Chapter 9

Quaker

Hannah Gurney 1804–1820

Our next witness is another agonised introspective like William Windham, with an added feature that we do not see very much in other Georgian witnesses; religious fervour. Hannah Chapman Gurney was a member of the tight-knit Quaker community in Britain. Her father was the private banker Joseph Gurney. Her mother was Jane Chapman, daughter of Quaker bank and ship owner Abel Chapman. Hannah went on to marry the Quaker banker Jonathan Backhouse and moved to Darlington in 1811. She was interconnected with all the major Quaker families, including the Frys. Elizabeth, the prison reformer, was 'my dearest Betsy' to her.

Hannah's diary was printed privately in 1858; it was never meant for publication of any sort, and was only printed to show others how a dedicated Quaker thought and behaved. It was never available as a commercial publication; then, as now, there was no commercial public appetite for such an intense piece of writing. The work consists, unfortunately, of preselected extracts chosen by her relative, Jane Gurney Fox, but we can be reasonably sure that nothing self-incriminating was left out; indeed, it is much more likely to have been put in. Strict examination of weaknesses was a Quaker habit.

Like the work of William Windham, the diary was an exercise in self-improvement and self-criticism. The man of feeling could have written this entry:

Resolved to be industrious and get up in the morning and knock Latin into me as almost every other hour in the week is employed.

It is not easy reading to the modern eye, but it is worth the effort. It gets into the mind of a dedicated religious devotee, and this phrase is not a figure of speech as the diary is mostly an internal monologue. There are external events, but they are all evaluated intellectually, religiously, and internally.

Hannah's diary starts on 11 March 1804, when she was aged nearly 17.[2] She describes her childhood in a few paragraphs; loving parents who would chastise her when necessary (with words); summer holidays in Cromer with other famous Quaker families; healthy outdoor play and a rigorous education.

It seemed that her early life was not particularly religious or even that intellectual, but the diary starts when things are about to change. She learnt to love learning in about 1800, aged 13, and this started a lifetime of activity; you could not be happy without work and intellectual effort. Like many nonconformist groups, her key tenet was working, getting things done and *achievement*.

She now wished to learn Latin, but had to create the time to do so by getting up early. She fought constantly against sloth, like she did with all the deadly sins. She hated time wasted, and sometimes despised people who wasted time, although she tried not to, as this was the capital vice of pride. Once again, this could be Windham thinking.

In the busy month of March 1804, she had a day of mathematics, some instruction on sketching and enjoyed reading philosophy ('I had a delightful hour reading Locke'). She also read the Bible every day and had read it through once by 1806. She had no problem with science – these were God's laws, to be discovered with the God-given intellect and God-demanded endeavour.

The next element of her diary is a profound introspection and constant scanning for sin, both in her actions and her thoughts, but mostly in her thoughts, as her most sinful action seems to have been what we might call a teenage tantrum. The best early example was her love of sketching. In September 1804, she drew an image of a hedger; she drew on the Friday and, on the Saturday, she liked it so much that she attempted some pride which led to a fall:

> I did so well that I felt most uncomfortably elated with it as I was self conceited beyond measure and did nothing but fancy I should be a great artist.

Quaker: Hannah Gurney 1804–1820

Sunday was no better; pride was not defeated and sloth made an appearance again

> Sunday – Like a fool I did nothing at meeting but dream about being an artist. Vexed that I have not the power of keeping my thoughts from wandering.

Hannah had desires – to be a famous painter, to go to London to see the gay life ('May I not savour it too well for my own good!') and to be clever. In her journal she writes 'my thoughts have been this week one continued castle in the air of being an artist.'

Like Windham, she saw reveries as a distraction and a temptation. A few years later, when a General Phipps was a guest at their house, her uncle requested a drawing but she was in agony again. She could not ignore a lawful order from her family, but did not wish to do something well and suffer the sin of pride – 'puffed up' was her usual expression – and she wished to give it up. 'A mind kept on the Christian's watch is I think little capable of entering into the spirit of the fine arts.' She then read the Bible in bed as a corrective for her behaviour.

Her attitude to life was theological. She had not seen much horror in the world, but she was very much aware that she was of the world, if not in it. She was visited by Jane C------- (much of her life consisted of earnest conversation with friends and relatives), who informed her that the world could be wicked, and Hannah's main conclusion was that there must be eternal life, and eternal separation from such good people like Jane would be unthinkable. The object of the human mind is eternal happiness:

> Today in parting with the C s with the greatest probability of never meeting again is there not a something that makes one feel it is not to be an eternal separation. It seems but a day since they came and now they are gone a few more and this busy life will be over and then I firmly believe the good we love here will be restored to us in tenfold measure for eternity.

Life was both important yet so very brief, but must be filled with action and improvement. She was particularly keen on early rising; on one occasion she lambasted herself for rising at 8.00 am; the next day she was more satisfied with herself when she rose at 6.00 am without, of course, being pleased with herself merely for doing the right thing, as that would be pride.

Hannah was very much aware of the seven deadly sins and the temptation of the world; happiness in eternity was the aim, but there was a lot of superficially more attractive world pleasures standing in the way and looking more alluring in the short term. Even a novel could run her off course; she wanted to see the world, but she knew that it could not make her happy and even worse, might be the antithesis of religion.

The world, as she said later, was probation. Another social event produced more internal religious monologue and a bit of snide:

> Sunday and C and C to tea. My reflection on the evening was; can these be immortal souls? What a great increase of happiness there would be if conversation were composed of better materials than it is.

The words that come to mind are puritan and judgemental; and wrath in the face of people who were not her intellectual equals – 'I cannot bear talking about trifles,' she said later. The next day, her friend Hannah Chapman told her of her faults in the form of a loving reprimand, which was very much part of the Quaker tradition. She thanked her friend for her help. She owned her faults. Life was a battleground, mostly fighting yourself.

She tried not to judge people, and not to use the words 'genteel' or 'vulgar'. This was pride, but pride sometimes won when she saw human beings showing their weak side. In October 1806, she visited a family noted only as ------ to save their embarrassment:

> What dull worldly people they seem to be. Having done nothing all day and being all assembled in the evening pervaded the whole room to such a degree that I wished I had been obliged to work for my bread that my duty might not lie in the listless inactivity of a parlour.

The Blanks came to tea on the following Sunday and Hannah maintained a judgemental sullen silence, which she later acknowledged as pride. She was 19; not 'so good as many but considerable better than some', she said, not knowing where she stood in the world.

She tried to be polite, even when tested by boredom, trivia or boring trivial people. She agonised about this too; if being polite was an act to save face or feelings, then it was a dissembling lie; politeness had to spring from Christian love, but how could you tell which it was? Part of the answer was forbearance. When faced with annoying children, she realised afterwards that she had failed again; 'Patience was indeed a virtue; there was room for patience on our return home, which I did not entirely fill.'

There are no jokes in the diary. On her birthday, 7 April 1807, she did not plan her party but asked herself in which corner of her mind Satan was lurking, and why she so puffed up. Every birthday was another reason for introspection, but this was not too noticeable because every day shows the same state of mind.

She is tiresome to many modern eyes, and perhaps also a few contemporary ones; no day out is complete without some personal moral exhortation. On a visit to Windsor to see George III, Queen Caroline and three princesses, Hannah noted that the crowd had taken great pains with their dress and appearance, but were jostled and crowded in and not treated with much respect. The Royal Family themselves were prefaced with 'those astonishing human beings'. She concluded that it was an instructive lesson 'showing the infinite disproportion between the value and consequence we affix to ourselves and that which the world attaches to us.' They came out to make people envious but they were just pushed and pulled around; she found it all 'amusing', but in a didactic way, of course. Everything was a constructive lesson; and the main lesson was that the enemy is the SELF; at one point she said so explicitly, and in capitals.

Hannah saw danger in both her successes and failures, and, like Windham, even her successes were sometimes marred by her analysis of how she could have done better. In August 1806, her brother Joseph was ill and she attended to him, spending tedious days in the sick room. She noticed that her motivation was love and duty, but she also got bored. She attacked herself again for not being interested enough in somebody else's sickness. How could she ever be a good mother in the future?

On 21 June 1808, there was a turning point in her 'spiritual journey' – an expression she used herself. She may have been born into a Quaker family, but becoming a Friend would have been a conscious decision of her own taken with the help of her family; she would not have been 'brought up a Quaker.' It would have to be her own decision. Quaker girls and women had much more agency than most, but this brought more personal responsibility as well.

Hannah started to make this transition when she added the phrase 'first day' to the date in her diary instead of 'Sunday'. The objection to the traditional days of the week was that they derived from heathen deities. Most months of the year were equally pagan. September to December should not have been a problem and two generations earlier, they were acceptable to Quakers. However, the movement of the New Year from March to January in 1752 meant that, for example, November ('ninth month') was now a lie, like paganism. She described it correctly as the eleventh month. At first, Hannah was self-conscious about her usage; but knew that this was only the beginning; this was a principle and it did cause her to blush but 'may no self exaltation be the consequence.'

She had already moved to Quaker 'plain speech'. Distinction of rank engendered pride. Plain speech also demanded that you did not try to show off or shine in front of others. A fortnight earlier, she had resolved to address everybody as 'thee' and 'thou'. But it took all this time to use it only to her uncle; it took a week, till Seventh day, for her to use it to everybody. Had she met the King and Queen during her earlier visit to Windsor, plain speech would have obligated her to address them in the same way.

Hannah would always worry about her clothes and what they said about her. On a visit to London, she went to a milliner's shop and was neither impressed nor wished to take the matter further. She hoped to be 'entirely relieved from its perplexities'; these were the vanities of the world that were the enemy. She did not wear silk, instead she wore 'stuff' – a generic term for a cheap, utilitarian cloth. This was the right decision, she thought, as long as she did not feel better about herself as a result.

Fashion was wasteful and sinful when the poor were starving, but there is little about social conditions in her diary. She already knew a poor unworthy creature that took up much of her time, and that was herself. She did visit the poor after she married, but there is no evidence of any early interest in the social movements that Quakers were famous for.

There are few diary entries between 1809 and 1811. The editor tells us that the spiritual path continued along the same route so, in practical terms, it would have been more of the same. The culmination of this was her marriage to Jonathan Backhouse in 1811; he was another devout Quaker, most famous for financing the Stockton to Darlington railway, not for profit but to provide cheap coal to the poor.

Hannah wrote to her mother about her marriage from her new home at Darlington. She had a new role, one that was expected of all women, not just Quakers – 'Conjugal duties, the regulation of her establishment and the training of her children, constituted almost her sole occupation.' There was no time or place for recording the inner turmoil of her spiritual journey. One of her decreasing entries between 1811 and 1820 admits as much:

> It may be that the sweet and new objects of external love and necessary attention in which I have been engaged, have too much drawn my mind from internal watchfulness.

Being, in the words of Gilbert and Sullivan,[3] a member of a wealthy family ('At length I became as rich as the Gurneys') did not protect Hannah from the barrage of death and illness that is the experience of the twenty-first century person in their sixties and seventies, but happened a generation earlier in the nineteenth century. Her brothers Joseph and Henry died in the space of two years in 1816, followed by her sister Rachel. Hannah's own son Jonathan was to die aged 8 from an unknown illness which took a familiar course; weeks of weakness, a brief hopeful rally and a sudden death. At his funeral, there was a sermon by Elizabeth Fry and Hannah was able to stand at the foot of the freshly dug small grave and 'humbly return thanks for the mercies that had been received.'

Hannah's later fame rested on her public speaking and ministry. She had attended her first Quaker meeting in 1806. She learnt to admire some of those who attended because they were sweet, angelic and they were happy; Quakers were, in her mind, happier than most people and their minds could often be purer. She reflected deeply after the meetings, both keen to say that she had been improved by them but also reluctant to acknowledge it. She first spoke in 1820:

> Opened my mouth in Darlington meeting, on First-day afternoon. A mountain in prospect! The meetings now became very interesting to

me, as the reward of what I was induced to believe was faithfulness, often greatly refreshing.

Once again, she needed the persuasion of others to clarify her motives.

The last twenty years of her life were involved in Quaker ministry, both in Britain and in the USA, especially the Southern states, where she expressed her opposition to slavery and her support for education to the poor. She had, as her obituary in the Annual Quaker Monitor said, 'a character in which the woman, a Christian, and the Quaker were… fused into one.'[4]

Chapter 10

A Dull Year?

Fanny Chapman 1809

How did middle-ranking women of Georgian England fill their waking hours? Were they mostly bored senseless? We have already encountered the Austen sisters busying themselves, and another part of the answer comes from the diaries of Fanny Chapman of Bath. They exist in two parts – 1807 to 1812, and a hitherto unpublished section that covers the period 1837 to 1840.[1]

We follow her for most of the single year of 1809. The most obvious message is that she was an immensely privileged lady from a rich family, a cut above the Austens while being in essentially the same social class. She had been living in Batheaston Villa since 1801 with her two aunts Jemima Powell (Aunt P) and Mary Neate (Aunt N). The house was magnificent and still stands today as a beautiful example of Georgian architecture. The three women were allowed to live there by the owner John Hutton Cooper, who had inherited it after marriage to Phillis Neate, sister of Jemima and Mary and aunt to Fanny.

Her mother Kitty (Christiania) lived in Trim Street, Bath, with her daughter Emma, Fanny's sister. They had a large number of friends and acquaintances, some rich and influential. Her relationship with her mother was reasonable, but it deteriorated as the year went on. Sometimes Fanny would arrive on the off-chance and her mother was not there, on one occasion because she had gone to Chippenham; sometimes they met by accident on the streets of Bath and when they met, it could be for a few minutes, a half-hour or a whole day. Her mother was capable of pretending to be ill when she did not want company, or that is what Fanny said. So Fanny's immediate household was dominated by women, although as it turned out, it was a man who mattered in 1809.

Fanny did not need to do paid work. She was a gentlewoman, a member of a gentry household where money was rarely mentioned because there was enough of it. They had servants who glided anonymously in the background, and were only named (and shamed) when they failed to do their job. Despite this, the word 'work' and its variations appear eighty-four times in 1809. Some of it was actually 'work' – she made and repaired things, and was not above a bit of cleaning, but most of her work involved luxury items that needed to be looked after. The family bulk-bought candles and Fanny did the stock-take, fined their casks of malmsey with isinglass – they had casks, not bottles, a sign of their status. She broke sugar (sugar cubes were still 34 years away) and cleaned out the locked drawer where it was kept.

So it would be wrong to say that Fanny did not know the meaning of hard work, but her main task was filling her vast amount of spare time, especially in the housebound winter months. She made, repaired and altered clothes like Jane Austen did, with her motivation enhanced by making it for a special occasion, such as a ball, or for a favourite person. She made lip salve and a mob cap for balls and assemblies, just like Austen. Evenings could be spent mending stockings or cutting up old shifts for rags. She made shoes for dolls, lavender water and lots of different gifts for her mother.

She worked very hard making a shift for Aunt P, sometimes during the day but late at night as well; in November, she worked very hard on it for five days out of six, including an early morning. On occasions she produced clothes from start to finish, often spending the day shopping for materials and the evenings modifying them by candlelight.

> I cut out a scarlet cloak for Emma and promised to make it for her. She went out with my Aunt and me to several shops. At one we saw a beautiful scarlet and white trimming, which we fixed upon for Emma's cloak.

Then she sent for it to work on all evening: 'I worked hard all day new bodissing one of my morning gowns.'

After the inward activities of making and repairing, her next activity was socialising, which can be broken up into its component parts; eating and drinking, moving about, reading and playing games. She read books, and listened to others being read aloud. She wrote letters, she rode, and she walked in the garden and the hothouse when the weather permitted.

She played games like spillikins, mostly with her Aunt Jemima, and a game could take up a whole winter's evening.[2] Her spillikins set would have been a luxury item consisting of fine cut pieces of bone in different shapes. The set was good enough to lend to Mrs Vassall of Bailbrook, one of her neighbours, who could have afforded her own superior set, but these types of interactions were part of a bigger creation of a local community that made life bearable. Like the letters of Austen, her diary is a roll-call of persons present; all of them, not just the main ones.

Fanny was not stuck in one place; for a start, she spent eleven weeks of the year in Weymouth, like the Royal Family did, and the fashionable town of Bath was nearby. However, for much of January 1809, the cold and snow made it impossible to go into Bath safely, despite living only 2 miles from the centre of town, but you would not know that from the fuss involved in getting there. Each diary entry starts with a description of the weather, not because of the worry of food prices, but because the weather dictated what could or could not be done. The roads were often the problem and the weather was still awful in early April. It was dreadfully muddy, both in Bath and on the road. It did not have to rain for too long for the badly constructed local roads to flood. The main problem after a night of showers was that everywhere was dirty, rather than merely wet.

There was a lot of chess played in 1809. Fanny played regularly and noted the wins in her diary. Her aunts often played the game with male visitors. On one occasion in July, her evening consisted of watching five games of chess in a row, which kept her up until 1.00 am. She would often read while they were playing if there was no other company in the room. When there was company, there would be both chess and whist tables available, and sometimes musical accompaniment.

Apart from whist, there was gosh, piquet, backgammon and casino, played in company, and patience, played alone or in family groups. Fanny gambled moderately. She won 3 shillings from a gentleman on one occasion. She also lost 4 shillings on a game called 'Speculation'. On 4 October, she asked her Uncle James to buy her a lottery ticket (there was a national lottery in Britain from 1694 to 1826). He did so, but only sent her the number rather than the actual ticket – nobody in their right mind sent whole banknotes or similar valuables through the post. In October, they discovered that all but one was a blank, and that their £15 winnings did not cover their outlay.

The letter delivery service was quite efficient apart from the thefts, and Fanny could also pass messages to people who lived nearby via her servants. The servants passed notes quickly and would often wait for a reply – on 25 March, a note was sent but the servant ('stupid Gardener') lost the reply on the way home. Some notes were brief; others took half an hour to write and were part of the day-to-day activities. She never divulges their contents directly, even though she clearly acted on them.

There was also regular letter-writing. Despite being rich, Fanny and the family tried to avoid postage. Members of Parliament were allowed free use of the postal service, just as they are today, but the difference was they could give this 'frank' to anybody they wanted, and the Chapmans knew at least three people who could extend this privilege to them. One was Edmund Bastard, MP for Dartmouth and a member of the landed gentry, one of the Bastards of Kitley: 'In the evening I wrote a long letter to my brother Henry, as Mr Bastard had given me a frank.'

Sometimes, a promise of a frank would be important enough to delay the sending of the letter:

> I wrote to my Uncle James, but as the Workmans were so kind to say they would get me a frank, I shall not send the letter till Monday.[3]

The exchange of both tokens and substantial gifts was part of the social fabric of her life, and some of the gifts were literally textiles; nosegays, moss, seedling geraniums and mackerel were also sent, as well as seasonal foods like asparagus and strawberries. On one occasion there was a fine goose, and lobsters more than once. Aunt P received ham, vinegar and olives. Fanny's uncle John Hutton Cooper sent a hare and a couple of woodcocks on another occasion, and meat was regularly sent by post. These exchanges are one of the few clues to their wealth, not mentioned because it was all taken for granted. They were eating far, far better than 95 per cent of the population of Bath.

What about the ball, much loved by Jane Austen, with whom Fanny had a reasonable amount in common? She attended local balls in the same way Austen did, although not the same ones, as Austen had moved from Bath by 1809. She looked forward to Mrs Chalies' ball to break the tedium of a snowy and wet January, but it was postponed at short notice. She does not provide gossip about these occasions, but then she was not writing light-hearted letters to a much-loved sister. She had the same interest in what made a good ball – an equal gender ratio, a good supper and adequate transport there and back. On more than one occasion, she felt the same sense of obligation people feel today when they relied on a lift to get them there:

> As Mrs Stevens was so kind to send us there and home, we were obliged to stay her time. I did not find it half so pleasant as the first Ball we were at.

The same Mrs Stevens sent her carriage two weeks later and they stayed out until 1.00 am. A great number of the guests sent excuses and they had only nine gentlemen to fifty ladies, the sign of a poor dancing assembly. Fanny went to Mr Rodber's ball in Weymouth in September, and summed up the point of them; where 'we met a great many people we knew.'

Was religious observance a large part of her life? The answer seems to be not excessively. Sundays would always include prayers and Bible reading, but the bad weather would stop them going to church. If life was busy, they would do ordinary manual work on a Sunday, although the diary was a little apologetic. On Sunday 15 October, the Sabbath did not stop them packing up their belongings as they prepared to move house. On the national fast day of 9 February, she followed the rules, more or less:

> I eat nothing but dry bread for breakfast and luncheon and salt fish at dinner and did not drink any wine till supper.

It seems that not drinking alcohol during the day was seen as a personal sacrifice.

In the second half of the year, while living in Bath itself, she visited Mr Jay's Chapel, not as an act of devotion, but almost as a piece of religious trophy tourism, as Jay was a famous local preacher. She knew the singing was good, and presumed the sermon was as well, but could not come to a final judgement because she did not have the knowledge, and because she stopped listening before the end because it was too hot. While in Weymouth, she visited a Quaker service, and was neither negative nor positive, but just moderately interested. Her own view of the local parish church was one that would have been shared by many; 'My Aunt P and I went to church at Bath Wick, which is very refined and comfortable.'

Fanny had a relatively healthy year; she had an inflamed eye in April and put a leech on her temple; the next day, she was worse with a swollen forehead; the following day, she recycled the leech, which was too satiated to suck her blood. It must have improved eventually as she stopped talking about it.

Was this a dull life? It's hard to say, but probably not. Fanny was an unmarried 34-year-old, and this array of time-consuming social activities may or may not have been enough, but we need to be careful not to judge by our standards. Individual days were very, very dull; the highlight of Friday, 6 January was the delivery of offal to the house:

> We did not see a creature the whole day. My Aunt P sent a piece of brawn to Mrs Jones. My Aunts played cards after tea. I worked at my gown. A very uncomfortable evening.

The reason why it was not a dull year was two-fold; she was in love with her uncle by marriage, Dr John Hutton Cooper, which was completely unrequited. Cooper was also breaking his long-standing promise and selling Batheaston Villa, which meant the three women would be house-hunting by the end of the year.

Cooper had his own accommodation in the Royal Crescent but life at Batheaston revolved around his presence and his needs. He more or less lived there and people called upon him as if he did. His ever-changing moods and requirements were a central part of Fanny's diary; absolutely nobody else received remotely the same treatment. This could be because he was central to the women's continued standard of living, but it was clearly much more than that in Fanny's case.

On 19 January, Cooper arrived at Batheaston with his good friend, Edmund Bastard from Bastard's ancestral home at Kitley. Cooper's mood, as ever, was noted but not appreciated. He seems to have had his head turned by Bastard's life of even more luxury and elegance than theirs:

> He talked of nothing the whole evening but of the 'princely stile' in which Mr Bastard lived, not even inferior to the Prince of Wales. We did not go to bed till after twelve...

The Prince of Wales's excesses were common knowledge but were regarded as admirable and enviable by Cooper and Bastard. Cooper was uncomfortable at leaving all the magnificence and grandeur of Kitley to come to a humdrum family circle, and he probably kept the ladies up with his drunken boasting and complaining.

The next day, they received the news that Cooper was to sell the house from under them. Fanny blamed the Bastard family for Cooper's decision. She needed to be treated far worse by Cooper before she deflected the blame elsewhere. The elder Bastard, John, the man who wanted to break up the happy family, had to go to town and Fanny was overjoyed. The Bastards were a powerful family – John was the MP for the county seat of Devon and Edmund for the town of Dartmouth (which had a population of 3,412 in 1801 and only forty voters).[4] There is no evidence that Cooper was under any pressure from them; it was the myth that Fanny needed.

Then events happened quite quickly. On Sunday, 22 January, Fanny recorded a conversation as her only entry for that day. Cooper had brought up the letting of the house, and was in an uncommonly good mood:

> He said if he could get 450 pounds a year for it, he should have 1,500 a year clear to spend, 'but I can't afford to marry on that Fan can I?' 'Marry' I replied 'You don't want to marry' 'Yes, I do'. 'You would not marry except the Lady had a large fortune' 'No, I could not afford to do so without, but if I had ten thousand an year, I would ask **you** to marry me'. O said I (laughing), that's very pretty talking, but I don't believe a word of it. 'I would upon my honour as a man' he replied in the most solemn manner.

It was not the ten-year age difference or the fact that she was his niece that was the problem. It was money, and by extension, social status. Love did not conquer these things in the mercenary Georgian marriage market. Fanny was in agony; she felt that Cooper was drifting away from her and that, despite her solicitude, she was still a victim of his moods which she could not influence

> When Cooper came down he never took the least notice of me, any more than if I had not been home, except to desire I would give him the ink stand and to be angry that there was not more ink in it.

It was sometimes hard to believe that Fanny was not a stroppy youth. This outburst was on the same day:

> Cooper shook hands with me when he got out of the coach, but did not offer to kiss me. I do not know anything I have done to offend him and I am sure I do not care.

If he smiled at her, she was glad. If he was nice to her when drunk, she let this go. If he was present but not at her side, she could not cope. Even the good moments were tinged with bitterness:

> 25 July – He walked to the bath with me, an honour he has not conferred this year before.

Cooper had a large library and he tasked Fanny to paste his coat of arms into his 1,500 books, cutting out the plates first. A whole day, 6 March, was devoted to this, as were the whole of the next two days. Stroppiness did not preclude working for Cooper, although her resentment intensified when he showed no gratitude. Cooper was in Weymouth for much of March; when he contacted the family again on 3 April, the event was worth three exclamation marks.

Cooper also expected them to help him evict them from their own home. The method of letting out the house was odd and long-winded. Any interested person could come and see the house on a Thursday only, if in possession of a ticket from Cooper's agent, Mr Clarke. Most Thursdays started with a sigh of relief that nobody had turned up to do a viewing. On Wednesday, 8 February, a man called Sir Hugh Bateman came to see the house, claiming that he could not come on another day. He was told by the servant Kitty that it was not a Thursday and, as a day of general fasting, praying was taking place in the house.

Despite this, and having no ticket, Bateman barged in when the ladies were in the drawing room. One of the aunts manoeuvred him and his carriage away, but Bateman and his family turned up the next day. They sat them in the library while they made up the bedrooms to make them clean and respectable. Fanny, who was quite capable of making judgements about people but did not do it often, called the Batemans 'weak', perhaps an odd choice of adjective.

Fanny deeply resented anybody who took Cooper away from her. The Bastards were high on her hit list but the main bitterness was reserved for the two 'rival queens', who were, in order of Fanny's blind hatred, Mrs Henderson and Mrs Williams:

> Cooper and Mrs Henderson came home together about twelve o'clock. She came in here, but I did not go down to see her, feeling very indignant at her having kept Cooper all night at Henningston, that she might have the pleasure of returning with him alone in the carriage, which was literally the case.

For most of the year, there was a full-scale guerrilla war between Fanny and Mrs Georgina Henderson, with some help from the rest of the family. The two rivals were rarely in the same space as Cooper at the same time, but Fanny was ever vigilant when it happened, and she hated it:

> As disagreeable a day as could be. Indeed, it always is to me where Mrs Henderson and Mrs Williams are.

This happened on Monday, 7 August. It was a whist and speculation evening, after a day of shopping, walking, eating, drinking tea and listening to the band at the Esplanade; a typical day, busier than usual, spoilt by the rival queens who:

> sat one of each side of Cooper but Mrs W was in the dumps because he did not play the same tricks with her as he did with Mrs H, who sat almost in his lap.

A week earlier, with only Mrs Williams present, Cooper had been altogether nicer to Mrs W, according to Fanny:

> He was obliged to coax and caress her to bring her round.

The rivals were mortified when Cooper did not sit with them at supper; Fanny knew this because she must have scanned their faces all evening.

The pen-picture of Mrs Williams presented by Fanny is unalluring. She was horrible to her husband – she made him go out in the snow and rain on more than one occasion. She was vulgar; on one visit Fanny and her aunts declared themselves not at home to the Williams and they barged in anyway. Mr Williams without his predatory wife was acceptable. In March, when he had to get the two-day coach to London for an operation to restore his sight, Fanny hoped most sincerely' that it would be successful (it was, but he was blind for a month afterwards). Mr Williams would send treats over and they were accepted.

Mrs Georgina Henderson was a different matter. According to Fanny, she schemed with malice to always be in the same space – preferably alone – as Cooper, and the accusations ran thick and fast. It was much more of a vendetta:

> Mrs Henderson drank tea here, but as Cooper was not at home she went away directly afterwards.

On 3 July Fanny and the family left for an extended visit to Weymouth. It was just about do-able in a day by private chaise if you got up early; early for private transport meant 8.30 am. They did so, but were frustrated when they had to wait for three hours for fresh horses at the coaching inn. They got as far as Dorchester by 10.30 in the evening – an effective speed just above walking pace, booked into an inn, had tea and went straight to sleep.

Fanny usually loved Weymouth; but not this year. When they returned home, on 19 September, she commented 'that she had passed the eleven weeks there as unpleasantly as I ever remember to have spent any.' She was determined to hate it and it was about Cooper again. Cooper had decided, or been persuaded, to sell rather than let Batheaston Villa and so take the house out of the family. She was still avoiding him and Mrs Henderson was still on manoeuvres.

In Weymouth, they were not on holiday in any sense we would understand. They had simply relocated to the resort, arguably for the sea and air and, perhaps, for a change of routine, although there was not much of a change, especially in the first half of their visit. It was Bath with a slightly different set of people. They visited and were visited. They met; talked, walked, had tea, played whist and ate some very large meals. Each meal had a roll-call of who was present, and who was absent. There was a stupendous amount of chess played.

Novel activities included visiting the warm baths (rather than sea-bathing), walking to the pier with her aunt, hearing the band play on the Esplanade, and a brief ride on a pony – just a few days before her thirtieth birthday. On 12 August, she celebrated the birthday of the Prince of Wales. She visited the Cavalry barracks at Radipole to see the horses of the 16th Regiment. On 19 July, a Miss Cussons promised to show her how to make shoes, although she did not need to make anything; on 28 August she noted, 'I went upstairs and practiced shoemaking.'

She was still obsessed by Cooper, and filled with resentment for the two other women who were getting more of his time than she was. Indeed, she was getting none of his time. After five weeks, on 16 July, she was both thrilled and irritated to be invited on her first walk with Cooper since they arrived. On her birthday, 18 July, she was discontented and grumpy as Cooper had played five games of chess with her aunt. Chess, she believed, was Cooper's excuse for not talking to her. It was not as nice as her birthday last year, but then nothing was as nice as when Cooper liked her:

> Mr Bussell went on the box with us, Cooper and Mr Atkins in the other carriage. Last year it would have been different.

It was still all about Cooper; his comings and goings, and his moods and tempers were recorded and resented:

> Cooper went out before breakfast and did not return till just time enough to dress for dinner.

His location was regularly noted, sometimes in stalkerish detail. Fanny once recorded that Cooper was dining 16 miles away. Whether he stayed up late or went to bed early, it was all diary-worthy, and the latter was clearly more disappointing. Then she listed who he ate with; when she was in the same room as him and other women, she took a great deal of interest in his behaviour.

> Cooper, whose conduct with Mrs Williams was very extraordinary!! not to say indecent.

Her campaign against Georgina Henderson continued. Her 'rival' had always been vulgar and disagreeable. In both Weymouth and Bath, if they met on the street, they would never quite manage to acknowledge them.

> We saw Mrs Henderson while we were out, but cut her as soon as we could.

If she invited herself to the house, Fanny's aunt would uninvite them; her four children were stupid brats but Mrs Henderson was always plotting:

> My Aunt Neate played Chess with Cooper till Mrs Henderson sent for him. Rather an extraordinary manoeuvre I think for a woman alone to do. He stayed about half an hour with her.

It reached a denouement on 9 August when Mrs Henderson paid them a visit in order to postpone a later social engagement – inevitably, another meal. It was clear that Mrs Henderson was doing this because she knew that Cooper would not be present. Aunt Neate contemptuously accepted the postponement, and Mrs Henderson became sycophantic and apologetic. Fanny triumphed; 'at last we got rid of her.' The day remained bad; the evening was filled with whist, chess and music, but Fanny declared it 'stupid'. Days like this were the worst thing that could happen to her, but then she was privileged. Her idea of a social problem was a party of fifteen on a table for twelve attacking a huge lunch in Weymouth, and she was so cramped that she had to turn sideways to chew her meat.

Cooper was still punching the bruise, according to Fanny. On 12 August, 'he took leave of us with tolerable kindness, but not with half the affection he did with Mrs Henderson.' By September, Cooper was plaguing her again with his comments – 'If I had had fifty thousand pounds I would have tried to persuade *you* to have shared Batheaston with me.'

They were back in Bath in mid-September and it was overwhelming gloomy news, with one bright moment. On 22 September, this was regarded as diary-worthy:

> I kissed him when I wished him good night. Cooper received me very kindly and kissed me, but not as he used to do.

The next day, Fanny got up very early to say goodbye to him as he returned to Weymouth. He had the demeanour of a man who was sorry to be selling the house, according to Fanny, but he was still doing it and Fanny knew why; 'he is that kind of disposition that nothing unpleasant makes a lasting impression on his mind.' This key phrase suggests that she knew exactly what he was like.

An auction was arranged. The advertisements appeared in the newspaper in August for an auction in September, not in Bath, but in London at Garraway's Coffee House. She still blamed the Bastards, but the family was the last to know and that was Cooper's doing.

Fanny was melancholic. One of the preparations for the move involved rationalising possessions and it reminds us where much of our written history has gone; 'evening looking over and burning old bills, some of them dated near a hundred years back.' While he was taking away their home, her uncle gave them some gifts – 'Cooper gave us all some uncut Brazil Diamonds, two half guineas, a dollar, a silver coin and some new half pence, that were my Aunt's.'

Now they had to find somewhere to live. It would be a rental rather than a purchase, not uncommon at the time even for the rich, but the choices available to them were limited. It became an urgent matter and three possibilities were seen in two days: a miserable cottage in Bathford, another house near Midford Castle, and another with a fine garden that was unaffordable. All three women were in very low spirits; perhaps it was at this point they remembered that Batheaston Villa had been their family's property until the marriage to Cooper, and the lack of a legal protest at his inheritance may well have been because of his promise to look after them.

The news from Weymouth was not good. Cooper had recovered from his grief about selling the house and organised a party. It was large and gay, and finished at 4.00 am, and Mrs Henderson was there – 'I don't think we shall hear anything of the party from Cooper,' predicted Fanny correctly. Fanny heard that Mrs Henderson had moved nearer Cooper in Weymouth; 'she sets the opinion of the world in defiance,' warned Fanny, but with the bitter knowledge that this was not stopping Mrs Henderson getting her own way.

The family started to look for lodgings in Bath and settled for one in Henrietta Street, after looking at fifty, said Fanny sarcastically. Their servants went with them but it was still a retrograde step, but at least they had the house entirely to themselves; the cost was 4 guineas a week for a month; the nominal rate for a month at Batheaston was 8 and a half guineas a week. They had gone down in the world.

The packing continued. They worked all day through Sunday, 15 October; Fanny was tired and fractious and this was almost like real work. The next day was 'black Monday'. Fanny got up early to look around, made easier by the fact that she had slept in her clothes the night before after more exhausting packing. The day got worse when they took a packed public coach to Bath. When she invited her mother to the new lodgings, she refused to go; her mother would not enter any house where Aunt Powell lived. Fanny was aghast; she thought that her earlier objection to going to Batheaston Villa was because of Cooper. She had been completely unaware of this feud. Perhaps it also reminded her that without Batheaston Villa, there would be much less John Hutton Cooper. Fanny was very low and hysterical in the afternoon, and slept her first night in her new house with her Aunt P as the sheets had not been aired.

Late October was miserable. Aunt Powell had gout, alleviated by laudanum given to her by Fanny. Life remained the same, essentially chatting and tea, but on a smaller scale. They were reading the newspapers at the circulating library at Gibbon's and Savages; at the same time, the new owner of Batheaston Villa sent a message via a servant enquiring how they used to buy their newspapers. Whether houses or newspapers, they were now renting things that they previously owned, although with the newspapers they could now read them when they wished without waiting for the men to hand them over.

Money was tight and it made the relationships in the house worse:

> My Aunt P came into my room when we went to bed and said there was no necessity for my burning a light, as she had one in the next room, so for the future I am not to have one.

This was a family who at the beginning of the year had bulk-bought candles and did stock-takes of their luxury items. Aunt P also resented the amount of time Fanny spent with her mother 'despite it only being three visits'. It was only now that Fanny had any inkling of the poor relationship between her aunt and her mother.

Henrietta Street was temporary, and soon they were house-hunting again in appalling weather and the subsequent dirty and slushy roads. On one occasion they had to take a sedan chair to travel around. They were also packing again and visiting houses without prior invitation. They seemed to have forgotten how inconvenient this was, but then their lovely life in the villa of three months earlier must have seemed a long time ago.

On 28 November, they went house-hunting in Taunton and, by December, they were living somewhere dirty and unsuitable. Fanny described her pre-Dickensian and pre-Victorian Christmas Day. They tried and failed to find a suitable church service nearby, so it was prayers at home, followed by a Christmas meal. 'Neither the beef or turkey were half done enough, but the oyster sauce and plum pudding were excellent', then almsgiving to the poor.

Fanny and her family did what was deemed socially necessary when helping the less privileged, but seemed to have no strong empathy for the poor and certainly no belief that change was necessary. We know that she read the newspapers but she makes no comments on their contents. The sufferings of war and the poor are far away, even though both would have been visible in Bath. On one occasion in Weymouth, they found a poor woman on their doorstep with a husband in the army and gave her somewhere to sleep for the night, but that was as far as it went. The draconian penal system also brought few mentions and no thoughts, apart from one, which sounds a little more than a missed sightseeing opportunity:

> A man stood in the Pilloury in the Market Place today, but I do not know what for. The crowd was so great that Mrs Jones said they had difficulty in getting through.

So this was 1809 for Fanny – tea and travelling, walking and talking, meals and games, and a constant stream of people, both welcome and unwelcome. This may have been dull but it is hard to say; the unrequited love and the disastrous eviction by the unrequited lover probably meant it was not a dull year at all.

There were more years. Fanny remained unmarried, living comfortably in Bath with her sister Emma on the bequests of her two aunts. Cooper married into money in 1821 and became friendly with the Duke of Clarence who was the future King William IV. Cooper would have become very influential if he had not predeceased his royal friend. Fanny died in 1871, outliving Cooper by fifty years.

Chapter 11

Body Snatcher
Joseph Naples 1811–1812

Who were the lowest of the low in Georgian Britain? Who were the most morally bankrupt? The men who stole recently buried bodies and sold them to the medical schools for dissection would be high up on any list. It is, of course, an activity shrouded in darkness, but we have a remarkable piece of evidence about their activities. It is a diary, in beautiful, accomplished literate handwriting commonly attributed to Joseph Naples, one of the most famous London 'resurrection' men, as they were called.[1] It contains facts, figures, dates and incidents concerning the 'Borough Gang' of body snatchers.[2] The first entry is 28 November 1811, and the last 5 December 1812. It is almost certainly a fragment of a bigger document compiled over many years. When witness 'C.D' (almost certainly Naples) was examined before the Committee on Anatomy in 1828, he gave statistics to show the number of bodies obtained, and stated that the figures 'were taken from my book.'

The third entry in the diary sums up the business model:

Saturday 30th November. At night went and got 3 Bunhill Row, sold to Mr Cline, S^t. Thomas's Hospital.

Bunhill Row was one of their favourite haunts – it sounds lovely but the name was derived from the sixteenth-century 'Bone Hill' when the area was full of remains from charnel houses. The robbers visited other 'cribs' as well, stole recently interred bodies and then sold them to surgeons at the major London teaching hospitals, St Thomas's in this case, but also Guy's and St Bartholomew's, as well as to smaller anatomical schools, who would use the corpses for dissection while teaching students.

The customer in this case was Henry Cline, who worked both for the hospital and the College of Surgeons. In the twelve months of the diary,

Cline bought nine adults and three children (two of them large, over 3 feet), paid £4 4 shillings for one adult and £12 1 shilling and 6d for two adults and a child. This was the same doctor who attended William Windham when his hip injury turned malignant. Presumably, he learnt something from his dissections that he used to operate on Windham's tumour.

The body snatching game was very lucrative. This crime *did* pay, and not just in money terms; Henry Cline's fame as a lecturer in anatomy would have been impossible without men like Naples. The surgeons and hospital establishments were grateful customers and protected men like Naples when they were caught. Dr Cline was a fervent radical of the period, a supporter of the French Revolution and the Rights of Man, although he seemed to make an exception for dead ones.

Naples was an educated and literate man; his grammar and spelling were excellent, and so was his mathematics. Naples' diary was essentially an account book making note of prices and division of the spoils, so facts and figures mattered. It was not a written confession or a salve to the conscience; he was the body snatchers' bookkeeper.

Thursday 16th Jan (1812) The party met at the Hartichoak. Settled the above, each man's share £8 4s. 7½d. At home all night.

Body snatching required teamwork. A tally had to be kept of who did the work, and what size of corpse was robbed, so that the cash generated could be distributed fairly to hardened criminals, who would be quick to violence if their sense of justice was disturbed. In this case, it was calculated to the last halfpenny.

One of the implicit achievements of Naples' record-keeping was that this notorious group of criminals rarely fell out over the division of the spoils. His colleagues were volatile, drunken and desperate. There was not much love lost between the resurrectionists themselves; there were rows and reconciliations and revenge. On one occasion, their leader 'Ben' seemed to have spoilt the bodies when he fell out with Naples.

Ben was Benjamin Crouch who, like the diarist Naples, had direct experience in the graveyard/hospital trade. He was famous for being sober when digging up bodies; drunkenness partly explains how others were able to do it. However, when drunk, Ben was to be feared and Naples monitored his behaviour particularly carefully.

Naples was in his second decade, at least, of body snatching. He was imprisoned for some ghastly crimes in 1801 when he was a gravedigger at Spa Fields in Clerkenwell, and later as a servant at St Thomas's Hospital dissecting rooms. His grave robbing took place during the day, easy for a gravedigger or anybody else who worked in a churchyard; he worked with one other person and had to store bodies and body parts at home while looking for a buyer. He may also have made the mistake of stealing property from graves, increasing the chances of a custodial sentence.

The set-up in 1811 was completely different; the business of grave robbery had been 'professionalised'. It became an organised team activity with some degree of specialisation and different roles. The key job was to dig out and around the coffin, as shown in this entry when something went wrong:

Tuesday 10th. Intoxsicated all day: at night went out & got 5 Bunhill Row. Jack almost buried.

They would break open one of the small sides of a rectangular coffin and haul out the body by placing a rope around it. Gang member Jack Harnet would have been tunnelling towards the coffin when it collapsed around him. It may have been deeper than they anticipated; they preferred the bodies of the poor because they were often buried near the surface. Either way Jack was safe as he was part of a watchful team, and Naples' entry was probably light-hearted. He may have had the accident at the end of the digging, when one of the key tasks was to tidy up after themselves because relatives would be watching over the graves for a few days. It would have been too late for their loved one, but they would raise the alarm and make the burial ground too dangerous to plunder again for a while.

A cart or carriage would be ready on the other side of the wall or fence to take the bodies away in sacks. You were more likely to be stopped on the street with a suspicious package than apprehended in the graveyard. Occasionally, the peripatetic constables would come across them or they would meet members of the public who raised the alarm, but they were not in much danger:

Friday 17th. Went & looked out: came home met at 11, party except Dan[l]., Went to the Hospital Crib (graveyard) & got 4, was stopt by the patrols, Butler, Horse & Cart were taken.

When Butler was arrested, he was not in serious danger. Money was no object for bail; sometimes the surgeons and doctors would go down to the court and pay it themselves. Butler was released the next day and celebrated by getting dead drunk for two days.

Butler was also in no danger because he had not committed a serious crime. There was no property in a dead body and therefore no draconian punishments. This was the reason that the bodies were hauled naked into sacks. No grave goods or clothes were stolen, and in any case, they were of no value compared to the bodies. Caps, pillows, shrouds, nails and screws were worthless; metal coffin plates may have been a temptation, but that would have been a felony with a possible punishment of imprisonment, transportation and (theoretically) execution.

On this occasion, the gang lost Butler and their transport; and it was the latter that put a temporary halt to business. When the cart broke down, it was worth a notice in the diary:

> Friday 31st. Went to look out, at night went out, got 2 Guys & Thomas's, same night 3 Harps 2 small: same night the Cart broke down, took 2 to Guys.

Stolen bodies could not be stored at home for obvious reasons; the industry had moved on from leaving incriminating corpses at home. Bodies would have been stored in a convenient outhouse with the agreement of the hospital, sometimes even before the bargain was agreed; hence various references to 'Took the whole to ——,' and the next day, 'Removed the whole from ——'. 'Shovils', as Naples called them, were also stored at the teaching hospitals, as it was rather obvious walking the streets with them at night.

The 'whole' was one of the many alternative descriptions for 'dead body'. These were coarse men, but they still felt the need to employ euphemisms to hide the reality of their trade; bodies were 'things', decomposition was 'bad' and bodies were split into large and small, rather than adults and children; although the stillborn were called 'foetuses'.

Another coded phrase was 'looking out' for 'blacks' – following funerals in the street to see where they ended up:

> Wednesday 26th. Went to look out. Could not go out Jack and Tom got drunk. Ben^n. taken very ill.

They 'looked out' thirty-eight times in the course of the diary. It was a useful daytime activity. There was a degree of trust and teamwork; on most occasions, only some of the gang looked out; on two occasions they split up and presumably reported back their findings and trusted each other to be accurate. They tended to fall out only after they had succeeded in finding bodies.

Like many jobs, specialised clothing was needed. Clothes used for grave robbing would not be used for anything else. The same set of clothes would be worn for every grave robbery; they would be covered in clay and would have been a giveaway if worn during the day:

> Tuesday 20th October 12 Went to Bathol^w. Bill had got P^d. for the above Male I borrowed of him £1 10 0, went to Lamb^h. came home at night met at the White [Horse] Hollis myself Jack & Tom Light, Bill not with us could not find his clothes.

Business was also seasonal; there are no entries in May, June, and July 1812 because the long nights made successful thieving from graveyards impossible. The anatomy schools were open from October to May; they avoided the summer for more traditional reasons, but it was still a useful coincidence. This was also a deed of darkness; body snatching started at 11.00 pm on most evenings, but the long winter nights made an early start both safe and more productive.

> Saturday 28th December. At 4 o'clock in the morning got up, with the whole party to Guy's and S^t. Thomas's Crib, got 6 took them to S^t. Thomas's. Came home and met at Thomas's again, pack^d. up 3 for Edinbro, took one over to Guys.

Full moons were usually avoided. On the back of the diary was pasted a ready reckoner to work out the phases of the moon.

> Tuesday 25th. At home all day, at Night met at Jack to go to Harps. The moon at the full, could not go.

No actual body snatching took place on other full moons of 1812 either, except the full moon on 28 January 1812, when they started work at

2.00 am, a few hours later than usual. On Thursday, 20 February 1812, the diary tells us that fifteen large bodies and one small were obtained from St. Pancras. No doubt this was made easier by the custom of burying several paupers in one grave.

Naples' ledger shows the gang to be running an efficient 'just in time' logistics organisation. The main problem was that they had only one consumer who demanded high standards. Bodies had to be fresh; which is why the gang would actively scout for 'blacks'. There were other problems. Even *post mortem*, both rich and poor kept hold of their dead relatives for a long time in unrefrigerated conditions, so the window of opportunity was tiny. Time was money, so the industry had to be efficient. It was not often that they came home with nothing, but on occasions they were too late.

Friday 7th. Met together me & Butler went to Newington, thing bad.

Decomposition was unacceptable, as were bodies of people who had died of infectious diseases. In August 1812, they were able to sell a body to Brooks that had died of yellow jaundice: easy to notice, impossible to catch and medically interesting. but that was an exception. A decomposed body found *in situ* would be abandoned – newspapers often reported that one common aftermath of grave robbery was decomposing bodies having been left behind, but if one was discovered to be bad afterwards, Naples would cut off the extremities (or 'extras') and sell them separately to compensate them for the risks already taken.

Thursday 27th. Went to St. Thomas's, sold the extremities.

Teeth were a valuable asset and their absence was of no importance to the dissector, so they could be pulled out and sold separately. If an adult body in the coffin was too decomposed, they would rip out the teeth. Naples recorded a guinea for each set but prices seem to have varied immensely.[3] As these teeth were to be put in the mouths of the rich who had blackened their own with sugar, quality seemed to be everything. Canine teeth were the mostly highly prized. Jack Harnett sold some for five guineas to a Mr Thomson, a man not mentioned elsewhere and who was probably a dentist. By 1817, Harnett specialised in robbing teeth, a sideline for the gang in 1812. Butler actually became a dentist in later life; he was well qualified for the job.

Part of the business was to sell effectively. It was on a knife-edge; one side had the monopoly of supply and the other had the monopoly of demand. One side had a product of diminishing quality and the other had students who had paid for a lecture on dissection and would be angry if it was not provided There was no licence or regulation of anatomy schools; the profession was open to anybody who could get the bodies, but it tended to be people with a link to London hospitals.

Both sides had a form of trade union. Naples worked with his gang, and part of the problem was to keep them together as the solidarity only lasted so far. Dissectors formed the Anatomical Club for their own protection and to agree a fixed price for bodies. When monopoly met cartel, there were bound to be problems but, in the end, they needed each other.

They were very much aware of the competition. It was Ben Crouch who went to confront a rival gang known not by their name, but as 'the Jews'. This was almost certainly Israel Chapman, who set himself up and did business with the same people. There were consequences:

Understood the Jew had brought a Male to Barthol^m. Met by appointment at the above place, had a row.

Georgian-era anti-Semitism was a gentler but more insidious version of what we have today, with fewer conspiracy theories, but the same need to identify Jews in all contexts even when not relevant. They were accused of undercutting and of poor business practices, which shows both an anti-Semitic meme and a lot of brass neck.

The Borough Gang tried to cultivate other customers, namely the anatomy schools of Edinburgh; they exported dead bodies to Scotland, mostly by sea but with some attempts to send them by stagecoach, marked (accurately) as 'perishable goods'. The last diary entry records Naples sending bodies to the wharf in London ready to be moved to a port that served the Scottish capital – possibly Leith – by sloop, the same type of vessel that Thomas Lucas would have watched from his home in Stirling in Chapter Fourteen.

Did Naples become rich? It seems not. He was unable to retire from body snatching, and only gave it up when the Anatomy Act provided a legal source of bodies. The diary shows that he borrowed money regularly, for reasons unknown.

Some of their money would be used for bribes and rewards for useful information, or to persuade the single night-watchman – an old man with a lantern – to look the other way, or be absent. Much of the cash made seemed to flow into the local public houses, including the Blue Lion, the same pub patronised by James Hardy Vaux fifteen years earlier:

> Sunday 29th. Went Look out at Blue L^n. &c. did not go out Jack Bill & Tom Drunk the reason as Ben said for not going out.

Naples did not come to a sticky end, no matter how much that might have been desired. He continued in the business until the Anatomy Act destroyed his livelihood and was then employed as a servant in the dissecting room of St. Thomas's Hospital. A man of that name died in Southwark in 1843. If this was our body snatcher, he would have been 70 years old, a ripe old age in the nineteenth century, and by then, his body would have been safe from people who carried out his former trade.

Chapter 12

Weaver, Luddite, Criminal
Thomas Holden/Holding 1812–1820

Stealing dead bodies was not a crime; destroying machinery was. Our next witness is Thomas Holden, a handloom weaver from Lancashire, semi-literate and completely obscure, who would have remained unknown even after his conviction and transportation to Australia if his letters to his family had not survived.

Holden was part of the Luddite movement, machine breakers who destroyed new technology and intimidated those who owned it. He was prosecuted because of the need to make an example of those conspiring to take illegal oaths and attending illegal meetings. He was a criminal, in the sense that he broke the laws extant at the time, but it would require a heart of stone not to sympathise with him. Unluckily for him, the establishment had such a heart, worried as they were that revolution, not just protest, was in the air.

His collection of painfully constructed letters to his family starts on 27 May 1812.[1] He and his brother John were in the cells of Lancaster Castle awaiting trial; in his own words – 'the sises did not Bigin till tusday Morning.' The only unrecognisable word here is 'sises', Thomas's version of the word 'assize'. Assizes were county-based court sessions that were held four times a year to deal with the more serious criminal cases. The brothers were in big trouble.

The Holdens were from Bolton-le-Moor and the county town was Lancaster, which is why they were a long way from home. Some of their fellow Lancastrians had already been found guilty of riot, conspiracy, theft and arson in an attack on the Westhoughton Mill near their home. Holden was clearly part of this general movement to stop in their tracks the machines that they believed were taking their jobs and starving their families. He never destroyed property or used violence, and was being charged, and later sentenced, separately. The brothers told their wives that they were in good spirits – this was a white lie – and addressed their letters to a public house in Bolton, the Golden Lyon, to be picked up by John Holden of Hagend, Thomas's father.

Whether Thomas ever had any real hope that he would be acquitted is debatable, but guilty or not, the odds were stacked against him. The next letter was dated two days later and was about money. Even if they were found not guilty, then they would need £2 15 shillings in recognizance. They told their wives that they had hopes of being released but would have to stay in gaol if they could not raise the money. Other people who had been acquitted had not been able to leave because they owed other fees to the gaoler, Thomas reported. Thomas tried to find out what these gaolers' fees were, but left the sentence unfinished.

The third letter passed on the news that he had been sentenced to be transported to Australia; it was from Thomas only. The words of the judgement were seared in his memory – 'Seven Years Transportation beyond the seaz'.' He was heartbroken to leave his family, and there is the first mention of his child. He could have coped with prison, but the English system did not favour locking people away locally. It wanted to get rid of them – in his case, for seven years, but sometimes for fourteen. He was very, very naïve and understood nothing about the system stacked against him – he hoped his father, another powerless weaver, could get the sentence remitted.

The crime didn't sound too heinous. He was accused of administering an illegal oath to Isaac Compton at an equally illegal gathering on the moors outside Bolton on 21 April, after a week of social unrest and protests about starvation. Crompton was almost certainly a paid informant or an agent provocateur. Thomas may well have merely been present when the events happened, but that was enough – this was an attempt to form a trade union. He was not the only person involved – there were five others there including Arthur, James and William Holden. These other three were released on a technicality.

What was this oath that caused the authorities to treat him in this manner? The *Lancaster Gazette* of 6 June 1814 has a report of the proceedings and the judge Baron Thompson made the nature of the crime clear. The oath was 'not to reveal or discover persons who were involved in such practices, and binding yourself to be associates with them.' This was a conspiracy, initially against owners of machines but ultimately against the state itself. The meeting on Bolton Moor, with its watchwords and elaborate and solemn declarations was proof that Holden was twisted in with the Luddites. It's hard to imagine the incomprehension of a man who was trying to feed his family and was then told that he was a traitor. The weavers of Bolton were starving; they sent a petition to the Commons in 1812 saying so. This was not an unforeseen emergency.

Holden's defence was that that he went there out of curiosity. This was rejected, probably correctly. The judge's view that this gathering was a prelude to the attack on Westhoughton Mill was a possibility. The next thing Holden would have heard after his own sentence was the condemnation of those people to be executed. At the end of the Assizes, eight people were sentenced to death, one a boy of 16 who had been complicit in the destruction at Westhoughton, another a woman of 54 who had stolen bread and potatoes.

Holden was now in the most desperate of situations, and that was *before* he arrived at Botany Bay. He pleaded in his letters for his family to collect two debts for him and get the money to him as soon as possible, as he was going to need it in the English penal system. One of the debts came from an Arthur Holden, the same name as one of the defendants in his trial who was released on a technicality.

In the next letter (14 June), the desperation and loneliness were palpable. He was receiving very few replies to his letters. The next letter was to his mother and another to his wife; he had not heard from her, or from anybody else who might help him. Throughout this period, he received seven letters in return for his seventeen. Had he been forgotten so soon? he asked directly. He still hoped for a remission of his sentence, and enquired about the work people were doing to make this happen. He mentioned a Mr Fletcher (and later a Mr Walkden) as somebody who might be able to help. Fletcher was no radical lawyer or reformist, but a highly respectable conservative colonel in the Bolton militia; Holden may not have had a radical bone in his body, except to take actions to defend his standard of living.

He knew that anytime soon, he would be moved to a prison hulk and then transported to Australia, but he did not know the timeframe for these events. Part of the cruelty of the system was that inevitable events like these could not be predicted, either when they happened or how long they happened for.

The second part of his letter was to his wife Molly. Holden asked her to go into exile with him; he was amongst strangers and feared for the future. Most people transported never returned, so this was not really a prison sentence but an effective termination of their marriage. At this point, we find out that he was a weaver, as he enquired about one of the looms. One of the problems with documents such as these is that they omit to mention what was blatantly obvious to people at the time but is vitally important to people using it as evidence later – in this case, that they were poor weavers and weaving meant eating. The fact that his wife had sent him a mere 4 shillings rather proved the point.

The next letter was 15 June and had a rushed and panicky tone – 'Dear Wife i take this opertumity of Righting a fue Lines' – other convicted prisoners were being sent to the hulks, the ships permanently moored on the south coast to hold prisoners prior to transportation. Now would be the time to send some money – but not clothes. They were not allowed to wear their own. 'if you are for Sending me any muney you must send itametitley'. He was so panicked that he failed to write his own name correctly; as his world collapsed, he signed himself Thomas *Holding*.

The second of his two letters (in the same envelope) was to his parents, mostly clinging on to the idea that somebody could get his sentence remitted. He requested help from his 'dear brother' and hoped that he continued in the attempt to free him; he had seen none of his family since his time in prison and the letters themselves had become the pathetic link between them. There seemed to be some regret too, as he advised his brother to stay at home and keep good hours:

> I have kissed this Letter a thousand times and i hope you will do the same and may the Loard bless you all and so no moa[r] at Present from your Ever loving and Efecned Son Thomas Holding I lefe you all.

Three days later (18 June), an almost identical letter was sent; nothing had improved, no news, no money and no chance of help. He made the first comment on his sentence – it was a false charge. He failed to spell his wife's name:

> Molly Old
> Molly Holding
> to be left at the Golden Lion Church Gate Boulton

Thomas was away from Lancaster by 20 June.[2] A lot happened in the next ten days; by 28 June, he was writing from Langstone Harbour near Portsmouth, which only meant one thing; a prison hulk, the HMS *Portland*. Langstone was a shallow harbour only suitable for a substantial vessel if it did not move, and so was suited to a prison hulk. He had arrived there via London, and spent four days there but provided no details. It would have been uncomfortable because he would have been fettered, or worse still, double-chained, on the journey, with none of the substantial meals and semi-deference enjoyed by radical leader Samuel Bamford in Chapter Fifteen.

He implored his wife not to visit him there as she would be shocked by what she saw. He was not in any case receiving any correspondence from her. He had been in the same clothes, day and night, for eight wet and uncomfortable days, and he had 'lost' the money he had.

The second part of his letter is a little cheerier, announcing that he was working (presumably in the government shipyards) from seven to five and that the captain was very good to the prisoners under his charge. Yet the neglect by his family still seemed to rankle a little – 'I am very sorry that my father mother & brother did not come to the New Bailey to see me.' He had spent four months on the hulk; this would have been a below average amount of time. It could be days or a year, part of the lottery of the justice system.

There seems to have been a lot of understatement about the horrors he was going through. The most eloquent expression of his own feeling was the admission that he could not say he was in the best of spirits and now he claimed 'He had the good luck, he said, to be at the best place of its kind.' He was now 'Thomas Holding' again.

The next letter showed the private enterprise judicial system at its worst. He now had a pound from his family. It was almost certainly a whole banknote – it was much safer to cut them into two and send them separately, but there was no time to do that. It was two weeks' poverty wages for a weaver – and it was now in the hands of the captain, who doled it out at 3 shillings per week. This was far better than having it stolen from him. He needed money because the meals were terrible; extra food was available at extortionate prices – a quart of flour was 10d and it was a short measure.

Holden provides no details of the horror of the hulk and he was certainly hiding many things from his family. James Vaux, writing for a different audience, provides more detail; 600 men, double-ironed in a small, squalid and noisy ship. Vaux also noted that it was every man for himself, and that all former friendships and connections were dissolved, something that Holden complained about as well. There is no reason to think his experience was untypical, or that Holden's was any better.

Holden's captain may have been pleasant, but he would not be in charge of Holden on a day-to-day level; that was job of the overseers – 'most commonly of the lowest class of human beings, wretches devoid of all feeling, ignorant in the extreme, brutal by nature and rendered tyrannical and cruel by the consciousness of the power they possess' as Vaux said. Vaux witnessed murder, suicide and sexual abuse; if it was a nightmare for him, it must have been something truly unspeakable for the soft-spoken, innocent weaver, whose only criminality was to make an oath to protect his family from starvation.

On 22 November, he replied on the same day to a letter received from his Molly. Will she be accompanying him to Australia? The answer was no; and it was never really going to be yes; she would have had to pay her own passage, leave her family behind and possibly endure a life worse than the one she had, although that would have been difficult in 1812.

He was on board the *Fortune* by this date, and it would have been unpleasant even before it left the land; he tells his wife that he had been ill, and now was better; it was probably another reassuring lie. The company was unpalatable; 'we are among a deal of differnd Soarts of people', he commented to his wife. He once again asked for money; a note rather than a post office order which would be impossible to use on a ship. He also asked her to prepay the postage. He had nothing.

On the third page of the letter (each one begins 'Dear Wife') he asks if they continued with the 'pertisones' that may get his sentence cancelled or mitigated. He needed to know any good news before his ship left, but the whole business of petitions was a waste of time. It seems that the Prince Regent had already rejected them. Escape and returning home were nearly impossible, and, in any case, very dangerous; it was a crime that carried the death penalty. His spelling and grammar were deteriorating under the strain. There was absolutely no hope, and perhaps he knew this by now.

Sometime soon after writing the letter, Holden was one of 200 convicts about to leave on the *Fortune*. On 29 November, he reports that he had yellow jaundice for a fortnight, so was not being entirely honest in his letter of 22 November when he said he was ill, but improving.

Holden was in close confinement and the only person helping him was John Fisher. Fisher was tried at the same time as him, and they left Lancaster Castle together, but he reports no help at all from the other Boltonians on the ship. He was able to tell his wife that his letters were not checked by the captain; before that, they would have been regularly checked by the prison and hulk authorities but now it was not necessary. He was no danger to the state now, if he ever was. He didn't think he was – 'not Doing the smallest Injury Either to Government or subjects.'

Conditions on the ship were appalling. They were allowed one hour on deck per day, and spent much of the time in leg irons (at this point, he admits that he was in leg irons on the hulks too) and slept in the same bedding, wearing the same shorts for seven weeks; when they protested, the captain believed that they could not be dirty yet. Holden didn't eat for three days, whether due to illness or poor conditions he did not say, and suggested that he would not make it to Australia alive.

The next letter is dated 12 December. He was somewhere along the journey and the messages were the same. Where are the letters? Where is the work towards his pardon? Where is the money he will need? He turned down the offer of flannel shirts, something his poor family could provide easily; they did not understand what the climate would be in Australia. He did want writing paper, though. His friends and acquaintances from Bolton had been no help to him at all, something that the authorities would have been very glad to read as destroying their solidarity was one of their aims.

He was worried that letters might be going astray – 'in the Next Letter you sends to me please to put my Christian Name in full as follows, Thomas Holding.' The next letter is dated 23 June 1815 and headed 'No 13 letter and only one Answer.' The address given as Sydney, Port Jackson, New South Wales, New Holland. He had been in Australia for two years – since 11 June 1813.

Communications were still poor, for many reasons, but there was a ship every three months from Portsmouth and there was never anything for him. He went down to the port to check and was always disappointed. His one letter seems to have been from his father asking about the fate of the other Boltonians on the ship; he had already told him that he had ignored them, so he was neither taking notice of his letter nor asking anything about him. He had enough to do to ensure his own survival, and told his father that.

Holden knew that the war in Europe had finished with an English victory and wanted to know if life was any easier for the Bolton weavers, and wondered if he could have earned an honest living – he could not. They were starving and rioting but not, thanks to the draconian punishments meted out to people like Holden, smashing machinery. His letter is sad and desperate to the end:

P:S: Kip my Dear little Wife & Child for me my Dear Mother

His wife and all other members of the family had not written to him. He wrote to his wife a week later. The same themes and phrases are repeated, and the same question asked. Why was the family ignoring him, and why no letter from her in three years? He reminds his wife, that, bearing in mind the ship's timetables, her commitment was one letter every three months. He seems loathe to draw the obvious conclusion. He hints at his fidelity, perhaps in contradistinction to hers:

But I will ashure you I have never Cept Company with any one Sins (since) I Left my natife Contry.

His ambition was to keep body and soul together and gain a pardon, but he was rapidly coming to the reluctant conclusion that they would only meet again in a 'World Where there will be no parting'. He gives details of his wages and prices. He earned the equivalent of £12 a year and the prices of shoes, stockings, hats and textiles were higher. Butter was 7 shillings a pound. He had met the indigenous population and was not impressed:

They are Blaiks and they go naked Just as they Came into the world and they live on Nuts of trees Snouts or aney oather Creeping thing and Children goes all naked.

In a later letter, he goes into more detail:

> I have no particular News here to Relate Excepting that the Native Blacks are Continually Murdering the White People in the Interior of the Country the Soldiers where font in pursuit of them A few weeks back & Shot 14 of them.

His next letter (19 March 1816) is the most demanding and hardest to understand. He wanted some Coulters Bouls; a coulter is a form of plough and a boul was possibly something on a coulter. It suggests that he was an agricultural labourer, by far the most common occupation. Many of the other requests seem to be linked to making bed covers, like the ones he was making in Bolton. Most of the other words are incomprehensible because he would never have seen them written down, but it looks like he was trying to sell the things he was asking for.

His penultimate letter of 30 May 1816 looked and felt very different. Grammar and spelling had improved; it had become far, far worse in exile. This one begins 'Honorde parents', and contains, correctly spelt, the words 'procured', 'governor' and 'emancipation'. It was clear that he was confidently looking for a pardon as early as 1816, but as ever he was overconfident, expecting it in December. It did not come until 25 February 1817.[3] The pardon was due to his own efforts, not those of Colonel Melcher or Isaac Crompton. If he got back to Bolton, he never wanted to hear their names again, although it is unclear who the first person was.

His last letter was brief and makes no mention of pardon – he enclosed a parrot feather (from a bird that he shot himself), some Australian newspapers and a plea that his daughter should go to school.

The end of this story has traditionally been an unhappy one. 'There's no way of knowing if he ever came back to Bolton,'[4] says an archivist at Lancaster Castle, but that seems not to be the case. A check on the 1861 census for Bolton shows a Thomas Holden of the correct address and correct occupation (counterpane weaver), with his wife, Molly. All of the families in the road were weavers, either by hand or machine, and next to each name it tells us which. Thomas, nearing the end of his life, died as a hand weaver. His wife, Molly, was also still a counterpane weaver, then a domestic servant. She lived past 1871, but had become blind. He lived in a street full of people called Holden, so it is fair to say that he did, in the end, live and die with his family doing a job he wanted to do.

Chapter 13

Trophy Tourism
Elizabeth Chivers 1814

Our next resource is the brief travel diary of Elizabeth Chivers (1796–1858). She is not Byng, Moritz or Warner, and perhaps the better for it as she is more representative of the Georgian travelling classes. For the most part, her diary is a tick-box list of the sites of London with a few tantalising personal details thrown in and it rather suggests that trophy tourism was as common as it is today.

Elizabeth was 28 and unmarried when she set out with her younger sister Sarah and an unnamed uncle for a twenty-day visit to London in March 1814. Her diary is mostly, but not entirely, a list of every tourist site that she saw in London.[1] Most of it is less informative than a normal tourist guide; the more interesting part is the glimpses of her life, family and experiences that appear in the gaps between the common destinations.

The weather was reasonable on the day of departure, not because Elizabeth said so, but because they would not have left home otherwise. 1814 had been one of the coldest winters ever, and the snows were just beginning to abate in the south of England by spring. The trio left their home town of Bath at 9.00 am for the beginning of their long journey to London, which was a two-day stint in 1814. Their day did not start at an unearthly hour from a grubby coaching inn; this was a late start because they were using private rather than public transport. They were in the same travelling class as Chapman and Byng and, occasionally, Austen.

They were using their uncle's own carriage and horses for the first part of the journey, with the rich relative leaving his vehicle in Devizes and then renting a post-chaise and horses for the rest of the journey. The alternative was the stagecoach; it was not much slower (the journey would have started at an inn at 7.00 am) but it was much less exclusive – the problem was not that the lower classes used them, as they mostly were priced out, but that you could not be sure exactly who was on it, sharing your cramped space and invading your privacy.

Elizabeth and her companions travelled on the Great West Road, probably the best road in the country at the time, via Marlborough, Hungerford and Speenhamland, changing horses at every stop. Horses could not pull a chaise for more than 15 miles. They arrived at Newbury at 5.00 pm, having done the 65 miles in 9 hours – an average of 8 miles per hour. Most of that would have been actually travelling – food breaks were short and new horses and carriage would be expected to be ready without delay.

They had a typical inn repast, the kind that Byng would have turned his nose up at, but Jane Austen would have regarded as acceptable – grilled food, wine and local Newbury apples, presumably as a dessert. Elizabeth liked her bed; as Byng and Austen also knew, that was not always the case. The fact that it deserved a mention shows the dangers of dampness, dirt and lumpiness that were the hazards of hiring a bed that, unlike a private carriage, would not be checked and cleaned before use.

On day two, they approached London via Reading, Maidenhead and Hounslow. Elizabeth seemed quite serene. She looked out of the window and checked off all the places she could see on the way; while she did so, she passed through Maidenhead Thicket and Hounslow Heath which, a mere 20 years earlier, would have brought fear to even the most hardened traveller. Elizabeth knew this to be the case; 'we passed over Hounslow Heath which is notorious for the numbers of robberies formerly committed upon it.'

Elizabeth continued to collect the names of places and rarely had anything to say about them. She passed Windsor Castle, was glad to see it, but seemed satisfied with that. The village of Bray reminded her of a childhood song; she often mentions places if members of the family were connected with it.

> We went through Longford, changed horses at Cranford Bridge and left the Village of Harlington about a mile on our left which parish the late Reverend Thos. was Rector of.

Thomas, clearly a relative, was curate (1798) and rector (1805) in this small parish until his death in 1809. Escaping the modest role of curate and gaining promotion to some extent on merit was a reasonable achievement.[2] Elizabeth did not elaborate because she already knew and did not envision an audience for her diary. She did exactly the same later on the subject of her murdered uncle.

They arrived at Godfrey's Rainbow Coffee House & Hotel, Kings Street, Covent Garden at about a quarter past five 'after a safe and pleasant journey'. Their uncle had hired some rooms for the month of sightseeing – a very common arrangement, and much more usual than hiring hotel rooms.

The trio had ended up in the most interesting and potentially dangerous place in the country. They were opposite the West Piazza and, to say the least, all human activity at its most sleazy would have been available by looking out of the window. It was, perhaps, the most vibrant and unregulated corner of the capital. But, after a tiring day, 'after making a good dinner and drinking tea at eight we retired to rest, soon after ten'; you would not know that they were in central London from the cosseted and Panglossian diary entries.

Day three – Wednesday, 16 March 1814 – was the first of many exhausting days of tourism. Elizabeth wanted to see everything but had nothing to say about anything. She lists seventeen tourist attractions in a row, without comment, including 'Black flyers bridge' and the 'Gild Hall', before she gets around to mentioning human beings. The unnamed uncle made some business visits and showed his two nieces places with family connections: a house 'where our late Uncle (William) Chivers' lived (more about him later); a house in Fenchurch Street where her mother Sarah Jalland and father Thomas Chivers first met (and later the church of St Andrews in Holborn where they married); and a house where the unnamed uncle previously lived. The fuzzy feeling of this undemanding tourism feels very modern. Another similarity is the cake shop as a highlight:

> We saw Leadenhall market then came to Birches the pastry cook's where we eat a charming cheese cake.

Eating 'artisan' cheesecake in cafes was an activity of the privileged lady – two other Bathonians of the same social class, Fanny Chapman and Jane Austen, did the same. Elizabeth had been to the shop of Samuel Birch, pastry cook to the Lord Mayor and purveyor of sweets to the Mansion Hall feast, who was to become Lord Mayor later in the same year. This was not just any London pastry shop, and Elizabeth knew it; it was the oldest and most prestigious in the capital. This was trophy tourism, just as much as the great houses and buildings they had seen. They were to revisit the pastry shop on day twelve.

Day four began in Charing Cross 'and the black man on the black horse and the golden crop'. Elizabeth's point of reference was a nursery rhyme from her childhood:

> Ride a Cock Horse,
> To Charing Cross,
> To see a black man,
> Upon a black horse.

She either did not know or think it was important that it was Charles I, the only English monarch ever executed after a public trial. Politics and history, or indeed anything contentious, was not part of a genteel woman's education.

Something she *would* know about was social drinking of tea, and the party spent time at the Twining's Tea and Chocolate Ware House; like the day before, she had sought out the best. Warehouse sounds a little staid and functional, but they were places aimed at the relaxation and enjoyment of the gentry and nobility; tea and chocolate were available at moderate prices everywhere, and were free in their own drawing rooms, but this was meant to be an 'experience'.

In the evening, they strolled across the piazza, two streets away from the Covent Garden Theatre, where they saw the highly popular *Artaxerxes* by Thomas Arne, and a farce called *Love Law & Physic*. Elizabeth did not tell us where she sat, as she would have been seated in a place appropriate to her class and no comment would have been necessary. They would not be in the pit, like the poor traveller Karl Moritz.

Covent Garden Theatre was not a gentle or genteel place to be. It was only two years since the OP (Old Price) riots in which people reacted violently to an increase in admission prices. The mentality and general behaviour would have been similar to that experienced by Moritz twenty years earlier. Moritz described in great detail because, as a foreigner, he was shocked and surprised. Elizabeth does not mention any unpleasantness; she may have taken much of it for granted.

Day five started at Leicester Fields as it was called then, and the unknown uncle visited Charles Howard, the 11th Duke of Norfolk. The evidence rather suggests that this would identify him as Noah Chivers. This is all very matter-of-fact, and Elizabeth had no need to boast; she was merely describing her life as it was. After the 'succession of noble squares', they ate at four and played backgammon all night until 11.00 pm.

The next day ('our sixth days march', as she called it, correctly), they ventured away from the aristocratic centre to Kensington via stagecoach. It was here that she saw the houses of the new commercial classes; as rich as their own class, but who worked for their money:

> We were astonished at the vast number of very elegant houses we passed which were chiefly inhabited by merchants and those who have acquired large fortunes in town.

It becomes clearer that Uncle Noah had come to London on business. They 'called on Mrs Hardwick who lives in one of these charming houses which are situated at Battersea Rise.' This was Sister House. Mary Hardwick had inherited the property from a William Francis, which seems generous as she was merely the bachelor's housekeeper, a word that can probably be put in inverted commas. Noah Chivers was to occupy the house itself from 1817. It had been owned by William Chivers, wine merchant, who was Noah's uncle, and Elizabeth Chivers' great-uncle.

Fanny fails to mention the context of the visit, although she could not fail to have known it. In January 1807, William Chivers had been murdered in his garden by his servant William Duncan, who hit Chivers with a spade. Chivers had been abusing him for ruining a vine and threatened to smash his skull. Unfortunately, the 82-year-old Chivers only had his walking stick to back up his threat; Duncan was the worker and had the tool, and he smashed the sharp end into his employer's face between the right cheek and eye. Chivers languished for three hours and then died, said one newspaper – 'languish' often being euphemistic shorthand for an agonising death.[3]

Duncan then went through the random pantomime of the Georgian justice system. Initially, he was due to hang; it was likely that this would be reprieved because of the lack of premeditation and presence of provocation, but he had to wait ten days on death row before finding out. The scaffold was actually built and ready for action at Horsemonger Lane Gaol and Duncan would have heard the banging and hammering. The public loved a hanging normally, but the decision to respite the sentence was popular. Instead, he was transported to Australia and would have experienced the same journey as Thomas Holden and James Hardy Vaux. None of this was in Elizabeth's diary, but as she toured the gardens and lovely prospects, she must have been thinking about it.

Did she see the poor? She had already seen them in Covent Garden and had nothing to say about them and, in any case, she had mostly seen the working poor. The London criminal classes and their rookeries and slums had no equivalent in Bath, and she mostly avoided them on her holiday. However, at this point in her journey, she visited places where the poor lived in great numbers because she wanted to tick the Archbishop of Canterbury's Lambeth Palace off her list. Lambeth High Street was neither mercantile nor aristocratic, but she was still very matter-of-fact: 'We passed through several little dirty alleys which brought us to the venerable Palace of Lambeth.' It reminded her of York; the same medieval building, but this was not a compliment like it would be for the modern tourist. It was dark, dingy and threatening; she resented going there.

The day finished when the light did because London was not always a suitable place to walk around in the dark, as Moritz found out and most Londoners knew. The evening menu and entertainment was the same – boiled meat in the hotel and backgammon in the rented drawing room.

The next day was another chance to see the poor. These were the deserving ones, blamelessly accepting charity in a context designed to satisfy the needs of the rich. It was a Sunday, but they did not go to church, instead going to gawp at pretty and obedient children at the Royal Asylum for Female Orphans in Lambeth taking part in a crowded chapel service. These 200 female asylum inhabitants were looked after until they could be guided back to their natural station in life, which was domestic service.

Elizabeth warmly commended the sermon, which told the story of Thomas, Second Baron Lyttelton, whose sinful lifestyle included gambling debts, duels, absconding to Paris with a maid and a prison sentence in Paris after a fight in a brothel. Conveniently for the preacher, less so for Thomas, he died suddenly before he could save his soul. He had been dead for thirty-five years but the moral was powerful and, in the nearest she ever came to an opinion, she agreed with it. She was clearly against sin, but it is doubtful if she had experienced much of it, apart, of course, from the murder of her great-uncle.

Afterwards, there was another visit to a pastry cook and a nice tartlet, and a visit to Hyde Park to tick off the splendid carriages of The Lord Mayor and Princess Charlotte from their tourist list. The young Charlotte, the only child of the Prince Regent and his estranged wife, Caroline of Brunswick, was now grown up and a public figure, looked after by another of our Georgian witnesses Ellis Knight (Chapter Sixteen). On day eighteen, they ventured out alone once more and lingered outside a royal carriage for a view of Princess Charlotte and the Duchess of Leeds. She was an exceptionally popular member of the Royal Court, the only one who could boast of that in 1814, and it did not do her any good. She would have been in agony about the wedding plans that had been forcibly arranged for her, her terrible relations with the Prince Regent and his determination not to let her see her mother. She probably did not smile for the crowds.

The trio finished Sunday with a visit to St Paul's Covent Garden (the Inigo Jones Church in the piazza, also admired by Karl Moritz) and another mention of the quality of the music and the sermon. The evening was the same as any other, but either without backgammon, or with backgammon, but not worth mentioning. Backgammon was doing the same heavy lifting of passing evenings indoors as whist or chess would do at the Chapmans' and the Austens'.

On Monday, it was raining; like tourism throughout time, enjoyment was linked to the weather. Noah Chivers was visiting contacts and the ladies were left looking out of the window, not going anywhere on their own. They spotted the hackney cabs and the drivers enjoying the fact that it was raining, because then, as now, it was good for business. It was to be a late evening as they got back to the Rainbow at 1.00 am, having seen *Hamlet* followed by a pantomime – quite an odd arrangement to modern eyes, but two completely different styles of drama on the same day were common and even expected.

The next day, the girls were left alone in a picture gallery while their uncle visited the Duke of Norfolk again. They were being informally chaperoned; their position had to be fixed at all times, whether at an exhibition or their hotel. Elizabeth had no view on the painting that was not a cliché. They were 'very well executed and fine specimens of their different merits', she said. The visit to Westminster Abbey brought only generalities; it contained the 'ashes of our monarchs and the remains of numbers of our most celebrated characters for many centuries'.

The evening was spent at the Drury Lane Theatre where she enjoyed *Wild Oats* by John O'Keefe, which is still revived occasionally today. One of the characters is the Quaker, Ephraim Smooth, who is uptight, over-serious and pompous; the reputation that the Quakers had, especially among people who did not know them, although a critic might regard that as fair comment about Hannah Gurney in Chapter Nine.

The next day, they visited St Paul's and had the same experiences as visitors were to have for the next 200 years – 'We saw the whispering gallery which is round the grand dome, where the vibration of shutting a door is like the firing of a cannon.' She also saw the monument to John Howard, prison and hospital reformer, much admired by John Byng and with whom Noah Chivers had been acquainted.

Day eleven was a let-down. Uncle Noah had to be elsewhere and they did not stray far from the Rainbow Coffee house – 'We had not courage to stroll far being afraid of not easily finding our way back again.' Both were women in their mid-twenties; it was their gender, not their age that restricted them, although they did venture out alone later on their tour. The evening was backgammon again – 'our everlasting amusement,' she said, possibly with a little sarcastic weariness.

Day twelve was a visit to the best collection of animals in the country at Exeter Exchange in the Strand (but not before Noah had visited his bankers). In the evening, there was the first family visit, to Captain William Chivers. The next day, Saturday, they visited the Tower of London after more banking interactions by Noah that they were only spectators to, being unmarried and female.

Sunday arrived once more, and like the Sunday previously, they combined piety with tourism by visiting the still-famous Foundling Hospital. The unfortunate children had been scrubbed up to loosen the pockets of the charitable; 'There are from two to three hundred of these poor deserted children male and female which is a very pretty sight.' The afternoon was spent in Hyde Park and then the Serpentine – 'which had been fatal to numbers' – said Elizabeth with vagueness and without much empathy.

The tour continued, as did the fine balance of business and pleasure. When the outside world did intrude, it was translated into tourism again. The apparent end of twenty years of European war and victory over Napoleon merited two lines:

> I must not omit mentioning that we had the pleasure of hearing the Park and Tower Guns firing on account of the Allies entering Paris.

The next day, they were going home; they took a different route, seeing the corn and grass fields of Knightsbridge turning green because of the recent rain. They stayed overnight at Speenhamland ('Spinham lands'). After dinner, they had a little conversation with the landlady, 'a very clever genteel woman and she was well acquainted with Yorkshire.' That was novel but the evening wasn't; they played backgammon. On the second day they arrived at Bath; both mother and father were in good health. Throughout our diaries, this was something that was always worth saying. Weather and health were always news.

What happened to the trio? Noah died aged 79 in Bath, in May 1826, much lamented in the obituaries, although in the tradition of the time, anybody worth mentioning when they died would also be worthy of praise. He was a charitable man, on one occasion giving £325 to a charity for distressed manufacturers.[4] Elizabeth did not remain single for much longer. She married John Bower in Doncaster in 1818 when she was 31 and he was 51. They had a son, Edward Chivers Bower, who became Justice of the Peace in Yorkshire and attended the Carlton Club when in town. They also had daughters, but they were harder to locate. Perhaps they played backgammon and ticked off tourist destinations. Elizabeth's sister Sarah never married. Elizabeth died in 1858, aged 71 and Sarah a year before, aged 67.[5]

Chapter 14

Respectability
Thomas Lucas 1813–1816

Our next witness is Thomas Lucas, who lived in Upper Bridge Street, Stirling, Scotland, with his wife Isabella and (eventually) eight children. He was a medically qualified surgeon. His published diaries run from 1808 to 1821, only ending with his own death in the year 1822, aged 66.[1] The BBC website, announcing the publication of the diaries online in 2013, said that it was a chance to see what peoples' lives would have been like 200 years ago.[2]

It is, of course, absolutely no such thing. It would be an impossible task for a diarist, even if they possessed a detached, overarching view of society, which Doctor Lucas did not. Ninety-five per cent of the population of Stirling remained unrecognised by him, except when they did something stupid or immoral, which he often jotted in his diary out of a sense of outrage or condescension. To be fair, he would often condemn the rich and influential as well. He is an ideal witness because he felt able to judge everybody.

He was a surgeon who had a shop and sold medicines. It can be established that he performed dissections of corpses and was privy to the medical histories of prominent members of the town. Records exist of Thomas Lucas taking delivery of the executed corpse of Sarah Cameron (1784) and of treating (unsuccessfully) a local family's young daughter who had VD.

Lucas took a professional interest in the health of the town and his patients, and had a reasonably compassionate view of the poor. Like most others of his kind, he did not appreciate much of their behaviour, but he also knew that it was not their dubious morals that killed them. Like the modern undertaker or florist, he was acutely aware that death was seasonal. He noticed that death rates rose in the winter, something that still happens today. He also noticed when more children than usual were dying from measles, or contracting the chin cough (whooping cough). He was an observer of everything in his city.

He does not mention his family very much. His wife, Isabella ('Belle') née Whitehead, receives one mention in the whole of 1813, and that was only to say that she had returned home from Edinburgh. Together they had eight children – Mary (died 1803), another Mary, Jane, William, James, Walter, Isabella and Agnes. In October 1813, his eldest son went to study medicine at Edinburgh and, in December, Lucas sent £10 in part payment for accommodation. His wife had returned from Edinburgh and the family were well: 'William and Mr Lucas's family all in health'. In a very uncertain life, when existence could slip away easily and quickly, continued good health was always newsworthy. His approach to family life tended to be pragmatic. In March 1813, he received a letter from Mr McNaughton of London informing him that his uncle Walter had married a young woman of 35, his age being upwards of 70. Lucas waited a fortnight and then sent a letter of congratulation.

Like most diaries, it was not an analytical document. He related events as they happened, obviously with no knowledge of long-term importance but no attempt to contextualise either, so the trivial and important coexisted. This explains entries such as 30 March 1813, which mixed his hobby of gardening and the war to the death in Europe:

My peas appear above ground. The accounts from Germany are favourable.

No matter what the state of his garden or the balance of power in Europe, the first entry in his diary would be about the weather. Poor weather ruined your plans and outdoor hobbies, no matter how rich you were. The Lucas family lived in a large house called Marieville with a large garden in the back for Lucas's pastime of growing food. Unlike most of his neighbours (the poor district of St Mary's Wynd was a street away), food was a pleasant distraction, not a daily struggle.

His interest in the weather was also linked to social stability. Poor weather and high prices meant social disorder, and Lucas noted the prices of bread, meat, sugar, eggs and oatmeal at regular intervals, and constantly worried about safely bringing in the harvest:

The harvest is not yet begun the weather being rather rainy.

Sometimes it seemed that a good supply did not guarantee the modest prices that would normally be expected. In January 1816, he noticed that:

all the necessaries of life although abundant are very high priced.

The price of bread was vital, literally, and Lucas knew it. He did not live on bread and potatoes but many of the locals did. He monitored the price of the quartern loaf; he did not have to enquire far because it was noted in all the newspapers. It was 11d in February 1814 and 2d more in August 1815. Like most people, he thought the bakers were conspiring in a cartel to keep prices high, although he never explains how that manipulation would be possible with a large number of small producers. He shared the odd notion that they could defy economic forces and charge what they wished:

the bakers have got the quartern loaf to 1/1.

On 12 April 1813, he suggested that the bakers were actively opposing the iron law of supply and demand:

The markets are on the decline but the bakers have not yet lowered the price of bread.

In 1808 Lucas had been part of an enterprise to undercut the bakers – the Society for the Furnishing of Bread – but the fact that this could only be done by subsidising ingredients rather proved the bakers' point. Food was in such short supply that distillers were from time to time forbidden to use grain and, when they did, it was an optimistic sign

The distillers have begun again to distil spirits from grain.

Lucas was very much aware that the price of bread was also being kept artificially high by the action of the government. In mid-1815, with the weather poor and the harvest a long way away, he noted that cheaper foreign imports were impossible because the ports were closed. In March

1815, he commented that there were 'warm' debates in the Westminster Parliament when a protectionist Corn Law was introduced, banning imports until a very high domestic price of 80 shillings per quarter was reached. He noted that there were riots in Glasgow and that members of Parliament had been insulted and windows were broken. He understated the amount of violence in London but was correct about one thing – the petitions of the voiceless, voteless poor could be ignored with impunity.

Lucas was living through a climate crisis that made harvest worse. Much of it he was unable to recognise, but some of it was, literally, visible to the naked eye. From late June 1816, sunspots were almost frighteningly clear. Lucas noticed them too:

> Several spots or holes in the sun has been observed by astronomers this summer and the summer has been uncommonly rainy but it is not pretended that the great and almost incessant rains that we have had of late is on that account.

Lucas was right; the sunspots and precipitation were different phenomena. What the people observed was the result of low sunspot activity called the Dalton Minimum; this was responsible for a small reduction in global temperatures but it was the eruption of Mount Tambora in present-day Indonesia in 1815 that caused the darkened skies, incessant rains and low temperatures, and led to 1816 being 'the year without a summer'. This was Lucas's entry on the last day of 1816:

> This year has been a very uncommon one. The spring was exceeding cold and backward or rather there was no spring, the summer was cold and wet, or rather we had no summer. The crop was very bad and unproductive. The harvest was very late, the crop was not well got in.

Lack of food caused social instability, and abundance of alcohol did the same thing. Our ancestors lived much nearer alcohol-fuelled anarchy than we do today. Lucas knew that New Year's Day was a critical flashpoint, and commented on it every year. The entry in 1813 starts with his main obsession, the weather (mild) and the sense of relief that there had been 'no riots on the streets this New Year's morning'. It was a good year; in

1816 he recorded 'several people drunk and quarrelling on the streets *as is usual* on the first day of the New Year'.³

Drinking and social disorder was almost hard-wired into the calendar. He notes a few of these occasions in the four years covered in his diary. This is from January 1816:

> Being old Handsell Monday was observed by the lower classes with the accustomed scenes of drunkness riot and confusion which is customary on celebration of that ancient festival.

Religious celebration and drinking seemed to go together. Lucas notes in his diary that people would even turn up 'drunksome' in church.

Christmas was different in Scotland. It is well known that Christmas was banned by the Puritans in England for a decade in the 1640s, but this had happened in the 1580s in Scotland and continued to have some influence afterwards. Some of the traditional English nativity celebrations would have been regarded as superstitious. The difference that survives today is the extra emphasis given to New Year celebrations in Scotland.

Old Handsell Monday was the traditional Hogmanay celebration in Lucas's part of Scotland. It was originally at New Year and was encouraged as an antidote to a 'popish' Christmas. It was now stranded in early January rather than the beginning by those who refused to accept the modification of the calendar in 1752. It was meant to be a lively and friendly celebration – Handsell is the practice of putting a coin into a purse given as a present, a tradition that persists to this day. There was also first footing, another New Year's tradition, but Lucas reported that there were more spirits in people's hands than coal.

Lucas was opposed to the drinking of hard liquor, even amongst his social equals, and he had the knowledge to back it up. He knew what cirrhosis of the liver could do to people; his medical background, rather than abstract morality, was his main prop when judging people, although he was capable of class prejudice. Later in his diary, in 1820, he noted that while the poor were drinking and causing havoc, the better classes were merely 'feasting'.

Lucas was dismissive about the inability of the lower classes to celebrate without degenerating into drinking, fighting and animal cruelty. In 1820, Lucas condemned the practice of throwing at cocks ('that noble bird,' said

Lucas, despite not believing that many of the humans of Stirling deserved that adjective), which was part of an increasing condemnation of the cruel sports of the poor in the late Georgian period. Critics would say that these were the same activities interpreted differently through the prism of class prejudice. It was the same with new animal cruelty laws, which punished the rustic farmer throwing rocks at chickens at the fair but not their betters who were hunting foxes.

Another place where the lower orders could not contain themselves was at markets and fairs. In late spring most years, Lucas went to Stirling May Fair, one of six annual gatherings that punctuated the year:

Was the May fair. The town was very throng, the day was fine. There was a few quarrels as usual, some broken heads and black eyes.

A level of violence was always expected. In 1815 he commented that the amount of pick-pocketing was less than normal – but that people would get drunk and pick quarrels was regarded as a given. John Byng came to a similar conclusion about English fairs and markets; both men were aghast at the lower classes' lack of rationality in the use of their spare time. Lucas and Byng accepted that the other entertainments would be morally dubious as well. A flagrant example were the blind fiddlers, wheel of fortune men, ballad singers, learned pigs and excessive gambling at the October races. In February 1816, Lucas noticed St Valentine's Day for the first time:

The Custom of sending Valentines among the young people was carried to excess this year, 'tis reported that upwards of 400 passed the post office. Several young people received them by dozens.

Each August, Lucas noted in his diary the number of strangers and tourists passing and re-passing through the town. On the whole he was not impressed: 'the rage or madness of going to see the Trossachs this year seems to be much abated.' He also understood that they were mostly the elite, travelling for the sake of their sensibilities or their health and the chance to see the trophy destinations of Scotland.

The war with Napoleon was another fixed and regular point in his diary. He was no fan of Napoleon or the French ('No oaths or promises can bind a French man!!!'). The French emperor was a usurper, a coward and an enemy of peace, and when the newspapers reported that he was to be exiled to St Helena, Lucas grumbled that he should have been put to death.

His war news was not as illuminating as the rest of his journal because it was mostly quoted verbatim from the local newspapers. It would already be old news by the time it arrived in London and would have taken another two or three days to reach Stirling by stagecoach. On occasion, the news took over two weeks to arrive. The Battle of Leipzig, a major defeat for Napoleon, finished on 19 October 1813 and was celebrated as good news in Stirling on 6 November with a twenty-one-gun salute from the castle.

On 30 November 1813, there was a celebration of Wellington's victories in Spain that involved illuminating houses with candles; Lucas spent 16 shillings and seemed to resent every penny of it. He noted that the mob behaved tolerably, referring to the habit of smashing the windows of anybody who did not take part with sufficient enthusiasm. Windham and Farington had the same problem with the mob as Lucas, which was more likely to be dangerous when it was patriotic than when it was revolutionary.

Another fixed event of the year was the annual celebration of George III's birthday on 4 June. There seems to have been little enthusiasm for this in Scotland. In 1811 Lucas noted that the celebrations were muted – 'the guns of Stirling Castle had been fired and there was no public guzzle as usual by the magistrates and their friends' – but this was because of the death and illness of some members of the corporation, not the insanity of the king, which had been common knowledge since the end of 1810. The next year there was still an eleven-gun salute, but no bonfires, no drinking to His Majesty's health at the Cross, and not even any guzzling by the corporation. In 1816, there was still only perfunctory bell-ringing and cannon-firing but no spontaneous joy at all. At this point, Lucas believed that the old king had been forgotten.

The monarchy generally left him unmoved. There were great debates in London about the behaviour of Queen Caroline:

> The parliament have been occupied in disputes about the Princess of Wales, which have been most shocking but which have come

to nothing, the princess's character being neither cleared up nor established to be infamous.

It wasn't so much that the jury was out, but that he did not care about the existence of a jury at all.

High bread prices led to the social instability that Lucas feared. It was exacerbated by commercial practices that put profit above people. In 1813, Lucas witnessed the departure of the first division of the 70th regiment from Stirling Castle to Montrose, because grain was being exported while people were going hungry. Soldiers had to be used when large-scale rioting was threatened, as local law enforcement could not cope with large numbers of violent protestors. Lucas would have known what was happening in Montrose; the Georgian bread riots were all very similar and, in the Regency period, they were happening more frequently. He was also able to predict the result. Discontent had come to a head after a month of grumbling; the local constables had held them at bay for a while and then, as Lucas says, the professionals were brought in.

The ringleaders were put on trial in April, accused of things that people would do to stop grain being exported: blocking the sea routes; attacking the granaries; and intimidating the owners and any workers who cooperated with them. It was common for the leaders to be women and, in this case, Elizabeth Beattie and Jean McMillan were accused of all of these things and of successfully raising a mob outside the Town Hall to liberate five women. James Ruxton was accused of threatening to smash out somebody's brains if they tried to apprehend the women, blocking the road with boats and being the leader of the mob. He was transported for seven years for riot, and the two women received gaol sentences of less than six months, being seen by the judge as more raucous fishwives than hardened criminals.

Lucas, a property owner and supporter of the status quo, could not have any sympathy at all for rioters, but this did not mean that he did not understand what was going on. The radical reformer Samuel Bamford (Chapter Fifteen) would have agreed with Lucas's end of year summary in 1815:

> The people everywhere are groaning under the pressure of enormous taxes, in Britain the taxes are excessive and collected

with rigour. Useless places and pensions are multiplied without number, bankruptcies are numerous, no specie in circulation, but the necessaries of life are at moderate prices, however many of the farmers are broken and have given up their farms. Some proprietors have been wise enough to give an abatement of rent to their tenants.

His own tax position was improving – he paid his last income tax bill of £5 4s 2d. Income tax was to be abolished in 1816 by a government that regarded it as a war emergency tax, and the shortfall was met by taxing malt and other commodities that hit the poor harder. Many decades of successful work had made Lucas a rich man and much of his diary describes how he managed his money; he expresses no regret that the poor were paying the price for his reduced tax burden. In March 1816, he noted that there were petitions in London against the abolition of the tax but does not mention the widespread riots; like many people, he believed income tax encouraged the creation of sinecures and payment of pensions to the undeserving rich.

As Lucas mentioned in his summary of 1815, the country was living through a currency crisis. On various occasions, gold and silver currency would disappear from general use and copper would become scarce, making the small-scale transactions of the poor impossible. Richer people would simply establish long lines of credit, and Lucas would have extended such credit to his own customers, but lack of specie-metal currency-was becoming a problem. In August 1815, Lucas, with his regular interest in military matters, noticed a soldier of the 42nd regiment with the Waterloo Medal, with a red and blue ribbon and about the size of a Spanish dollar, a foreign coin that would have been in circulation as a makeshift form of currency to make up for the lack of guineas. Lucas explained the problem:

> Banks multiplied to an excessive number and forgeries of their notes are become very frequent. A Guinea in Gold is not now to be seen and is worth about 28 shillings. Silver is worth six shillings and Eleven pence per ounce.

The reason why the twenty-one-shilling guinea had disappeared was that it was now worth more than that in its nominal value. The coins would be melted down and sold on. Bank notes could easily be forged, and banks that failed would take their clients' money with them.

Lucas believed that corrupt government was the root of all these problems. He had nothing good to say about his Member of Parliament for Stirling Burghs, Alexander Campbell. He had been elected in October 1812 with 75 per cent of the vote; that is three out of the four votes cast. English parliamentary seats were small and corrupt, but paled into insignificance with the Scottish seats, where almost nobody had the vote. Had he lived in an English town of the same population, Lucas would have had his democratic say.

Lucas had no time at all for the town council, the people who feasted and guzzled their way through the celebration of the poor king's birthday. No respectable people would join the council so they were left for corrupt nonentities competing to be Provost and Baillie. Just like in London, the town council and their acolytes prospered on taxpayer-funded sinecures. When one of their number died, it produced an unseemly and premature clamour for his job:

> Thomas Wingate died. This man possessed the places of Collector of the taxes, Clerk to the Trustees of the Turnpike Roads, Collector of Cess, Keeper of the Register of Seizens There is a Keen canvassing begun for his places some time previous to his death.

Lucas also witnessed the work of the justice system.

> the Justiciary Judges came into town. One man from Tillicoultry was sentenced to one year's imprisonment and to be whipt through the town of Clackmanan for striking a Constable and deforcing an Exciseman who endeavoured to take his Whiskey still. Another for illegal Distilling was sentenced to 9 month imprisonment. A Sheep Stealer was sentenced to 14 years Banishment to Botany bay. Another man was sentenced to six months imprisonment for attempting to commit a rape.

The sentences handed out were indicative of the Georgian bloody code and the different value given to persons and property. A man guilty of attempted rape was imprisoned for six months while a sheep stealer was transported to Botany Bay for the maximum period of fourteen years. Any attempt to undermine the tax-raising power of the state was regarded very seriously; an attack on an exciseman was an attack on government revenue, and you could expect the painful humiliations noted by Lucas.

His view of religion was tinged with moderation. He attended the Church of the Holy Rude, near his home, and was a member of the established Presbyterian Church of Scotland. This was an area where anti-Catholic prejudices ran high, but Lucas was mostly matter-of-fact on the subject when it came up in his diary, and the tone was more weary than angry.

On the subject of religion, like all others, he was as even-handed as anybody who was a product of their time could ever be. His interests were wide-ranging, and there has not been enough time to cover them here. Lucas's diary is also one of our more readable accounts of Georgian Britain. He was a unique voice, much different to the rulers, radicals, gentlewomen and criminals in the other chapters.

Chapter 15

Radical Reformer
Samuel Bamford 1815–1819

Samuel Bamford (1788–1872) was in some ways similar to Thomas Holden. They were both weavers and they were punished by the state for defending their standard of living in the face of mechanisation. That is where the similarity ends.

Holden is obscure while Bamford is famous; as Wikipedia says, 'his *Passages in the Life of a Radical* (1840–1844) is an authoritative history of the condition of the working classes in the years after the Battle of Waterloo.'[1] He was highly literate, being both naturally gifted and having been given a school education by his ambitious parents. The key difference was that Bamford's protests were based on political principles that Holden would not have understood; Holden feared starvation and poverty while Bamford believed that suffering would end when politics was reformed, a view that would never have occurred to Holden.

There was misery in Britain at the beginning of the century, hardly noticed by most of our Georgian witnesses, and this was no better after the war ended. Bamford's autobiography opens in 1815; the 'laurels were not cool on the brows of our victorious soldiers', noted Bamford, giving credit for victory where it belonged but high food prices, unemployment and climate change made life intolerable for the poor.

Traditionally, unemployment or high bread prices led to rioting or destruction of property, such as Westhoughton Mill (which Holden was involved in) or the bread riots mentioned by Thomas Lucas. Bamford listed the places where people rioted; in Bridport, because of the high price of bread, and in nearby Bideford where grain was being exported despite scarcity at home. Other riots took place against mechanisation. Luddite activity reappeared in Nottingham; starving weavers protested in Preston; and there were bloody confrontations against low wages, high bread prices, mechanisation and unemployment in South Wales, Dundee, and Bury.

Bamford's solution was to improve the quality of government, rather than rioting or revolution. He knew that neither would work against a well-resourced state that had just defeated Napoleon. This put him in a grumpy confrontation with all of the revolutionaries and many of the reformers that he encountered. His plan was to agitate peacefully for reform, hold fast the law and organise the working classes to pressurise the establishment into change. He formed such an organisation in his home town of Middleton, near Manchester. It was full of workers who had learnt to read, write and speak at Sunday schools; its headquarters was a working Methodist church with political meetings on Saturday and Monday evenings. It was a world of resolutions, discussions, delegates and persuasion. On 1 July 1817, they made their views clear; they wanted:

> the right of every male to vote who paid taxes ... males of eighteen should be eligible to vote ... that parliaments should be elected annually ... and that talent and virtue were the only qualifications necessary.

The existing system, as well as creating bad laws, produced violence, mob rule, civil unrest, bribery, corruption, intimidation and drunkenness, and that was even *before* anybody was elected. The whole electoral system was rigged against the poor. As proof, Bamford could point to the London riots in 1815 when the price of bread was deliberately kept high by lawmakers who were also landowners and rich farmers with a vested interest in high agricultural prices. So the answer was reform of parliament.

Bamford did not demand voting by secret ballot, which would end the kind of corruption he deplored, and also made no demands about the abolition of church tithes, payment of members, controlling factory conditions and allowing a free trade in food. He believed that a reformed Commons would be the gateway to these other changes 'and all these things shall be added to you', he said, biblically, referencing Mark and Luke, and making it clear that Christianity was his main motivating factor.

The Home Office – newly formed to protect the security of the state – was deeply alarmed. It did not see these bureaucratic, penny-a-week subscription clubs as moderate gatherings spreading the Good Word of Reform, but as conspiracies, and wanted to know what was 'really' going on. Spies were used but they did more than pry; they provoked people into action so that the authorities could both arrest people *and* justify their draconian actions. Thomas Holden believed that he was a victim of such men. Bamford called them 'incendiaries' and we know them better as agents provocateur. For the rest of his life, he was paranoid about espionage, but at times the establishment *were* out to get him, as subsequent events proved.

When he travelled to London ('the great Babylon') as a representative of his Middleton club, he met other political reformers, but there was always a class issue. Bamford was a weaver like Holden and, in common with Holden, he owned nothing but his own labour, which was absolutely not the case with most leaders of the reform movement.

These included William Cobbett ('no man could enjoy a bit of sarcasm better than he') who was, in class terms, a Hampshire gentleman farmer; and Major John Cartwright, ('the father of reform') who had been agitating on the issue since the 1780s in parliament. The movement was led by 'Orator' Henry Hunt; 6-foot-tall, well-dressed, vain and haughty and the owner of 3,000 acres in Somerset and Wiltshire. He was the undoubted inspiration for the noisier side of the reform movement. Hunt was Bamford's hero until he met him, and afterwards he liked him less and less. This was a fair assessment of Hunt's character, but Bamford tended to like people less the more he met them, as they inevitably failed to reach his own very high standards. He thought that people needed reforming as well as government, and was happy to tell them so. His autobiography is mostly very readable, but he could be preachy and insufferable as well.

Bamford was not on direct speaking terms with these elite reformers. He did have a brief conversation with Sir Francis Burdett, who was a rich baronet, married into the Coutts banking family, and had two decades of radical action behind him. Burdett did not talk to weavers with ease and Bamford noticed that 'he was submitting to rather than seeking conversation with men of our class.' The visit was short, Burdett was distant and still in his slippers and what looked like a dressing gown. His household did not provide the customary refreshments. Bamford's hero worship was strained again – 'he was one of our idols, and we were loath to give him up.'

Bamford was far more politically radical than Burdett. Bamford wanted universal male suffrage, while Burdett wanted a form of householder suffrage that would deny the vote to most of Bamford's weaver friends.

One discussion was particularly fraught; despite not deigning to turn up, Burdett's view was still considered by a meeting of prominent reformers. The radicals did what they would always do for the next 200 years: fell out about detail, translated the fallings out into matters of principle, and split and weakened the movement they all supported.

One particular morning in late January 1817 illustrated the ambiguity. In the House of Lords, the Prince Regent was giving a half-hearted speech in which he showed zero empathy for the plight of the poor. In the same building, Bamford was watching while Hunt delivered a petition to the House of Commons on parliamentary reform; later that morning, the Prince Regent's coach was attacked by a mob of hissing, stone-throwing plebeians. These two different but related events highlighted the reformers' dilemma. They were split on their demands *and* their tactics – was it to be petitions or threats of violence, and if neither, what was the way forward?

Bamford was no strategic genius, and his self-importance and naivety often put him in tricky positions. Soon after the attack on the Prince Regent, he took it upon himself to visit the barracks of the local footguards in Knightsbridge with his radical friend Joseph Mitchell to discuss politics with the ordinary soldiers. Bamford could not see the harm in some low-level chat about the reform of parliament and handing out a few newspapers; it did not occur to him that radicalising the state's armed forces could be seen as insurrectionary intent, and it also feels a little self-important:

> Very soon after this a law was passed making it death to attempt to seduce a soldier from his duty. Could it possibly be that the occurrences of this evening led to the enactment of that law?

He met the revolutionaries of Regency Britain and did not like them one bit. They did not have discussions and resolutions in austere church halls; they gathered in the pubs of London with a half-pint of porter, smoking tobacco from long pipes emitting abominable odours that were worse than the fog in the streets. They banged the table, shouted across to each other and were not silent until the main speaker arrived; sometimes, the main speaker was an even worse influence than the alcohol and the solidarity.

Bamford was worried that their rhetoric was highly regarded by some of the working men, but the actions it encouraged made them no better than government spies. Specifically, he met James Watson and Thomas Preston, members of the Spencean Society of Philanthropists, which, despite its name, was dedicated to the violent overthrow of the state. In December 1816, the Society had attempted a coup d'état. This 'Spa Fields Insurrection' was laughable. Bamford despaired:

> Preston had mounted a wall of the Tower and summoned the guard to surrender. The men gazed at him, laughed [and] no one fired a shot and soon after he fell down or was pulled off by his companions who thought no doubt he had acted fool long enough.

The attempt to overthrow a well-armed and organised state was so poor that the soldiers did not even need to fire. He was amazed that their childlike play-acting and big words had so much support, but knew that lack of reform would encourage similar madness. The authorities did, indeed, react by suspending habeas corpus. This would allow the government to arrest people and imprison them without recourse to appeal. All this was made possible by reckless radical action that gave the government a pretext, thought Bamford.

He continued to 'hold fast by the laws'; the rule of law was fine – the problem lay with those making them. He went to visit the House of Commons like Karl Moritz had done twenty years earlier and was deeply shocked. The MPs did not debate; they howled like a kennel of dogs at feeding time; they shouted, screamed, gossiped, snorted into their napkins and lolled about amidst chaotic scenes and wild hubbub; some were stiffened immovably by starch or pride, or both. Lord Brougham, a reformer and a Bamford favourite, was shouted down; one MP pretended to cough so convincingly that it turned into a real one. One of the subjects under discussion was the moral weakness of the reformers; this irony did not help Bamford's mood; 'Are these, I thought, the beings whose laws we must obey?' His mind turned to Oliver Cromwell and what he would have done to such a corrupt parliament. He returned home in March 1817, disillusioned with everything except himself and those who agreed with him.

Back in Manchester, he was still being sought out by desperate people organising madcap schemes that totally ignored the overwhelming power of the state. One of these was his friend William Benbow, who told him that he was going to lead a group of men in blankets to London to present a petition to the Prince Regent. Starting in Manchester and building up support on the way, it would converge on Carlton House, the prince's palace in London, and ask him for help. It would be a petition with menaces, the new peasants' revolt, or a version of it, for people who did not know how the original in 1381 ended. Bamford was aghast; a half-starved, unarmed, unorganised group marching day and night would fail and, indeed, would never arrive. The army would stop them. They would be infiltrated by spies beforehand, stopped by the army during the march, and punished severely afterwards. Benbow was sent away with a flea, and a condemnation, in his ear. Bamford 'left with a lowered opinion of my former comrade.'

Bamford's predictions were accurate. The blanket march went ahead and it was even worse than he predicted. Their numbers never increased, disproving their main premise. There was physical violence and an innocent person was killed. Bamford was in despair, but proud to be right; nobody from Middleton had gone (Benbow did not go either). Like Winston Churchill, who famously said that history would vindicate him because he would write it, Bamford's description of events has become a key historical text on the blanket marches. This would have made him even prouder.

Bamford thought that huge outdoor meetings of men, women and children in families were a better way to make a political point than rooms of beer-swilling revolutionaries. These monster meetings took place usually in large empty spaces in the countryside, in this case Cronkyshaw Moor. They were advertised in advance, open to all and not conspiratorial. There were speakers, speeches, and resolutions around a husting similar to those used at election time by those who had the vote. The aim of these meetings was usually to find a way to 'obtain a reform on the Principles of Universal Suffrage, annual Parliaments and election by ballot.'

Sometimes these meetings, publicised in advance, could become tense. Soldiers would be under arms in the towns, the local amateur gentry militia might be called out and violence was a possibility. It didn't happen in this case. It rained so much that their muskets were saturated; the good-natured crowd joked that they could only squirt them. The meeting finished with a big dinner at the Rose Inn, Rochdale, and Bamford accepting 4 shillings in expenses. He was, after all, a weaver and could not spend time at his loom if he was speaking at meetings. He often worried about the madder spirits who were on the hustings with him, and these people still pestered him. He did not worry that peaceful protestors would be killed by the authorities and when this did happen in August 1819, the sense of betrayal was great; these people had held fast by the law, and look how the law treated them.

He was still being invited to overthrow the state; whether by iterant revolutionaries or agent provocateurs. On 11 March, Bamford met a stranger in a pub who proposed that he lead a contingent of men from Middleton to Manchester, draw away the soldiers from their barracks, take possession of the arms there when they weren't looking, set fire to the houses of their enemies, and rescue the blanket marchers from the New Bailey Gaol. He said no, of course – it was unlawful, inhuman, cowardly, and bloody stupid. Yet Bamford never turned down an opportunity to go to a pub with a deranged stranger to put them straight, a hubristic habit that brought him to the attention of the authorities. Like the blanket march, this insurrection took place without his blessing but left him with a problem. He was still implicated; a critic might say that he implicated himself. He needed an alibi, in the strict meaning of the word – *elsewhere* – so Bamford and friend 'Dr' Joseph Healey, who had initiated the meeting, decided to leave home and stay in the house of a female reformer (his first mention of women radicals).

Reformers were now in great danger; they were being picked up and imprisoned everywhere. Strangers came to Middleton and told him that King's Messengers were in town to arrest him. Spies informed on people; scores were settled by false allegations; open political activity disappeared and some reformers buckled. Formerly sympathetic people withdrew their support; their chapel-keeper turned them out and ended their peaceful meetings. William Cobbett escaped to the United States. The government could not arrest everybody, but could scare everybody, and it did. The plan was working.

Bamford and Healey decided to leave home until the crisis was over, although it is hard to see how a few days would make a difference. They left 'with light purses and heavy hearts' and, as they tramped through the moors, his friend Joseph Healey ('the doctor' as we must now call him,' said Bamford) told the story of his life. His father, like Bamford's, was a devout Methodist but also believed in witches and the supernatural. He would treat sick cows with spells, drugs and herbs, and Healey's mindset was the same. Healey had become an apprentice cotton-weaver when his father died and left him nothing; there he learnt his business but also learnt – like William Hutton and James Vaux – to hate the tyranny of the 'apprenticeship'.

He followed his father's interests and became self-taught in simple drug and herbal medicine, vein breathing and tooth-pulling. Bamford worried that Healey had done what quacks always did – sold worthless drugs at high prices, telling people they were very ill and he had the cure, and pulling sound teeth when he could find no decayed ones. He was also deeply concerned at the ambition of his friend to deliver babies.

Healey was tall, swaggering and often drunk; he had 'too much wind in his sheet'; he was odd like his father who, he recounted, had thrown himself from a barn into a dung heap, expecting faith to save him. Healey bought books but did not read them, and had opinions that were not supported by extensive thinking. He was generous and supportive but complacent and self-obsessed; later, his negative qualities corrupted his better ones, although it has to be said that Bamford thought that of everyone he met. At the moment they were friends, looking like unemployed men tramping the countryside.

They stayed, as promised, with some relatives of Healey's and then moved on Bolton. As they walked the moors, they enjoyed a prospect and a view just as much as some of our other travellers, but they were political refugees. When they found a spring of water, they made three toasts – to their friends and family, to the suffering brethren and the imminent downfall of tyranny.

They now had no money. Healey's relatives had not paid for any board and lodging, and they had spent too much of their own money in the pub (there seemed to have been very little 'temperance' around; it was a decade and a half too early). When Healey's promises of a helpful relative turned out to be worthless, Bamford considered hiring a loom to make some money.

However, a better opportunity to make money presented itself when, in the kitchen of yet another public house, they were served by 'a rosy cheeked lass with cherry ripe lips and arms as red as apples'. She also had a raging toothache. Healey offered to take out the tooth, after a nudge from Bamford. The mother was reluctant, saying that Healey did not look like a doctor. However, the choice was Healey or crossing the moors to buy an expensive palliative from a quack. A deal was struck.

So the tooth was removed with the pliers that Healey carried in his pocket for this eventuality. Bamford knew the type of pain that was imminent and retired to the yard, but he still heard the sound and the screams of bone being pulled out of living flesh. When he returned, he noticed that the young woman was covered in blood, and cream from a mug that had crashed to the ground. Tooth-pullers would encourage the patient to move violently to add to the momentum of the pulling pliers. This had backfired spectacularly. Worse than that, the 'doctor' had pulled out two teeth.

The constable arrived remarkably quickly, and the accusations flew. Local dialect was one of Bamford's interests, and he provided a phonic transcription of the outrage that gives a great insight into the Lancastrian accent:

These ar um she said yo seen what havock theyn made an iv ye hadno comn they met ha kilt us for owt I kno. That little devil pretended to be a docthur an put a pair o pincers into th wench's meawth an has very nee poo d her yed off an th tother's no better nor him. Beside theyn brokken my mug an shed my kryem.

Going in front of a magistrate was the very last thing that Bamford and Healey wanted, so they met with beer (warm ale and grated ginger) and pipes for a peace conference. The young victim of Healey's dentistry was brought in and the tooth was stuck back in her mouth. A face-saving deal was reached, no pun intended, in which the compensation for the damage would be slightly more than the cost of the operation; Healey was down sixpence. Healey continued to drink, and show off – 'sprozing', as Bamford called it – and Bamford continued to fret that some of the locals were near starvation, when the word came through that government agents were nearby.

They were back on the road the next day, trying unsuccessfully to get meals at inns – 'they had something better to do than cook steaks on a Saturday night', avoiding the king's agents on the main roads and taking directions from strange old women that they met on the way. The pair took refuge in an inn, and Bamford gives us a very detailed description of what must have been a particularly poor house. The table was, in fact, a door that had been taken off its hinges and placed on bricks; it was dark and smoky with tobacco, with ten drinkers, mostly sitting on bricks and wood. They were weavers, farmers and factory workers; and there was another room which was the same, but with more card-playing and swearing.

When they arrived, the crowd stood up threateningly and asked them who they were, where came from and what they wanted. They assumed that the pair were informers or excise man; either way, it was the repressive state that was their enemy. When they revealed themselves, they were welcomed and Bamford then describes a boxing match – it was Doggy versus Poacher, and Doggy was nearly killed. The damage is described in great bloody details and with interest rather than condemnation. Boxing was universally popular in the Georgian era amongst all classes – the weaver Bamford and the Cabinet minister Windham both appreciated it.

They went home after their wanderings, making it only a matter of time before the government caught them. Bamford was still being invited by strangers to covert meetings where the conversation turned to assassination of the cabinet, the uprising of the people armed with sticks with a pike on the top, and pistols wherever they could be found. Bamford was prepared to help those who had not been as wise as he; he advised Healey to flee; another reformer, John Lancashire, had a pike in his house and Bamford had it taken away. It was when leaving Healey's house that he was finally arrested by the infamous Joseph Nadin, the deputy constable of Manchester, and about six or eight police officers all well-armed with staves, pistols and blunderbusses.

There was no charge but there was no legal right to challenge the arrest since the end of habeas corpus. The formalities took place in Healey's house and a hostile crowd gathered outside. As they left, a brick was aimed at Nadin's head so Nadin grabbed a soldier's blunderbuss, threatening to shoot into the crowd. His threat was believed as he was already infamous in Manchester. Nadin was corrupt, or to put it in the polite language of

Bamford – 'he housed a good harvest while the sun was up' – retiring to his Cheshire farm later in life:

> His head was full sized, his complexion sallow, his hair dark and slightly grey his features were broad and non intellectual his voice loud his language and illiterate and his manner rude and overbearing to equals or inferiors.

After a stint at the Assheton Arms (it was common to detain those arrested for any crime in local public houses), Nadin offered Bamford a beer and made no attempt to intimidate him. Then a coach arrived, protected by a party of dragoons, and visited pubs in Manchester to pick up other radicals. Once gathered, they crossed the river to the New Bailey, Salford, the local gaol. The whole of the creaking Manchester judicial system was waiting for him. He was told the crime was high treason; this would have caused him to pause, as he had once witnessed an Irish lad being executed for merely stealing a square of material outside the very same gaol.

For the moment, he was in a filthy 9-foot by 5-foot stone cell, with a rickety bed and a stone ledge below a small shuttered window. Later, four more common criminals were added to the cell, perhaps as a form of intimidation. Bamford diplomatically shared his bread and cheese ration.

The next morning, the party was heavily leg-ironed and put on coaches for London. Nadin had also wanted neck and arm restraints but was overruled by the King's Messengers. Bamford's other problem was the company he was keeping; it included the incautious pike man John Lancashire and his erratic friend Healey. Healey still looked grubby after his night in a dirty cell, despite being allowed to wash under a cold tap. This was not a punishment – most people would wash their hands and face in the morning, and that was it. Healey now looked ready to perform the Moor of Venice, thought Bamford, showing off his education again.

Bamford was soon aghast – these were men who had definitely not held fast to the law and now he was literally chained to their fate. Their journey south revealed more disturbing news for Bamford. They were being called the 'Manchester Rebels', not a useful nickname to save yourself from the noose. There was better news for Healey. The state provided its prisoners with better food than they could afford when they were free but poor. Healey wished that he had been a state prisoner years earlier.

Bamford thought he was a cut above the others and the King's Messengers agreed, as they offered to remove the leg irons if he vouched for all of them; that he could not do. They remained chained, and one of the prisoners' legs swelled enormously. After a day's travel, the prisoners had a chance to talk (and sing) among themselves, and it revealed the greatest weapon the state had. It wasn't the irons or the gaols but the fear that the prisoners would inform on each other and turn king's evidence to save their own skins. The ultra-upright Bamford, who could not lie to save them from painful leg irons, schooled them in untruths; tell the same story, he said sagely, and agree to say that the meetings they had attended were to raise subscriptions for the families of prisoners, and then say nothing more.

There *was* a legal process and there *were* rules; the problem was the people who made them. They were to be interviewed by the Home Secretary Lord Sidmouth, but as he was not available, they were put up in the Brown Bear Inn opposite Bow Street. First, they ate and Healey showed off, but later they were chained together in twos for the rest of the evening and slept in the same way, except they were chained to the bedpost as well. They had no objections to their treatment at Bow Street; generally, the further away from Manchester and the rule of Nadin, the better the treatment was.

The first meeting with Sidmouth and Lord Castlereagh was a non-event. Bamford was expecting the Spanish Inquisition, but all he got was a legal notice that he would be incarcerated for a week and interviewed 'this day se'ennight'[2]. He was reminded that he could make requests and was not legally required to say anything. Bamford asked for clean clothes; this was agreed. He wanted to write to his family; this was allowed if he accepted the need to be monitored. No state prisoner had ever been given pen and paper to jot down his thoughts unsupervised and Bamford was not going to be an exception.

Healey could not make himself understood when spelling out his surname and became embarrassed when asked to write it out, so he handed the guard a printed label with his name and the instruction 'please take --- spoonfuls of this every --- hours.' The eminent statesmen were shown this and had a little laugh as they passed it round.

Their new home was Coldbath Fields gaol. One prisoner went to the hospital sick ward because of the effect of the chains and recurrent gout (he was a pub landlord). Another rebel, Robert Ridings, was ill with consumption exacerbated by a cold and damp night in a stagecoach. Their cells had three beds, some chairs, candles and a fire with wood and coal. It was a good prison cell. Bamford wrote out a sermon that was long, pious and didactic, worrying that his enforced friends were 'agonised by visions of the scaffold and the block.'

Breakfast was bread and butter, sugar and tea; dinner was pork, potatoes and vegetables, porter and pipe smoking. Ablutions were hot water, soap and towels; a garden, a sewer and a water tap. When they got fleas, the room was fumigated. Their beds were changed regularly. They were living better than most of the poor on the outside, but those people were not facing the prospect of a painful and public death and condemnation as traitors. When they asked for reading matter, they were expecting a Bible but were nonplussed to receive books of sermons 'for persons under sentence of death'.

The prison was mixed; it also contained a man who was convinced that he was King of Denmark and, worse than that, had been asking the Prince Regent for money. There were women in the next enclosure, and, in a reminder that the word 'radical' had changed over the centuries, Bamford and the others got them to do their washing and darning. As 'politicals', they were fed well, and threw legs of mutton and vegetables over the enclosure wall to the women. It was the prison version of the family power structure.

Bamford was amazed that the reformers were allowed to associate freely. He was convinced that he was in less danger than the other five, who freely admitted that he was not a party to their illegal plans; yet he wanted to help them, partly because they were his people, no matter how misguided, and partly because he could go down with them if the state dangled pardons in front of the more obviously guilty. So every evening, he catechised and drilled them into telling the same skeleton story with added personal details for plausibility.

On 16 April, the prisoners were separated and sent to different prisons, and a new set of prisoners arrived. A week later he was told that the case against him was not ready and he would have to wait another week – this was the glory (for the state) of lack of habeas corpus. Bamford put the Home Secretary's attitude down to ignorance, rather than malice. The ministers took their information from the higher classes, who were either too proud or too indifferent to examine the sufferings of the poor. On 29 April, he was offered the chance of being discharged. He was told that the present distress of the people was unavoidable and the government tried to help; Bamford bit his lip successfully. He was released on bail for £100, payable if he appeared again at the Westminster Courts within the next twelve months.

He left prison as a free man but a stranger to London; he was looked after by the two King's Messengers who had brought him to the capital. Before he left, he was given a tour of the worst of the metropolitan slums; the poverty would have been recognisable in Manchester, but the level of degradation would have been new. This was the uncontrolled urbanisation and social breakdown that Bamford would see in his own city twenty years later.

Bamford went back to weaving with his wife Jemima. But what was he to do next? The situation seemed hopeless. There was a reactionary government elected under a corrupt electoral system with enough strength to impose its will; and a divided and fractured reform movement, egged on by revolutionaries and infiltrated by spies. Added to that, people were *still* approaching him in the Dog and Partridge, armed with sticks and plans to overthrow the government that defeated Napoleon.

1817 saw more political discontent and madcap schemes, including the insurrection organised by Jeremiah Brandreth, and the subsequent execution of the ringleaders. Princess Charlotte had died in childbirth at the same time and it was expected that the grieving Prince Regent would spare the plotters; he did not. Ingratitude was everywhere – Healey returned, much richer and much more puffed up, and James Leach, another man Bamford had helped in gaol, returned much less terrified and a lot richer, as he had become a government agent.

In 1818, the monster meetings continued. Women who were in attendance started to put their hands up to pass political resolutions and, at first, they were laughed at but later less so. One of the trends in these meetings was for the masses to 'elect' a representative, usually a gentleman rather than a weaver, but the authorities did not like the idea at all. A meeting to do this was initially planned for St Peter's Field, Manchester on 9 August, and then rescheduled for 16 August.

This was to be a landmark meeting; it certainly was, but not for the reason that the organisers were seeking. It was to be highly respectable to counter the calumnies in the government press that they were a ragged mob who could not be trusted with their own appearance, never mind the government of the country. 'Cleanliness', 'sobriety', and 'order' were the first injunctions issued by the committee, to which, on the suggestion of Mr Hunt, 'peace' was added.

Order was to be achieved by drilling and marches, led by veterans. To Bamford, it was all romantic and harmless. It was all excellent health-giving exercise, and maidens would follow the men with pails offering milk fresh from the cow. Crowds of weavers would drill on open moors after they had done a day's work (you needed natural light to weave). The veterans were unarmed; their only weapon was 'a self approving conscience' in that most Bamford of phrases.

Hunt ordered that there should be no weapons at all and, at this point, Bamford thought he was being naïve; he was aware that there were special constables that had been armed and thought a few lightly-armed people would be a moderate response, but this was not to be. Parties of unarmed men and women set off for St Peter's Field on that fateful Monday, a day when, traditionally, domestic workers did not work. It was all very respectable; the Middleton contingent were 4,000 strong, led by the women a 'hundred or two of our handsomest sweethearts' who carried nothing more intimidating than stout sticks to help walk on the cobbles, singing along the way.

They carried banners which were political – 'Parliaments Annual' and 'Suffrage Universal' – but not threatening, although tragically it was the people with weapons who decided if the unarmed people were scary. This was the Manchester Yeomanry Cavalry – amateur soldiers that had been recruited by the Manchester magistrates, men who could never see the marchers as respectable, no matter how well the crowd behaved.

Bamford may never have expected the meeting to go ahead; it had already been forcibly postponed by the authorities. He expected to be stopped before they reached their destination, or have the Riot Act read to them and then dispersed by threat of lethal force. Later on, he saw his ex-friend Healey carrying a banner saying 'Equal representation or death'. One of those would come to pass that day.

Bamford was not a significant enough figure to be on the hustings; he knew the names of the men but not the women who were preparing their speeches there. Hunt took confident control of the crowd, estimated by

Bamford at 80,000. As Hunt spoke, Bamford went to get a drink; he knew the exact word for word formulation of these monster meetings and could fill in the gaps later. The blue and white livery of the yeomanry cavalry was spotted; there was an initial cheer, but then they starting cutting people; 'then chopped limbs ... gaping skulls were seen and groans and cries were mingled with the din of that horrid confusion.' The hustings were emptied and the soldiers ripped away the banners from the stage. The massacre lasted ten minutes:

> the whole field were strewed caps bonnets hats shawls and shoes and other parts of male and female dress trampled torn and bloody. The yeomanry had dismounted some were easing their horses girths others adjusting their accoutrements and some were wiping their sabres. Several mounds of human beings still remained where they had fallen.

There were more forces available to harass people as they escaped. Godly and pious Bamford threatened immediate violence to anybody who hurt his wife, and the atmosphere for the next few days was toxic. Bamford still held fast to the law, even after the massacre. He still dissuaded people from violence; it was not moral and they could not win, but 'Peterloo' was a betrayal and a huge step backward for people like him.

The government rode the storm; with parliament not in session, control of most of the media (Manchester being an exception), and the use of repressive laws, they survived the initial indignation and horror. Bamford continued his reformist work and lived long enough to see the start of the democratic process, but it was a hard road. It would be 99 years before the descendants of the men at Peterloo were allowed to vote, and 109 for the women; but it started with men like Bamford.

Chapter 16

Courtier

Ellis Cornelia Knight 1800–1814

Our next Georgian voice is the polymath Ellis Cornelia Knight. She was born in Westminster in 1757, but lived in Italy from 1776 to 1800, with spells in France and Vienna. She was highly educated; she painted (her work can still be bought today) and wrote poetry, knew modern and classical languages, and was the author of two novels. She was by no means the only educated and erudite woman in Georgian Britain, but Knight kept a diary and became a courtier, so it provides a unique insight into late Georgian Society and the highly dysfunctional Royal Family.[1]

As a girl, Ellis met Samuel Johnson, Edmund Burke and Oliver Goldsmith through her mother. In Naples, she was friendly with Lord and Lady Hamilton and Lord and Lady Nelson. In England, she was an established part of the *bon ton*, and met aristocrats, politicians and eventually the Royal Family. She lived in the same world as Farington and Gronow, but her descriptions were much less salacious and gossipy, largely because, unlike the two men, she had an official position in the court, so knew her stuff and did not merely 'suspect'.

She arrived back in England on 6 November 1800 at Great Yarmouth. One of the passengers was greeted by the Mayor and Corporation and given the freedom of the city, his carriage had the horses uncoupled and was moved by the power of populism to the Wrestler's Inn. This was Norfolk man and national hero Horatio Nelson, someone she had known well in Italy. When they arrived in London from Yarmouth, she dined with the two couples in a hotel in Albemarle Street. At the celebrations, her song for Emma Hamilton's birthday was sung (produced on a ship in a raging gale in the April) to the tune of *Hearts of Oak*. Knight was called the navy's (or even Nelson's) poet laureate.

Her acquaintance with Nelson started when he arrived in Naples after the Battle of the Nile in 1798, and he took an interest in both her and her mother, initially because the latter was a navy widow. Knight knew about the relationship between Nelson and Lady Hamilton at an early stage, and the couple were the subjects of her watercolours. It was a relationship with the couple that did not survive their return to England

Knight slotted effortlessly into the top 10,000 of British society. Her friend Evan Nepean was a Tory MP and Secretary to the Board of Admiralty (the same post held by Samuel Pepys), and this provided entrée into the British elite. She admired Castlereagh, and loved Pitt's speeches in the Commons. She mentions and approves of William Windham, who was very much in the forefront against Napoleon, and her anti-Jacobin views was one of the reasons she was so well received. She had already seen mobs and rioting in the South of France in 1789 while travelling, and knew their power. Knight remained a Tory and supporter of the French monarchy all her life, and this was one of the reasons she continued to prosper when the link with Nelson was broken.

It wasn't all perfect. This wasn't warm, easy-going Naples. She was not much impressed by the 'official gentlemen'; they were cold and satirical compared to the warm-hearted and open Italians she was used to. She went through the torment of the morning visit with the ladies, but did not enjoy them either:

> I observed that in morning visits, for example, it was not only the same style of dress, but that nearly the same topics of conversation, the same time of staying, and the same expressions would be used by almost every lady who made her appearance.

Our gentlewomen Elizabeth Chivers, Jane Austen and Fanny Chapman would have expected such a lifestyle, but Knight's own topics of conversation would have been classical languages, art and culture, history, geography and mathematics, and as one of the most educated women of the age, she would have stood out. This was not a positive in polite female company, but drinking tea and talking were never going to be enough in the long run. She had a friendship with the poet Elizabeth Carter, where the conversation would have been more rarefied and intellectually equal.

The other big difference to southern Europe was the weather – the gloom and the darkness affected her, and the Italians with her were affected even more:

> How do you like London? said I, one day, to my old Italian friend, Andrea Plaudi. I dare say, madam, he answered, that I shall think it a very fine city when it comes to be daylight.

She had been abroad a long time and was not used to London's short winter days. She also noticed how bad a state the poor were in, despite not being very close to their lives – it would have been very hard to miss. She had no analysis of the poverty and did not mention it again.

Knight was still on a tightrope with the Nelsons and Hamiltons. She had been under Lady Hamilton's protection since July 1799 after the death of her mother, which was part of the reason why she returned to England with them in 1800. It was embarrassing; not only did she know about the relationship between Lady Hamilton and Nelson, but most other people did as well. What could be winked at in Naples would not be allowed to go un-noted in London, so she endeavoured to move away from their public appearances. She was urged by friends to drop the acquaintance, but was deeply worried about looking ungrateful.

She tried compromise and had private dinners with the two couples, but would not go to the theatre with them. On one occasion when Knight absented herself, Lady Nelson fainted in the box; Emma Hamilton was the one who helped her home, and Nelson still felt able to stay and receive the plaudits of the audience.[2] He was there to make an appearance and he still did, showing scant consideration for his wife. Eventually, the Nelsons separated – a decision made by him rather than her. Knight believed that this outcome was never his intention when he arrived in England.

A new government was in place in February 1801, and Knight took lodgings in Whitehall to be close to her new powerful friends and to patronise music and opera. She had also met Lady Aylesbury earlier, and this was her entrée to the next level of society.

> Early in 1802 I was presented to their Majesties at a drawing-room by Lady Aylesbury, and was received very graciously.

It was Lady Aylesbury who informed Knight that she had a new job accompanying Queen Charlotte, the wife of George III, at Windsor Castle. She had already met the Prince of Wales, hand in hand with his first, unconstitutional wife, Maria Fitzherbert, while at her first concert at Lady Macartney's.

The only responsibility of the post was to be there when Her Majesty wished it. 'I should be present at her evening parties, when invited, and always on Sundays and red-letter days, and be ready to attend upon her in the morning when required to do so.' The post attracted £300 a year, lodging in the castle and a servant, and she would be free for two months of the year as she was not required on their frequent holidays in Weymouth. She had only been there in June for two weeks when the Royal Family took themselves to their favourite seaside resort for a ten-week summer holiday. Knight made a special point in saying that the post was 'quite unsolicited', which was telling. She had been asked by them. She was now a courtier and could get no higher.

The political power struggle at court was obvious; the original plan was for Knight to be the sub-governess of the 9-year-old Princess Charlotte; but it seems that Lady Aylesbury and the Dowager Lady Ilchester shared this service between them; the former, we are assured, was well-bred and amiable; there was no comment about Lady Ilchester. Knight was now part of the cut-throat world of courtier politics and the civil war raging in the Royal Family – and there was worse to come.

Princess Charlotte Augusta of Wales has been largely overshadowed by Queen Victoria, but had she lived there would not have been a Victorian age. She was the heir presumptive to the throne, and would only have been superseded by the subsequent birth of a boy, but there was no chance of that. The Prince of Wales and her mother Caroline were at war with each other, had been for nearly 20 years and had not shared a bed since the days after their honeymoon. Charlotte was born 270 days after their honeymoon (the average length of pregnancy today is 280 days) and was almost certainly the result of a single night of alcohol-fuelled Royal duty. Later, when he was Regent, the Prince of Wales was determined to separate Caroline from his daughter and take charge of her education; later on, this would be fatal for Knight's career at court.

For the moment, she was at the beck and call of Queen Charlotte, mostly at the oddly named Frogmore Cottage, no more a cottage then than it is today. Time was spent in the library, reading aloud in English and, in the Queen's case, also in German. Knight's diary breaks off and becomes fragmentary from 1806 to 1810 and the editor tells us that there was nothing interesting; 1810 *was* interesting but it was a calamitous year for the Royal Family. Three things happened: the attempted assassination of the Duke of Cumberland; the death of Princess Amelia; and, probably connected, the return of the illness of George III, 'a gloom that was never removed during the remainder of my stay,' said Knight.

The next scandal was the attempted assassination of the Duke of Cumberland, the fifth son of King George III. Despite being the victim, he did not come out of the event with his reputation fully intact. The Duke already looked like a villain. His face had obvious and permanent scarring due to war service, he had lost sight in one eye, and those who lived around him, including Knight, knew that he was foul-mouthed, lewd and politically highly reactionary in an age where the bar for that judgement was very high.

At 2.00 am on a late May morning, as Knight reported, the Duke was awakened by an unknown assailant. The Duke defended himself, but received several wounds from a frenzied attack using a recently sharpened sabre. A hue and cry ensued, and his Piedmontese servant Joseph Sellis was found dead in his room with his throat cut; but Knight (and many other people) was not convinced of Sellis's guilt. The pair of Sellis's slippers were perhaps a little too conveniently placed, with his name in French rather than Italian. Knight was also happy to point out some of the other weaknesses in the case. Sellis was left-handed and would have had difficulty making the slash wound. This was a common opinion at the time so Knight was breaking no confidences, and never did even when she knew some secrets – 'I never did and never will repeat what I then heard.'

The bloodied room was left open for people to visit with the grisly evidence of Sellis's apparent suicide, although the prim and proper Knight never went herself. Sellis was buried in an unmarked grave by night, but he didn't go unmourned. By giving him a suicide's burial, it was made clear that Sellis had killed himself after his plans had failed; the establishment rallied round, but it was not to be the end of the rumours about the Duke of Cumberland, which would include conspiracy, attempted murder and incest.[3] These rumours were known to all but not mentioned by Knight;

all she did say was that George, soon to be Prince Regent, looked after his brother for a month despite their 'differences', which was a clear understatement.

The death of Princess Amelia in November 1810 was the next sad event, leading to, and possibly causing, the relapse of the king into his final illness. She was 27, had never been strong, and the extended summer holiday in Weymouth had not helped. Knight met the Princess a few days before she died. The Princess asked her father to remember her but not to grieve excessively. Knight noted that the Princess died well, with dignity and Christian resignation, despite her relatively young age. Knight met the king on the eve of the sad event; George no longer recognised people or accepted reality, saying 'You are not uneasy, I am sure, about Amelia. You are not to be deceived, but you know that she is in no danger.' This opinion was held by nobody else.

The king recovered sufficiently to plan his daughter's funeral, despite his delusions. Knight was a key figure in the grieving and funeral formalities, taking part in one of the nightly vigils over the corpse, despite her position not requiring it. She was now at the centre of the court; but there would be no insider revelations. She would have seen much of the king's erratic behaviour but revealed almost nothing, apart from one occasion when his manic and powerful grip hurt her hand when he grasped it and she broke etiquette by gasping out loud.

The poor king disappeared from the public eye till his death, apart from regular and repetitive medical bulletins in the newspapers. The Prince of Wales became the Prince Regent on 5 February 1811, and the power structure of the Royal Family changed. Knight herself was more or less confined to Windsor Castle, ultimately taking orders from the Prince and almost becoming Princess Charlotte's guard from her mother.

Knight also attended the 17-year-old's lessons because her governess, Lady de Clifford, was unwell. Charlotte was allowed to dine once a fortnight with her mother at Kensington Palace, and Knight accompanied her. It was a surveillance operation; 'I was not to leave Princess Charlotte one moment alone with her mother, nor prolong our stay beyond a certain hour.' The Prince needed somebody to perform this task because his own aim was never to be under the same roof as his wife. The watchers were watched themselves:

On our way from Kensington to Windsor the carriage stopped, and Lord Yarmouth, who was at that time the most intimate friend of the Prince Regent, came up to the door to speak to the Princess. He, no doubt, afterwards informed the Prince that all was right.

She was now very much involved in the fate of Charlotte, and this proved an agonising place to be.

In January 1813, Knight attended the deathbed of one of her original friends from her arrival in London, who had put her on the first rung of the royal ladder. Lady Aylesbury died in the approved way 'with a calmness that had never forsaken her during all her sufferings.' The Queen came to town one day and sent for her and asked her, perfunctorily, whether there was any hope, but then moved on to the main business. Lady de Clifford had resigned; she had, in fact, been sacked, and it would have been impossible for Knight not to know that. It was intimated that Charlotte would have a new governess and 'a lady or two'.

Knight was certainly not going to be the governess; that would be the Duchess of Leeds, and it wasn't even obvious that she was going to be one of the ladies. Only Knight's advice was sought, or so it seemed. Later, Knight found out 'in my other letters from the castle' that these events were in response to a revolt by Charlotte herself. She didn't want the Duchess of Leeds giving her orders; she didn't want a governess at all, or to have the Duchess's 15-year-old daughter Lady Catherine as her companion in musical afternoons and social activities with young ladies who had not been presented. The two-year age gap was an unbridgeable chasm. Princess Charlotte did not want to organise children's balls; she wanted an adult court of her own with lady companions rather than supervision. Her enthusiasm for an adult court was understandable – it would be the first step to freedom from her bickering family.

This was technically an unconstitutional request even if the young Charlotte had been behaving well, which was not the case. She was poor at her schooling, a little slovenly and sweary in company, and was pretending to be a Whig to annoy her father, taking on Whig companions like Mrs Mercier Elphinstone, who helped her formulate her demand for independence.

The Princess was robustly told the law; the Prince even brought Lord Eldon, the Lord Chancellor to Windsor to explain. When asked for his opinion about how he would react, Eldon said that if she was his daughter, he would lock her up. Both Knight and the Princess thought that she was already incarcerated quite effectively anyway. Knight also knew that the Prince Regent was determined not to change his mind:

> Depend upon it, as long as I live, you shall never have an establishment unless you marry.[4]

A compromise was hatched. Charlotte was to have two ladies' assistants, later renamed 'companions', as well as being supervised by the Duchess of Leeds. Knight was not the first choice for these two positions and, in any case, she already had a position with the Queen. When the job was hinted at, she was positive, but protested (rightly) that she needed the absolute command of the Queen to do it; this was from a sense of loyalty and an equally strong reluctance not to make an enemy out of a formidable woman. She was in the middle of a royal war, but it was not really about Charlotte, but about the Prince Regent and the Princess of Wales scoring points off each other.

Using his physician Henry Halford as an intermediary, the Prince applied the pressure on Knight. The Duchess wanted her; she could have her own assistant; the Princess was pining for her; she should write to the Queen and explain that she would still be a member of the family. It was also in the national interest; the Queen's daughters – Elizabeth, Sophia and Maria – also wrote supportive letters. She had everybody's support, except the person that mattered. Yet the Queen was not going to let her go; she could not contradict the Regent, but she would not agree either.

As Knight visited Windsor in order to be persuaded, this received a passive-aggressive letter from the Queen, saying that she:

> doubted whether my health was equal to it; and, after intimating some displeasure at Sir Henry for the proposal, and great affection for me, she evidently showed that she wished me to remain with her till death. One of the expressions was, that Lady Aylesbury was the first, and I was the second.

It was blackmail with emotional manipulation, the same method she had used on Lady Aylesbury to block Knight's appointment with Princess Charlotte in 1805. Knight was sorry that she was ever involved. It was hardly surprising that the letter was taken from her by a servant after she read it. When the two eventually met, the atmosphere was icy. The Queen was in bed and stayed there during the audience, refusing to give Knight the release she needed.

Knight was a highly intelligent woman, physically confined at Windsor and mentally confined by the narrowness of conversation and the intrigues of an unhappy Royal Family. She wanted to work with Charlotte as it had to be more interesting than her present work at Windsor, which was trivial, unchallenging and monotonous.

There were more days of agonising commands, negotiations and letters. When, finally, a positive command from the Prince was received, she relented, miserably:

> The last thing I did before I left my old lodgings to enter on my new duties, was to write a respectful letter to the Queen expressive of the deepest regret at having offended her, and of the sincerest attachment. This letter was never answered.

Knight moved into Warwick House with the Princess in 1813. Carlton House was next door and physically connected, and Knight visited regularly and was not particularly impressed. It was magnificent, but really not much more than a nobleman's dwelling, expensively furnished. It was not that impressive on the inside – 'an old moderate-sized dwelling, at that time miserably out of repair, and almost falling to ruins.' It was a prison to all purposes. Knight described it as a convent; Princess Charlotte was not going to take on the role of nun and Knight was very much on team Charlotte.

Knight came into contact with the Royal court at the dinner table. She was formally introduced to the Prince Regent and she had her own view on him; he seemed to care little for Charlotte, and talked to her little. Her orbit was kept small. 'Every consideration was to be sacrificed to the plan of keeping the Princess Charlotte as long as possible *a child*'; for Charlotte, this meant a life that offered no independence, and despite the balls and events, was dull.

Nothing had really changed, apart from the meaningless compromise that caused Knight so much grief. Charlotte was still interacting mostly with children. The Queen was still distant; Knight was not allowed to sit in the Queen's presence, and she was told later that the sub-governesses were not allowed to do it. She was accustomed to being seated, and her new role was clearly flagged up as a demotion.

There was some good news. Knight insisted on a new title, as reported by the newspapers. On 30 January, the *Morning Chronicle* announced that she was sub-governess and this was corrected five days later:

> Miss Knight is not appointed sub-governess to her Royal Highness the Princess Charlotte. Miss Knight is one of the ladies companions to her Royal Highness, and is the daughter of the late Sir Joseph Knight.

The new title did not stick; it did not help that the Prince himself was unsupportive. Knight said that the Prince remarked that 'they might as well call me Lord Chancellor.'

In one of her many dinners with the court and members of the government, she encountered Lord Chancellor Eldon. He was not sober; it was, after all, the evening and he would have been drinking all day. Much of the business of the British state was done in a haze of semi-intoxication. He manhandled her and tried to convince her that the talk of Princess Charlotte's maltreatment was a fiction; this was the man who had suggested that the Princess be locked up. Once again, she had to use all of her diplomatic skills to get rid of him, while claiming no knowledge of the subject.

The screw was tightened on Charlotte. The rigid court etiquette made it plain that she was still a child; it was mooted that her visits to her mother should be reduced. She felt the stress and Knight felt it with, and for, her – 'I feel almost ashamed of spending ink and paper on such trifles,' she commented, perhaps thinking that her learning was clearly being wasted.

The Prince Regent felt the need to brief against his wife to Knight with anecdotes that she had to accept at face value. Caroline had neglected Charlotte, which was why there was a mark of smallpox on Princess Charlotte's nose, whereas *he* used continually to watch beside her cradle. The Regent also said that Caroline had threatened to declare that Charlotte was not a legitimate heir. Presumably, this was bluff and bombast as it was the worst accusation possible, and, of course, was untrue. The nearest that Knight got to criticism was that these were wild allegations and suggestions that she could only agree to 'in general terms', meaning not at all. She also said that she got no help to guide Charlotte into womanhood. It was not the Regent's priority and, in any case, it tragically never happened.

Knight was stuck in the middle with Charlotte, seeing the two sides vie for her affection, but not being able to believe either of them.

> Princess Charlotte said she had of late received much more kindness from her mother than from the Prince, but that their unfortunate quarrels with each other rendered their testimonies of affection to her at all times very precarious.

The briefing war continued on 10 February 1813 when the Princess of Wales's complaint letter to the Regent was leaked to the *Morning Chronicle*. The allegations were true; Charlotte was not being prepared for adulthood and was not allowed to see her mother. In response, Charlotte's next visit to her mother was cancelled by the Regent. As Knight noted:

> Poor Princess Charlotte was thrown into agonies of grief ... and always remarked that she could not have three days' peace, and trembled continually for what was to come next.

What was to come next was a moral condemnation of his mother, with Knight as a witness. In the presence of a miserable Charlotte and a clearly embarrassed Prime Minister, Lord Liverpool, the Regent told her that the visits had stopped because of the ongoing investigation into the moral behaviour of her mother. The conclusion, said the Regent, would be painful, but that he would not consider her accountable for the faults of her mother, although that was probably not how Charlotte felt.

Liverpool was dismissed from the room; and the Prince Regent walked on with Knight, hinting that his daughter was lying; he had, he said, made the same comment to Charlotte alone, and her reaction had been moderate. Knight knew this to be a lie and she swung against the Royal

Family, while still deflecting the blame from them. She believed that Royals coped less well with adversity than ordinary people because they had the problems of life smoothed over for them.

She was still dependent on the Prince Regent for her position, and his support was diminishing. When she was referred to as a 'sub-governess' rather than 'ladies' companion' by the Queen at Windsor, and she felt the need to appeal to the Prince, he ignored her. Unfortunately, relations with Princess Charlotte herself deteriorated, and Knight was now a victim of gossip herself.

The education of the child continued; English, French and German; singing, the guitar and violin, and the classics. The Bishop of Salisbury used to come three or four times a week, and 'do the important', which involved constant warnings against popery and Whig politics. Charlotte was bored and Knight found her waspish and ill-tempered.

And so it continued; the Princess probably realised that there would be no release from this until she was married and in July 1813, the hereditary Prince of Orange came onto the scene. It was mooted that he would marry her, but she was not having it. She had her own alternative thoughts and Knight was allowed to discuss them with her. The Princess suggested the Duke of Gloucester as a husband. She admitted that it was not a good match, that she never loved him and the age difference was great; but at least he would do her no harm and be kind, which were two things her parents had not managed to do.

The Prince Regent seemed reasonable in a passive-aggressive kind of way. He said 'he was himself too severe a sufferer to wish any other person, and especially a child of his own, to know the misery of an ill-assorted marriage', playing the blame game again. Knight clearly did not believe the Prince Regent, and she was right not to. By December 1813, Charlotte was engaged to the Prince of Orange; she had seen him in real life for the first time, not just pictures and prints, and her praise could not have been fainter; he was not as disagreeable as she expected. When Knight met him for the first time a few days later, she thought he was plain, sickly, tender, hearty and boyish. Appearance was not the deal breaker; Charlotte eventually changed her mind when she was told that she would have to live for much of the year in Holland.

The negotiations rolled on into 1814 and Knight was a bystander to Charlotte's increasingly desperate reactions. She asked to see the marriage contract; this was refused as it was the business only of the two fathers. When Charlotte called the marriage off, Knight was widely seen to be behind it. Others accused her of writing the letter of refusal, although she does not say this herself.[5]

Knight's career in the Royal court ended ignominiously on 12 July when she was summoned to Carlton House and summarily dismissed from service for lapses of judgement, without being given any details. She was well regarded by everybody until the enmity and jealousy of one powerful person put an end to her time in England, and she went travelling in Europe for the rest of her life. She was ill, worn out and demoralised by life at court, but once free of it, she prospered. She left England and died in France, aged 80, in 1837.

Chapter 17

Regency Man About Town
Rees Gronow 1812–1820

Rees Gronow (1794–1865) is our loose-tongued witness to Georgian high society. As with Farington, our task is to turn his gossip into historical evidence, but even if that fails, there are still the interesting stories of the Regency, most of which can be corroborated by other sources. Gronow was a member of the top 10,000 of British society like Knight, Byng and Windham, but he alone was also a member of the often capitalised 'Fashionable World' as well; only he would be mentioned in the arrivals section of the newspapers, so his perspective is unique.

He knew lots of famous people, or just knew people who knew them, and he enjoyed collecting stories about them. He was a gossip without a judgemental bone in his body, so the stories are rarely about him, but there is enough confessional material to convince us that he was an adventurous, devil-may-care individual similar to the people he wrote about.

His 1862 autobiography – *Reminiscences of Captain Gronow…Being Anecdotes of the Camp, the Court, and the Clubs, at the Close of the Last War* – sums up what he was selling.[1] The only downside is that he did his reminiscing to pay off his extensive gambling debts, so he may have embroidered them a little, but he probably did not need to do much as the prim Victorians already found his Regency characters shockingly attractive.

Like the Duke of Wellington, the man whose army he served in, Gronow started off as a soldier and when the peace was won, he became a minor celebrity. Until the age of 15, Gronow was educated at Eton, or to be more precise, he attended Eton College. His main activities would have been drinking, hunting, shooting and recklessly driving through the streets of Eton and Windsor, and avoiding the vicious floggings that were the only form of discipline.

After leaving Eton in December 1812, he moved with ease from public school to the first Regiment of Guards (known as the Grenadier Guards after 1815). He spent the first part of 1813 being trained very poorly and guarding St James's Palace, and then marching down to Portsmouth on the newly macadamised roads to join Wellington in Spain. In October, he was active at the Battle of Bidassoa, saw a Spanish soldier smashed up by a cannonball and came under intense French rifle fire. He was 19. He described both the horror and adventure of war, but his main interest was always people and their stories. His Sicilian servant was an accomplished forager ('ill natured persons might give him a worse name,' said Gronow, never a man to judge, especially when the benefit was his), who rode his mule for 20 miles a day to make sure that his junior officer had enough to eat.

Like Farington, Gronow specialised in the interesting pen-portrait. Examples include the Mayor of St Jean de Luz, who held a ball in Wellington's honour and almost nobody turned up. The mayor himself danced an English hornpipe that he had learnt as a prisoner in a Plymouth hulk. There was the Honourable W. Dawson, a fellow member of the Guards, who spent his fortune importing food from England and giving great feasts to the officers, including Wellington, and also ran a pack of hounds when he was there. There was another bon vivant, the Hon H. 'Bull' Townsend, taken prisoner mostly because he was too fat to run away. Gronow also had some personal stories but only recounted them when they were equally interesting. His stories show him to be both restless and reckless. While knee-deep in mud and exhausted while on duty at Bayonne, he opted to sleep one night with a knapsack as a pillow on top of a breastwork. He was an easy target for a sniper, didn't care at the time and boasted about it later.

Gronow largely disapproved of draconian punishments for the other ranks. One soldier was given 800 lashes for the crime of uttering – producing and passing off forged coins. He had stolen the regiment's pewter spoons in order to make sham Spanish dollars. These lashes killed him, of course, a much worse punishment than would have been inflicted in civilian life for the same crime. He saw other examples of harsh discipline for desertion, yet one gentleman, 'W.R', escaped any punishment for the same crime. He rode away from the battlefield and left for England, buying himself out of the regiment before a court martial could start. Gronow was aware that the rules did not apply to all, but never drew any real radical conclusions (although, later in life, he supported the Great Reform Bill of 1832 that gave the vote to a section of the male middle classes).

Later, he arrived to a friendly reception at the Royalist town of Bordeaux. Out of danger, his interests became wine and women; the wine was cheap and the women were attractive and well-dressed, and when they went back to England 'we left it with regret and the more youthful and imaginative amongst us said that we were wafted across the Channel by the gentle sighs of the girls we left behind us.'

In 1814, with the war apparently over, he was back in the Portman Street barracks and making the very best of the glory of the successful campaign. Without a proper war, he entered a new one – the struggle to be socially recognised and acceptable in the best of high society, and the best way to be so was to gain admittance into Almack's.

Almack's was the ultimate dancing establishment; provincials like Fanny Chapman and Jane Austen could only dream of attending, although the overall quality would probably have been inferior to any ball at Bath or Basingstoke. The building in St James's was nothing special; the music was often average and the food was regularly terrible – plain cakes, tea and day-old brown bread and butter. Alcohol and serious conversation were banned and the small room was often uncomfortably full.

The main attraction was that it was almost impossible to gain admittance. There were no more than 700 members at any time and it was four or five aristocratic ladies who made the rules about admittance, behaviour and dress. A ticket (a piece of cardboard) could be purchased for 10 guineas a year if you were on the approved list; in exchange, you could attend an evening of dancing every Wednesday during the London season.

In 1814, the quadrille and waltz revolution was yet to arrive; the entertainment was mostly English country dancing and Scottish reels. But Almack's was the place to be; most people could not get in; Gronow could. If you had a ticket, you had made it socially; as Gronow said, 'it was the seventh heaven of the fashionable world'.

He was seen in all the fashionable places; the *Morning Post* tracked his comings and goings as if they were news; when in town he stayed at Fenton's Hotel. He also patronised other prestigious yet slightly outré places like the Argyle Rooms; and who he danced with was also a piece of news. The C-list celebrity is not a new phenomenon.

How did Gronow gain admittance when many of his social superiors were turned away? Of the 300 or so officers of the footguards, it seemed that invitations were issued to Gronow and about five others. He was a handsome and well-dressed young man, a dandy like other Almack's regulars such as George Bryan 'Beau' Brummell. At Almack's, Brummell would use his good manners, fashion sense and personal appearance to impress the ladies, the gentlemen and eventually the Prince himself. Gronow did the same on a lesser scale. He was welcome because he fitted in with what Almack's was for: dancing, looking good, gossip and looking for a suitable marriage partner, although there was absolutely no evidence that Gronow was ready to 'settle down'.

Gronow was a second-division dandy, he was never one of the puffed-up gentlemen, led by Brummell, who sat in their own chairs at the bow window of Whites Club and made hurtful remarks about the passers-by:

Damn these fellows, they are upstarts, fit only for the company of tailors.

One of the haughty crew at the window was Gerard Frederick Finch Byng, the youngest son of John Byng who we last met being spoilt by his father in Chapter Four. By this time, he was an eccentric dandy, nicknamed 'poodle' at Eton for his long curls and later because of his pet dog. Gronow knew all of these people or knew of them.

Lord Alvanley, the second ranking dandy after Brummell was Gronow's favourite, and Gronow had stories about both of them. He is the source of one of the best-known Regency stories: when Brummell 'cut' the Prince Regent. This incident was the most famous and complete example of the art as it contained both an insult *and* ignoring somebody who was demonstrably your superior. The Prince had fallen out with Brummell already over the latter's poor attitude to his Catholic wife Mrs Fitzherbert, and cut him at a masquerade ball in July 1813. Brummell got his own back by ignoring the Prince and asking Alvanley 'who's your fat friend.' Later, they met again and the Prince took advantage of the fact that Brummell was drunk to send him home in disgrace. Royalty was always going to prevail.

Gronow liked Alvanley because the anecdotes were good, and it needs to be remembered that was the main point of his gossipy book. With

Brummell in disgrace, Alvanley became the source of the famous witty or bitchy remark, which impressed Gronow more than the clothes. Gronow professed to condemn the odious fashions that the Prince and the dandies spent time agonising over, but he was speaking for an 1860s audience who thought these Regency men an embarrassment at best:

> How unspeakably odious with a few brilliant exceptions such as Alvanley and others were the dandies of forty years ago. They were a motley crew with nothing remarkable about them but their insolence. They were generally not high born nor rich nor very good looking nor clever nor agreeable and why they arrogated to themselves the right of setting up their own fancied superiority on a self raised pedestal and despising their betters, Heaven only knows. They were generally middle-aged some even elderly men had large appetites and weak digestions, gambled freely and had no luck.

They hated everybody and abused everybody. They swore, talked in slang, and were sullen and invariably drunk in the evening. They effected to be bored; their ennui was fashionable. Gronow still recounted the stories to a shocked but receptive Victorian audience. Lord Fife, an intimate drinking and eating friend of the Prince Regent, spent £40,000 on jewellery, furniture, clothes and money for an opera dancer called Miss Noblett, in return for no more than 'her flattery and professions of affection'. Whether that last part is believed or not, it is still quite outrageous behaviour. The eventual bill for this platonic love was £80,000, paid for by the tenants on his farms in North East Scotland.

Another forgotten dandy that repulsed the Victorians was another of Alvanley's victims, Sir Lumley St George Skeffington. Skeffington, according to Gronow, used to paint his face so that he looked like a French toy; he smelt like a perfumery in an age when Brummell had decreed that the only smell should be of clean linen and country washing. 'You always knew of his approach by an avant courier of sweet smells.' Famously ugly, he was the most well-known example of the fop, the effeminate dandy. 'Skiffy' was a favourite with the ladies but was unmarried himself.

Skiffy was a poet and playwright. His only artistic success, a play called *Sleeping Beauty*, was a decade old by 1815 and he was still dining out on his fading reputation, both literally and metaphorically. Like Brummell (and the Prince, and Gronow for that matter), Skiffy ran out of money; rather than receive a taxpayer subsidy like the Prince or go into exile like Brummell, Skiffy went to prison. When he tried to reintroduce himself into society, Gronow reports that Skiffy's friends were very shy of him; what they meant was that he was ignored and insulted. On being asked, on one occasion, who that smart-looking individual was, Alvanley answered, 'It is a second edition of the *Sleeping Beauty*, bound in calf, richly gilt, and illustrated by many cuts.'

Gronow's own credentials with his Victorian readers were strengthened by his own war record. In 1815, when it seemed that Napoleon would need to be defeated in battle again, Gronow used his influence to get himself into the action. Mounting guard at St James's was too tame for him, and he put together a plan that went against all notions of military discipline with a confidence that came from knowing that people of his class would get away with it.

Gronow used his influence to get an introduction to Sir Thomas Picton and smarmed his way into the position of aide-de-camp, despite there being no vacancy. He needed a uniform and some horses so he borrowed £200 and gambled it into the £600 he needed. Gambling with borrowed money was highly reckless, and he did a lot more equally risky things without mentioning them. It certainly explains why he never condemned gambling in others; he knew it was a vice, but stories of aristocratic ruin were just anecdotes, and he was always ready to take mad risks himself. In this case, Picton's permission to accompany him was predicated on Gronow asking for leave of absence; this he did not do because it would have been refused. His plan was to get back quickly and not be noticed, or for nobody to care very much.

His admiration for his fellow Welshman Picton was obvious, despite Picton not getting on with Wellington and making that obvious too. Gronow admired his dress and energy, and his flirting in fluent French with a chambermaid at Ostend. It was not the flirting, which was expected, but the fluency that impressed him. Picton had a reputation for generally being rough and foul-mouthed and specifically for ordering the torture of a 14-year-old Spanish girl, Louisa Calderon, when he was governor of Trinidad and Tobago a decade earlier. Gronow would have known this.

Picton was personally impressive and brave; he was fatally shot through the temple at Waterloo and was the most senior officer to die on that day. Gronow did not see this; when he arrived at what was then the Netherlands, he was directed elsewhere when the practical implications of being given a non-existent job came to light. He was sent to fight with his own Guards regiment, who were amazed to see him there because he should have been in London, but they all decided to just get on with it. This was truly the insouciance of a ruling class.

Gronow provided one of the most searing and accurate descriptions of the Battle of Waterloo that stands up to cross-reference with other more famous ones today.[2] He delights in battle and victory, but he has real empathy; war was necessary and exciting, but it was not really good. He echoed the Duke of Wellington: 'Believe me, nothing except a battle lost can be half so melancholy as a battle won.' Gronow, while more familiar with the rich and famous, was concerned that the post-battle muster roll of fame stopped at the rank of captain and did not acknowledge the ordinary soldier. It was good of Gronow to do this as it was the enlisted men, rather than the officer class, who did most of the fighting, and he knew it.

On his return from war, his reminiscences lose any sense of narrative and become pen-pictures of famous people that he knew or heard stories about. One that came from direct experience was Percy Shelley:

> He was a boy of studious and meditative habits, averse to all games and sports, and a great reader of novels and romances. He was a thin, slight lad, with remarkably lustrous eyes, fine hair, and a very peculiar shrill voice and laugh.

Shelley would have stood out at Eton and their friendship is perhaps a little surprising, as almost no other Eton boy would have behaved liked this, Gronow included. Shelley visited Gronow's family in Swansea in 1810, sad over an affair of the heart. He met Shelley again in the year he died, in 1822, at Genoa, and was hailed as the friend that he was.

Gronow knew about the aristocratic hobbies of hunting, gambling and drinking; his Victorian audience would have been shocked by the amount of alcohol that the so-called respectable element of society put away. He knew of four-, five- and six-bottles-a-night-men, including Lord Eldon, who insulted Cornelia Knight in Chapter Sixteen. These bottles of port (or brandy) would be drunk slowly in small glasses, punctuated by other activities, and bottles would have been pints rather than the 70cl bottle of today, but much of the day would still be spent in a state of semi-intoxication. Fox and Pitt disagreed on everything but their alcohol intake was similar – 'the moderns would pronounce their ancestors fit for nothing but bed,' said Gronow.

He knew about food and that it was not very good; Byng and Moritz would have agreed. Even in their elite clubs, the food was monotonous. When they told the Prince Regent this bad news, he sent his own chef over and Gronow and friends formed a dining club, but it was the best of a bad job. Food was mostly solid, hot and temporarily tasty; it was boiled and roasted meat with roast potatoes and cold vegetables without sauce; it could be predicted with ease. Fish would be salmon or tench; the dessert would be an apple tart. The nearest people came to matching and mixing flavours was putting three different things in their mouth at the same time. People ate too much – taking wine with every course on top of the port or brandy. They got gout – 'the pill box was their constant bedroom companion,' said Gronow.

Gambling ran through Regency high society and, when mixed with alcohol, it was ruinous; however, it could be very lucrative when not mixed with alcohol. General Scott drank water while playing whist and at one point won £200,000. The two main games, faro and macao, were very fast-paced and allowed many games of alternating wins and losses, which meant many hours were spent at the gambling table. Faro was addictive because the house edge was tiny, and could be played for hours, with losses creeping up slowly but surely. Gronow recounts some terrible stories of a night's gambling destroying the fortunes and reputations of gentlemen at Whites or Brookes. Brummell had won £20,000 at whist from George Harley Drummond, who only ever gambled once in his life and, as a result, had to retire from the family bank

Gamblers who had reached the point where they could not borrow from respectable sources had the humiliation of applying to 'Israelite money lenders' to pay their debts. Gronow was anti-Semitic and this should be taken for granted; the racist trope is one still recognisable today: 'they do not create trade, but exploit the stupidity of others as an alternative to honest work, which they by nature would avoid.' He characterised them as humble and flattering to authority and rude and supercilious to those below them, and condemned both attitudes. He knew that there would be no Hebrew moneylenders without ruinous gambling, but he only resented the Jews.

He met Byron and Sir Walter Scott together on one occasion. His thoughts on Scott were unoriginal. He was a trencherman and drank a lot. Byron was all show-off and affectation, which he liked. Byron did not like to see women eat; this may have been because he wanted to think about them as ethereal creatures, or possibly because he resented them getting to the chicken wings first. It was an evening of excessive drinking, recitations and literary quips. They also stayed up late and get very drunk. It must have been an evening of great excess for this to be mentioned, as it would normally be taken for granted:

> A perpetual thirst seemed to come over people, both men and women, as soon as they had tasted their soup.

Gronow also presented his views on the Royal Family, written for a Victorian audience. The Prince of Wales's disastrous marriage to Caroline of Brunswick was rightly described as a way of paying her debts, rather than solving the root cause of his overspending. His view of the Prince's wife was uncharacteristically judgemental:

> The Princess of Wales was one of the most unattractive and almost repulsive women for an elegant-minded man that could well have been found amongst German royalty.

Her daughter, Charlotte, was tall and charming, (unlike her tiny and rather malodorous mother). Gronow rightly points out that she was the only member of the Royal Family who was nationally admired. She entered into a love match with Prince Leopold of Coburg after hearing about his bravery at the Battle of Leipzig. Gronow did not know about, or did not mention, the long painful story of Charlotte's failed engagement to the Prince of Orange. The tragic death of the Princess and her baby boy in childbirth (1817) removed the next two heirs to the throne, and led to a deep national mourning that proved Gronow's point about her popularity.

Queen Charlotte demanded total obedience and was manipulative and domineering, and was envious of Princess Charlotte's influence over the Prince Regent, a view that Ellis Cornelia Knight could have agreed with.

Gronow recounted his version of the famous scandal of the Duke of York and Mary Anne Clarke. As a 16-year-old, she had been invited to meet Frederick, Duke of York, the second son of the king. This is according to Gronow, but the facts are probably wrong. She wasn't 16 but older, probably 27, and they met in a place where aristocrats meet future mistresses – the theatre. Once, while sitting in his box at the theatre, she was mistaken for the woman he had just married. Mary lived in great luxury, despite Frederick not providing enough money, so she sold army commissions in order to help ends meet.

Gronow had other views on the Royal Family that he was very willing to repeat. The Duke of York was a big baby, not out of his leading-strings (when the scandal broke, he was 46). With the Prince of Wales, he hit the spot:

> an idle sensualist, with just enough of brains to be guided by any laughing, well-bred individual who would listen to stale jokes and impudent ribaldry.

Gronow was right to point out that it was the dispute with Caroline that made him unpopular and led him to rely on cronies and false friends. Gronow recounts the story of the Prince befriending a Captain Bloomfield in Brighton because he wanted somebody to accompany him playing the 'cello. Bloomfield was later involved in a scandal with jewellery and was punished with a peerage and an ambassadorship to Sweden.

These were serious criticisms, but Gronow also believed that the Prince was entitled to the same peccadilloes as other members of his class, and he also accepted that he had some redeeming features. Like most other observers, Gronow guessed that the only woman the Prince ever really loved was Mrs Maria Fitzherbert, and that love was heart-felt.

Today, the Prince's abiding weakness is seen to be his extravagant expenditure on clothes, food and houses, but Gronow believed that the main problem was his betrayal of his Whig friends when he took over day-to-day control of the government from his ill father in 1811. The

Prince's other weakness was that he would not follow his own rules. He understood the Prince well – he could act well-bred in public, but only if he wanted to.

Gronow believed that the Prince was imbued with petty royal pride, but this did not mean he had democratic leanings. After the Battle of Waterloo, the non-combatant Prince Regent had made himself Captain-General of the Life Guards and Blues as a reward for their brilliant conduct at Waterloo. Gronow recorded Wellington's response with approval – 'his Royal Highness is our Sovereign, and can do what he pleases.'

The story was far from over for Rees Gronow, as the rest of his writing shows, although his life was never as colourful as it was in the Regency. Gronow lived a long time, dying in Paris in 1865, and he had had an exciting life, rubbing shoulders with people like himself, having fun and taking risks. This seems to be an excellent description:

> One of the prettiest dandy officers of proud Albion Britain. He committed the greatest follies, without in the slightest disturbing the points of his shirt collar and would rather have blown out his brains than have gone to the opera in morning costume.[3]

Gronow was a reckless, self-centred, adventurous Etonian who broke the rules but still prospered. In that respect, the past does not always feel that long ago.

Notes

Introduction
1. The Life of William Hutton, F.A.S.S. (1817) via Google Books (books.google.com)

Chapter 1: William Hutton
1. Free edition used – brittlebooks.library.illinois.edu/brittlebooks_open/Books2010-08/huttwi0001lifof/huttwi0001lifof.pdf
2. The Breeching Ceremony of a Young Boy and His Rite of Passage: Jane Austen's World (janeausten.co.uk/blogs/fashion-for-children/breeching-ceremony-young-boy-rite-passage)
3. Whyman, S., *The Useful Knowledge of William Hutton: Culture and Industry in Eighteenth-Century Birmingham* (OUP, 2018)

Chapter 2: Karl Moritz
1. Vision of Britain | The travels of Karl Moritz (visionofbritain.org.uk/travellers/Moritz)
2. Dorchester in Oxfordshire

Chapter 3: William Windham
1. *Bury and Norwich Post* (6 June 1810)
2. *The Diary of the Right Hon. William Windham, 1784–1810* via Google Books (books.google.com)
3. Brougham, Henry, *Historical Sketches of Statesmen who Flourished in the Time of George III* (1839) via Google Books (books.google.com)
4. Sir Harbord Whyman elected (2305 votes); William Windham elected (1297); Henry Hobart (1233)
5. Details via The History of Parliament (historyofparliamentonline.org)
6. Windham, William (1750–1810) | The History of Parliament (historyofparliamentonline.org)
7. Details via The History of Parliament (historyofparliamentonline.org)
8. Felbrigg Hall, Gardens and Estate (nationaltrust.org.uk/felbrigg-hall-gardens-and-estate)

Chapter 4: John Byng
1. Vision of Britain | The travels of John Byng (visionofbritain.org.uk/travellers/Byng)
2. St John the Baptist
3. Church of St Mary, Eaton Bray | Wikipedia (en.wikipedia.org/wiki/Church_of_St_Mary,_Eaton_Bray)
4. Grimsthorpe Castle, Park and Gardens (grimsthorpe.co.uk)

Chapter 5: Joseph Farington
1. *The Farington diary: Farington, Joseph, 1747–1821* via Internet Archive (archive.org/details/faringtondiary01fariuoft)
2. *The Scotsman* (8 July 1926)
3. *Sheffield Daily Telegraph* (21 December 1922)
4. An Eighteenth-Century Love Triangle? – Cambridge University Museums (www.museums.cam.ac.uk/blog/2019/02/11/an-eighteenth-century-love-triangle/)
5. Sir Richard Arkwright died in 1792
6. Could be father or son – Philip (1749–1833) or Ramsey (1775–1862)

Chapter 6: James Hardy Vaux
1. *Memoirs of James Hardy Vaux* via Google Books (books.google.com)
2. *1819 Dictionary of Criminal Slang and Other Impolite Terms* via Google Books (books.google.com)
3. A public house of that name still exists, rebuilt in the 1930s

Chapter 7: Richard Warner
1. *A walk through Wales, in August 1797* (1799) via Google Books (books.google.com)
2. *The itinerary in Wales of John Leland in or about the years 1536–1539* via Google Books (books.google.com)
3. William Penn was a Quaker nonconformist who believed in religious freedom

Chapter 8: Jane Austen
1. Jane Austen and the art of letter writing | OUP blog (blog.oup.com/2014/03/jane-austen-letter-writing/)
2. *Letters of Jane Austen* via Project Gutenberg (gutenberg.org)
3. The expression is from *Pride and Prejudice* (1813)
4. As the Wheel Turns: Horse-Drawn Vehicles in Jane Austen's Novels | Jane Austen Society of North America (jasna.org/publications-2/persuasions-online/volume-40-no-1/ewing)

Chapter 9: Hannah Gurney
1. Hannah Chapman Backhouse (1787–1850) (durhamweb.org.uk/dclhs/downloads/HCBackhouseDBVol6.pdf)
2. *Extracts from the Journal and Letters of Hannah Chapman Backhouse* (1858) via Google Books
3. *Trial by Jury* by Gilbert and Sullivan (1875)
4. Quoted in Hannah Chapman Backhouse (1787–1850) (durhamweb.org.uk/dclhs/downloads/HCBackhouseDBVol6.pdf)

Chapter 10: Fanny Chapman
1. Sarah Murden, *The Diaries of Miss Fanny Chapman* (fannychapmansdiary.wordpress.com/author/allthingsgeorgian/)
2. Picking up small rods of wood (or bone) without disturbing the others
3. Mollands Circulating Library G.E. Mitton – Chapter 6 via www.mollands.net/etexts/
4. Dartmouth | The History of Parliament (historyofparliamentonline.org)

Chapter 11: Joseph Naples
1. *The Diary of a Resurrectionist* via Project Gutenberg (gutenberg.org)
2. Ben Crouch, Bill Harnett, Jack Harnett, Daniel Butler, Tom Light and Bob Holliss

3. Lennox, Suzie, 'A Short Tale Of A London Body Snatcher | Joseph Naples', Digging Up 1800 blog (31 January 2021)

Chapter 12: Thomas Holden/Holding
1. Lancashire County Record Office, DDX 140/7/12 (www.lancashire.gov.uk/libraries-and-archives/archives-and-record-office/our-collections)
2. *Lancaster Gazette* (20 June 1812)
3. New South Wales State Archives (www.records.nsw.gov.au)
4. Goodier, Christine, 'Living death of convict ship prisoner', *The Bolton News*, 28 February 2005

Chapter 13: Elizabeth Chivers
Much more information and the whole diary can be found on the Museum of London website (museumoflondon.org.uk).

1. Elizabeth Chivers' Journal | Museum of London (www.museumoflondon.org.uk/discover/noble-squares-charming-cheesecake-regency-tourists-london-diary)
2. theclergydatabase.org.uk
3. *The Ipswich Journal* (31 January 1807)
4. *York Herald* (20 May 1826)
5. Arksey Village, A History: Church Graves (arkvillhistory.blogspot.com /p/church-graves_4.html)

Chapter 14: Thomas Lucas
1. thedrlucasdiaries.wordpress.com
2. BBC News, 'Diary depicting life in Stirling 200 years ago goes online', (11 January 2013), (bbc.co.uk/news/uk-scotland-tayside-central-20984343)
3. Author's italics

Chapter 15: Samuel Bamford
1. *Passages in the Life of a Radical* via Google Books (books.google.com)
2. 'Se'nnight' is a week, formulated like 'fortnight'

Chapter 16: Ellis Cornelia Knight
1. *Autobiography of Cornelia Knight* via Project Gutenberg (gutenberg.org)
2. *Newcastle Courant* (29 November 1800)
3. A Life of Scandal: Ernest, Duke of Cumberland-Royal Central (royalcentral.co.uk/features/a-life-of-scandal-ernest-duke-of-cumberland-90688)
4. Charlotte of Wales – The triple obstetric tragedy-History of Royal Women (www.historyofroyalwomen.com/the-royal-women/charlotte-wales-triple-obstetric-tragedy)
5. *Lady C. Campbell's Diary*, vol. i quoted *in Autobiography of Cornelia Knight* via Project Gutenberg (gutenberg.org)

Chapter 17: Rees Gronow
1. *Reminiscences of Captain Gronow* via Wikisource (en.wikisource.org/wiki/Reminiscences_of_Captain_Gronow) (also available as a free e-book)
2. BBC News, 'Waterloo: Neath captain's memoirs depict battle', (25 May 2015), (bbc.co.uk/news/uk-wales-32868026)
3. Dandy days | York Press (www.yorkpress.co.uk/news/886415.dandy-days)

Index

alcohol consumption, 61, 66, 76, 200–201
Almacks, 196–97
Amelia, Princess, 186
animal cruelty, 44, 54, 73, 158–59
apprenticeship, 4, 5, 6, 7, 8, 14, 16, 72, 172
assemblies, 46, 55, 96, 97, 99, 101–102, 112, 116

balls, *see* assemblies
banking system, 18, 64, 162
Bath, 84, 103, 113–22, 124–27
Beckford, William, 61, 62, 63
beer, 5, 27, 29, 89, 92, 173
Birmingham, 7, 8, 11, 14
Blanket March, 170
body snatching, 128–35
Boswell, James, 61, 65
boxing, 37–8, 62, 174
bread prices, 63–64, 155, 156, 157, 161, 165, 166
breeching ceremony, 2
Burdett, Sir Francis, 167
Burke, Edmund, 34, 35, 37, 41, 66, 181
Burton-on-Trent, 7, 8, 29

calendar modification (1752), 110, 158
Caroline of Brunswick, 67, 151, 160–61, 184, 191, 202
Castlereagh, Lord, 176, 182
charity, 48, 51, 75, 152–3, 159
Charlotte, Princess, 67, 151, 178, 184, 186–88, 190–93, 202
Charlotte, Queen, 184, 187–190, 192, 203
childhood, 1, 2, 3, 4–5, 12, 48, 51, 53, 68, 111 *see also* orphans
Christmas, 4, 127, 158
Church of England, 26, 28, 84, 85
Clarke, Mary Ann, 203
climate change, 157, 165
Cline, Henry, 65, 128–29
Cobbett, William, 45, 167, 171
Constable, John, 69
Covent Garden, 74, 147, 148, 150, 151
criminal justice, 14, 127, 136–37, 140, 150, 163–64, 176

Cromford Mill, 68
Cumberland, Duke of, 185
currency crisis, 64, 162
Customs and Excise, 18, 59, 163, 174

dancing, 96–7, 98–100
dancing etiquette, 96–97, 98–100, 117
dandies and fops, 197–99
death and illness, 12, 13 14, 15, 118
death penalty, 4, 53, 131, 138, 149–50, 177, 178
Defoe, Daniel, 3
Derby, 2, 3, 5, 7, 11, 30
Derby Silk Mill, 3–4
domestic industry, 6, 11, 179
Duke of York, 203

Eldon, Lord, 188, 190, 200
elections, 5, 40, 119
Eton College, 23, 37, 62, 194, 200, 204

fairs, 51, 80, 159
Felbrigg Hall, Norfolk, 36, 42
Fitzherbert, Maria, 184, 197, 203
Flaxman, John, 59, 60
food, 18, 25, 45, 116, 201
forgeries, 47, 74, 75, 162, 163, 195
Fox, Charles James, 21, 33, 40, 201
framework knitting, 5, 9
French Revolution, 41, 42, 43, 129

gambling, 59, 115, 194, 199, 201
George III, 30–31, 48, 53, 109, 160, 186
George, Prince of Wales, 67, 151, 168, 184–7, 186–191, 202–203
Glyndwr, Owain, 91
Goldsmith, Oliver 29, 30, 61, 181
Grand Tour, 43–5, 87
Gretna Green weddings, 68, 98

Halford, Henry, 32, 188
Hamilton, Emma, 61, 181, 182, 183
Hayley, William, 59–60

Index

Healey, Joseph, 171–76, 178, 179
health and illness, 15, 111, 153, 154, 155, 156–57
Hoppner, John, 59, 60, 67
House of Commons, 20–21, 33, 169
Howard, John, 44, 51, 152
hulks (prison ships), 139–42
Hunt, Henry, 167–68, 178–80

income tax, 62, 161–62
inns, 7, 22–3, 24–5, 26, 29–31, 53–5, 146, 174

Jews, 22, 38, 134
Johnson, Samuel, 33, 34, 35, 61, 181
judicial system, 37, 127, 140, 149–50, 163–64

lead mining, 91–2
letter racket, 75–6, 81–82
Liverpool, 72–73
London, 10, 17–22, 45–46, 50, 145–153
Luddites, *see* machine breaking

machine breaking, 136, 138, 143
medicine, 4, 13, 14, 15, 32, 55, 98, 73, 172
Methodism, 50, 166, 172
militia, 25, 55, 170–71
Milton, John, 19–20, 23, 26, 60, 86
Mount Tambora, 157

Nadin, Joseph, 174–75, 176
Napoleon, 41–2, 62, 64, 87, 159–160, 199
Napoleonic War, 42, 102, 160, 165, 194–5, 200
naval prize money, 63, 77
Nelson, Horatio, 61–2, 181–82, 183
Norwich, 36, 40, 42, 63

Oak Apple Day, 45
orphans, 150, 152
Oxford, 26–8

pedestrianism, 23–4
Peterloo, 178–80
Picton, Sir Thomas, 199
Pitt, William, 35, 62, 65, 66, 67, 201
Portsmouth, 75, 77, 81–2, 140, 143
postal service, 52, 116
Prince Regent, *see* George, Prince of Wales
prison conditions, 82–3, 137, 176–77

private transport, 13, 36, 101–103, 122, 145
prostitution, 19, 20, 72–3, 79

Quaker calendar, 110
Quakers, 105–112, 117, 152

Ranelagh Gardens, 20
reform of parliament, 40, 166–68, 170
Reynolds, Joshua, 33, 37, 56, 59, 61
rioting/ mob violence, 5, 64, 160, 161, 165, 168
roads, 17, 36, 103, 115, 126, 195
Royal Academy, 57, 59, 64, 65, 69
Royal Family, 18, 23, 67, 109, 115, 181, 184, 185, 186, 202
Royal Navy, 63, 71, 77–8

schools, 3, 51, 68, 71, 99, 106, 148
Scotland, 44, 63, 67–8, 154–164
servants, 22, 23, 43, 52, 85, 114, 149
Shakespeare, William, 19, 28
Siddons, Sarah, 31, 34, 61
slavery, 41, 63, 72, 112
Spa Fields Insurrection, 169
Spencean Society of Philanthropists, 168–69
stagecoach, 22, 23, 28, 45, 103, 104, 134, 145
Stratford on Avon, 28, 29

theatre, 21–22, 61, 148, 152
tourism, 85, 93, 145–54, 159
transportation (to Australia), 70, 131, 137, 139, 142
travel problems, 22, 23, 24, 36, 55, 103, 112, 115, 146
Turner, J.M.W, 69
turnpike roads and tolls, 39, 86, 88, 90, 163

Unitarianism, 3, 26

Vauxhall Gardens, 19–20

Wales, 84–94
Walpole, Horace, 66
Waterloo, Battle of, 165, 200, 204
Weymouth, 116, 117, 122, 184, 186
Windsor Castle, 23–5, 109, 110, 186, 188–89
wool-combing, 1, 5